INDIA ILLUSTRATED

WITH PEN AND PENCIL

INDIA ILLUSTRATED

WITH PEN AND PENCIL

REV. W. URWICK, M. A.

EDITED BY

PROF. EDWARD P. THWING, M. D., PH. D.

GYAN

Published by

GYAN

Gyan Publishing House
5, Ansari Road
Daryaganj, New Delhi-110002
Phone: 011-47034999, 9811692060
E-mail: books@gyanbooks.com

Distribution Network
gyanbooks.com
India, USA, Canada, UK, Australia, France

ISBN : 978-81-212-9593-2 (HB)
First Published, 1891

2nd Impression 2023

Printed at: Gyan Press, Delhi.

INDIA ILLUSTRATED WITH PEN AND PENCIL
Author: REV. W. URWICK, M. A.

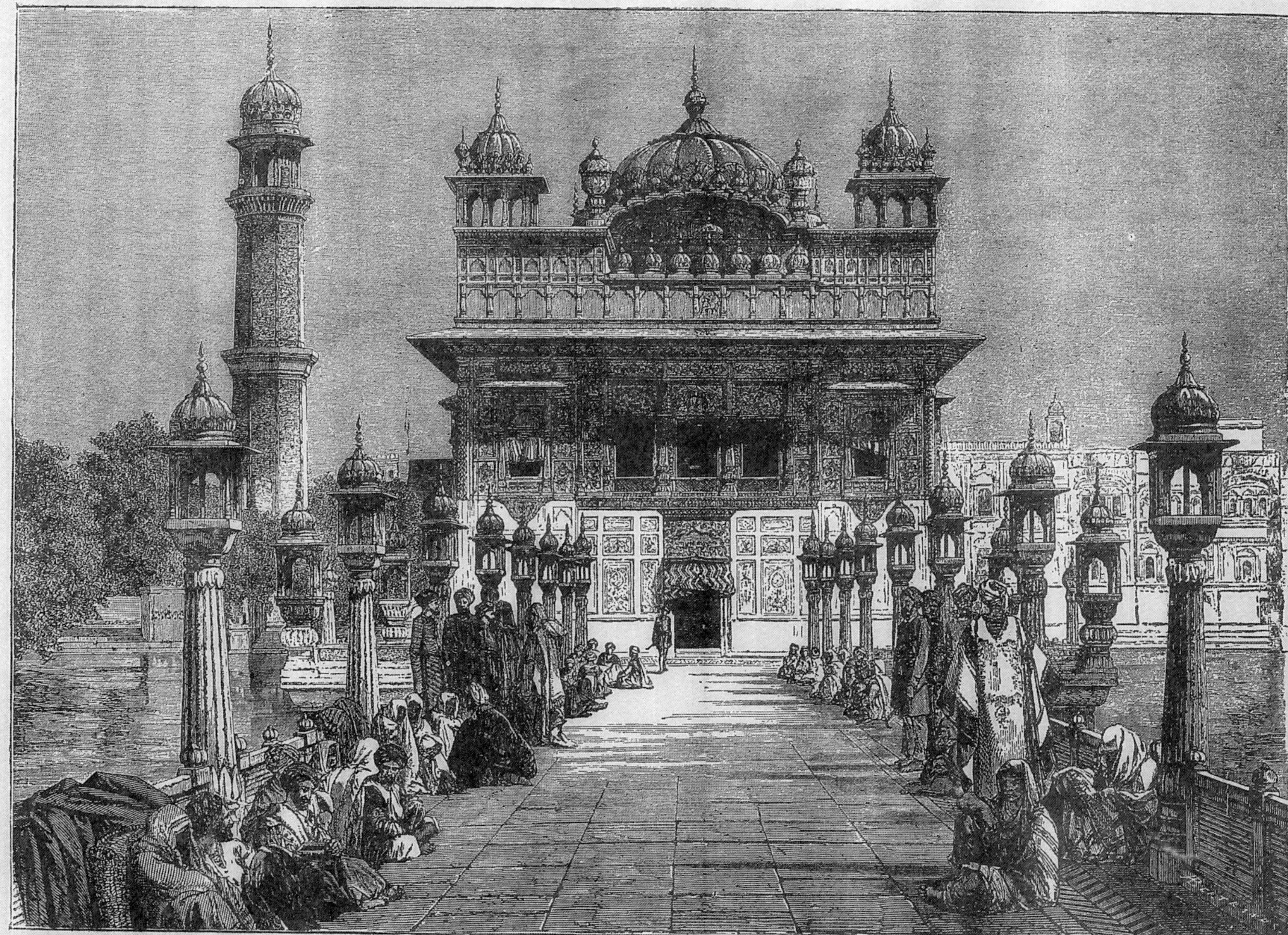

THE GOLDEN TEMPLE, AMRITSAR.

INDIA ILLUSTRATED

WITH PEN AND PENCIL

BY THE

REV. W. URWICK, M. A.

AUTHOR OF "INCIDENTS OF A TOUR AROUND THE WORLD," ETC.

REVISED AND ENLARGED BY

PROF. EDWARD P. THWING, M. D., PH. D.

MEMBER OF THE ROYAL ASIATIC SOCIETY, CHINA BRANCH; AUTHOR OF "OUTDOOR LIFE IN EUROPE," "OUTDOOR LIFE IN THE ORIENT," ETC.

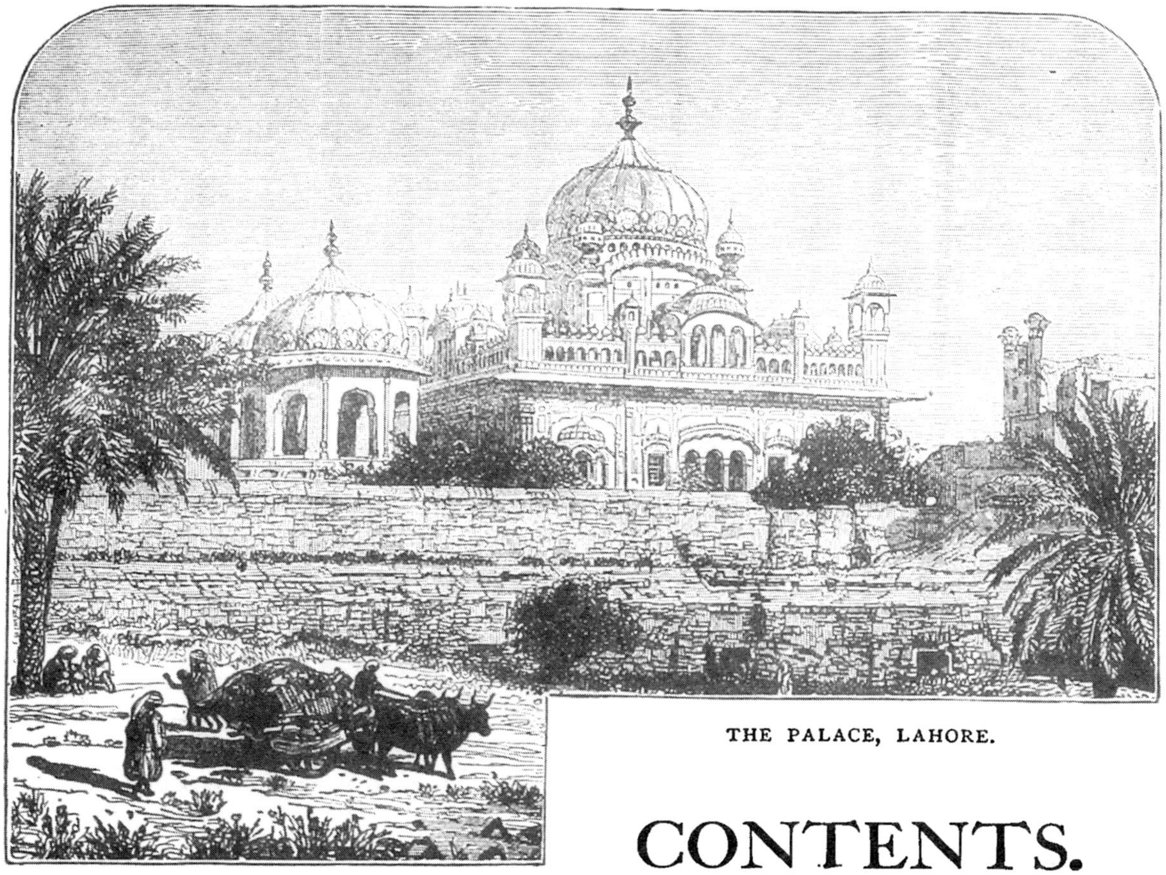

THE PALACE, LAHORE.

CONTENTS.

CEYLON.

Illustrations.

CONTENTS.

Madras Presidency.

Illustrations.

The Bengal Provinces.

Illustrations.

The Northwest Provinces and Oude.

Illustrations.

THE PUNJAB.

Illustrations.

RAJPUTANA AND CENTRAL INDIA AGENCY.

Illustrations.

BOMBAY PRESIDENCY.

Illustrations.

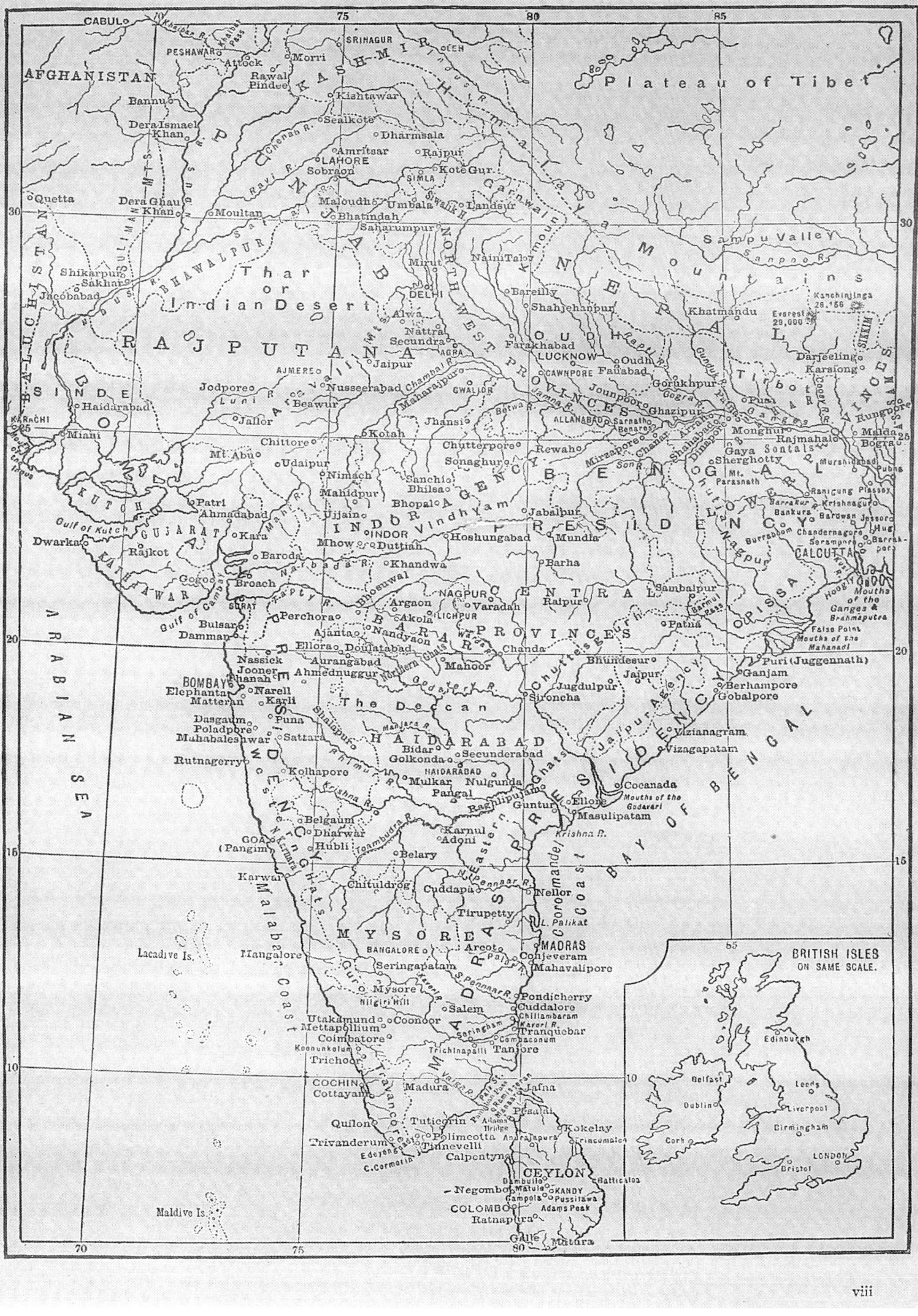
CABUL
PESHAWAR
Attock
Rawal Pindee
Morri
SRINAGUR
LEH
KASHMIR
AFGHANISTAN
Plateau of Tibet
Bannu
Kishtawar
Dera Ismael Khan
Sealkote
Dharmsala
Amritsar
LAHORE
Sobraon
Rajpur
SIMLA
Kote Gur.
Quetta
Dera Ghazi Khan
Moultan
Maloudh
Umbala
Bhatindah
Landaur
Saharunpur
Himalaya Mountains
Sampu Valley
Shikarpur
Sakhar
Jacobabad
BHAWALPUR
Thar or Indian Desert
Miruc
Naini Tal
NEPAL
Bareilly
DELHI
Shahjehanpur
Khatmandu
Kanchinjinga 28,156
Everest 29,000
SIKKIM
Alwa
Nattra
Secundra
AGRA
RAJPUTANA
NORTH WEST PROVINCES
OUDH
Farakhabad
LUCKNOW
CAWNPORE
Oudh
Faizabad
Gorukhpur
Darjeeling
Karsiong
Jaipur
AJMERE
Jodpore
Nusseerabad
Beawur
SINDE
Haidarabad
KARACHI
Miani
Jallor
GWALIOR
Jhansi
Jounpoor
Ghazipur
ALLAHABAD
Sarnath
Benares
Kotah
Chittore
Mt. Abu
Udaipur
Nimach
Chutterpore
Rewah
Sonaghur
Mirzapore
Chunar
Monghur
Rajmahal
Malda
Bogra
Gaya
Sherghotty
Mt. Parasnath
BENGAL
Sanchi
Bhilsa
Mahidpur
Bhopal
Jabalpur
Ranigung
Plassey
Krishnagur
Barrakur
Bankura
Burdwan
Jessore
Chandernagore
Serampore
Hugli
Barrackpore
CALCUTTA
KUTCH
Patri
Ahmadabad
GUJARAT
Gulf of Kutch
Dwarka
Rajkot
KATHIAWAR
Gogo
Kara
Ujjain
INDOR
Vindhyam
Mhow
Duttiah
Hoshungabad
Mundla
Baroda
Narbada R.
Khandwa
Barha
Broach
Bhosuwal
NAGPUR
CENTRAL PROVINCES
Raipur
Sambalpur
Argaon
Varadah
Akola
ILICHPUR
SURAT
Gulf of Cambay
Perchora
BERAR
Bulsar
Damman
Ajanta
Nandyaon
Ellora
Doulatabad
Chanda
Patna
Mouths of the Ganges & Brahmaputra
False Point
Mouths of the Mahanadi
Puri (Juggennath)
Ganjam
Berhampore
Gobalpore
ORISSA
Nassick
Jooner
Thanah
BOMBAY
Elephanta
Matteran
Narell
Karli
Aurangabad
Ahmednuggur
Mahoor
Bhundesur
Jaipur
Jugdulpur
Sironcha
The Deccan
Dasgaum
Poladpore
Mahabaleshwar
Puna
Sattara
HAIDARABAD
Bidar
Golkonda
Secunderabad
Vizianagram
Vizagapatam
Rutnagerry
Kolhapore
HAIDARABAD
Mulkar
Nulgunda
Pangal
Cocanada
Mouths of the Godavari
Ellore
Guntur
Masulipatam
Krishna R.
Belgaum
Dharwar
Hubli
GOA (Pangim)
Karnul
Adoni
Belary
BAY OF BENGAL
ARABIAN SEA
Karwar
Chituldrog
Cuddapa
Nellor
Tirupetty
L. Palikat
MADRAS
Coromandel Coast
Malabar Coast
MYSORE
BANGALORE
Arcot
Conjeveram
Mahavalipore
Lacadive Is.
Mangalore
Seringapatam
Mysore
Nilgiri Hill
Pondicherry
Cuddalore
Chillambaram
Salem
Utakamund
Coonoor
Mettapollium
Coimbatore
Tranquebar
Combaconum
Trichinapalli
Tanjore
Trichoor
COCHIN
Cottayam
Madura
Jafna
Quilon
Tuticorin
Adams Bridge
Polimcotta
Tinnevelli
Trivanderum
Edeyengoddy
C. Cormorin
Kokelay
Trincomalee
Anradjapura
Calpentyn
CEYLON
Negombo
Dambulla
Matule
KANDY
Batticaloa
Campola
Pussilawa
Adams Peak
COLOMBO
Ratnapura
Galle
Matura
Maldive Is.
BRITISH ISLES ON SAME SCALE.
Edinburgh
Belfast
Leeds
Dublin
Liverpool
Birmingham
Cork
LONDON
Bristol
70
75
80
85
30
25
20
15
10

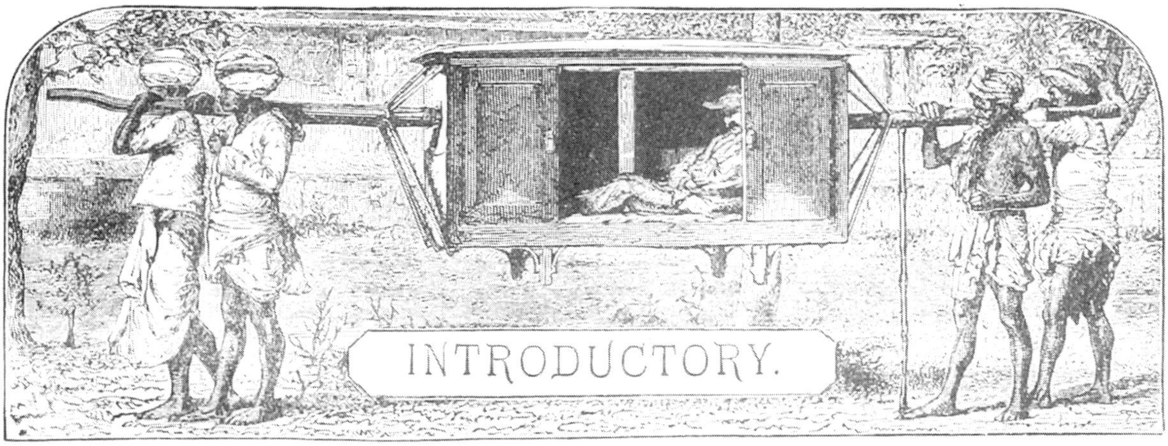

INTRODUCTORY.

INDIA, a stately and sonorous word! To the thoughtful scholar it suggests distance, vastness, wealth, scenic and historic charms, ancient art, barbaric wealth, as well as potential factors of national greatness. Sir Edwin Arnold has not unduly exalted the importance of a visit to India in any liberal education. No thinker can be an intellectual exile here. The student of language, history, ancient philosophy, or antique civilization finds a treasure house in the India of the past. She has been the nurse of useful arts, of subtle thought, and of epic verse. Fantastic mythologies, curious speculations, and occult sciences have here had their home. India has been the arena of chivalric deeds and of appalling tragedy, the battle ground of truth and error, the field of some of the most inspiring conquests of Christianity. But the India of the future is to be a nobler study still. We even now see a gradual unification of its many principalities and powers on a grander scale than that of Italy or Germany, with the gradual growth and supremacy of the English tongue and the surer domination of Western science and Christian thought.

We furthermore see the development of her industrial arts, and so the opening of hitherto unutilized natural products of this vast empire. We see rural communities changing into the grander features of civic life, swayed, as we believe they will be, by wiser legislation and purer morality than past centuries have seen.

We see, even now, the multiplication of schools, colleges, churches, and other features of Christian civilization, molded by Occidental ideas, yet adapted to Oriental conditions. In journeying forty-five hundred miles from place to place in India, the past year, the writer has been impressed by the intellectual ferment found, by the advances in science and by the urgency and promise of the missionary enterprise. That 8000 entries are yearly made in the official catalogue of vernacular and English works written mainly by Hindus, and on religion more than on any theme, is a notable evidence of that ferment. A pile of missionary reports examined, and personal inspection of work doing in schools and churches, satisfy me that Buddhist theosophy will never "tear Christianity in tatters." Whatever may be said of British rule in other days,—and its severest critics have been Englishmen,—I have a hopeful outlook for the future. Her thinkers are here and her men of science, in every department. A member of the Royal Asiatic Society at Calcutta, a numismatologist, told me of 5000 rare coins sent him yearly for examination. Wider and quicker weather reports—aided by a quadruplex telegraph system, by hard copper wire, and other improvements—are perfecting meteorological science. A vast and growing railway system,—surpassed by none, perhaps, outside America,—museums, libraries, industrial schools like the Technological Institute at Bombay, and other educational enterprises, inspire confidence in India's future.

These pages, therefore, possess a special attractiveness at the present time. . . . Rev. Mr. Urwick some years since made a wide tour, beginning with Galle, formerly the starting point, and proceeding, as his itinerary indicates, northward and westward. His pages are full of instruction. He avails himself of the helpful materials of Fergusson, Hunter, and other authors. The whole is profusely illustrated by pen and pencil. Foot notes have been added. The volume is offered to the thousands of American readers, young and old, to whom the past and the future of this land of romance presents a vivid and an imperishable charm.

EDWARD PAYSON THWING.

BROOKLYN, N. Y., *January*, 1891.

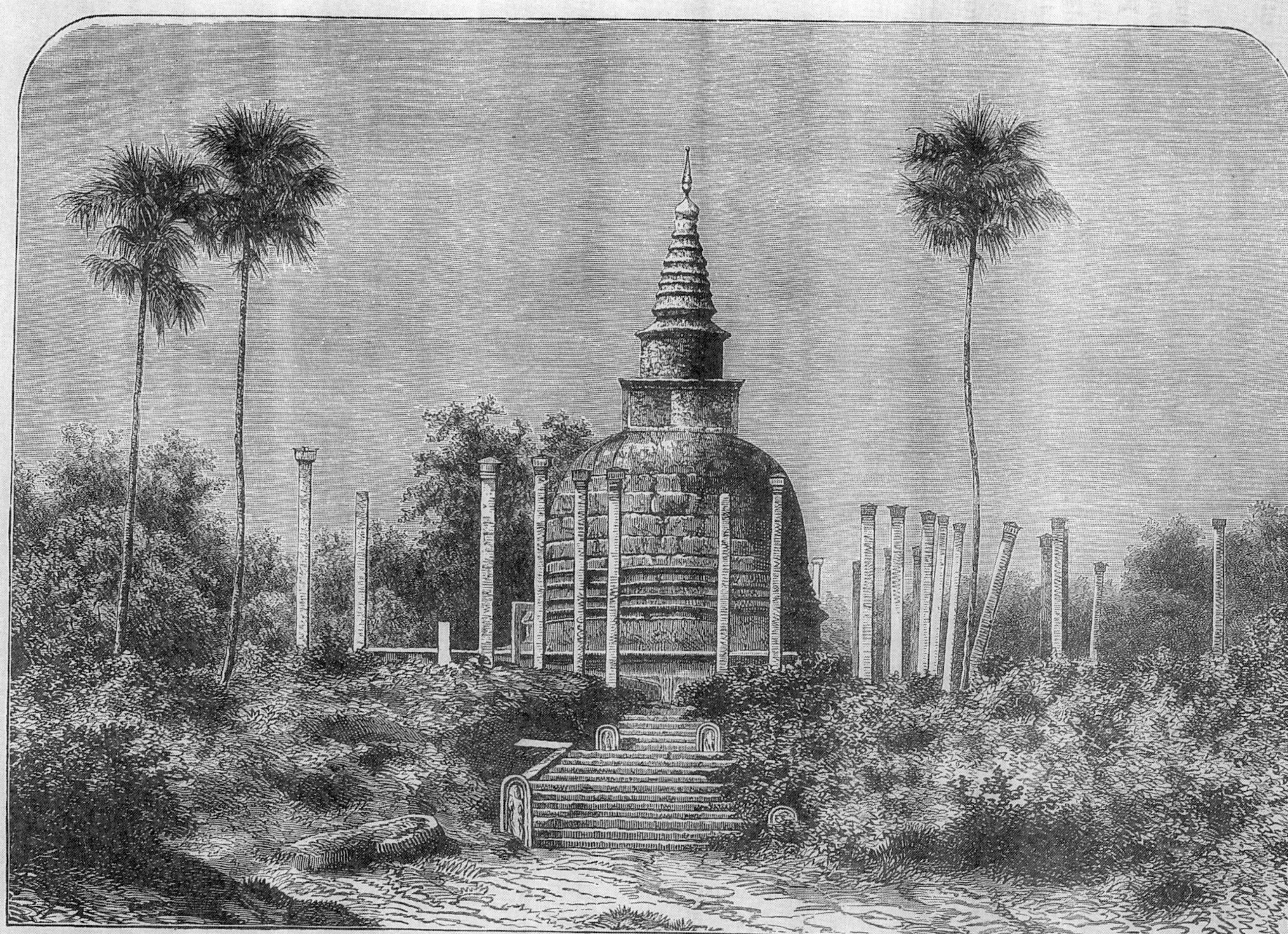

THUPARAMA DAGOBA, ANURAJAPURA.

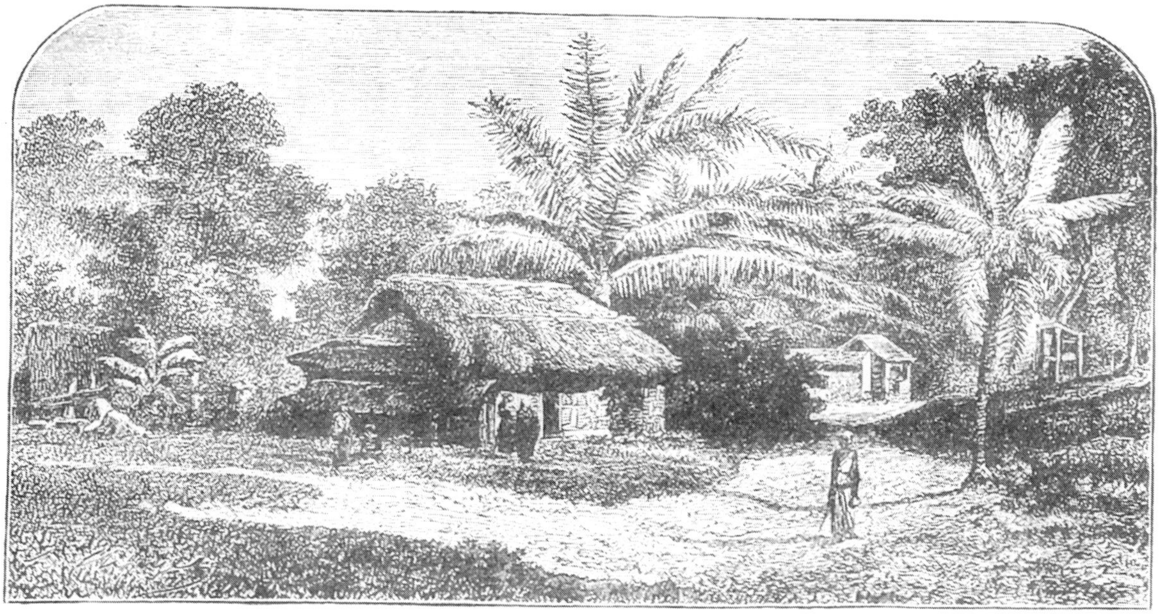

COTTAGES NEAR GALLE.

CEYLON.

POSITION AND ASPECT OF THE ISLAND—GALLE AND COLOMBO—NEWERA ELLIA AND PEDRO-TALLA-GALLA—ADAM'S PEAK AND KANDY—THE BO TREE—THE RUINED CITIES—ANURAJAPURA AND POLLONARUA—CHRISTIANITY IN THE ISLAND.

CEYLON in shape and position hangs like a pear from the southeast coast of the Indian Peninsula. The isthmus called Adam's Bridge forms, as it were, the stalk connecting the island with the continent; the name Adam's Bridge arising from the Mohammedan legend that on his expulsion from Paradise, Adam passed by this singular causeway into Ceylon. The northern portion, answering to the thin part of the pear, is one vast forest,—interminable jungle,—dotted sparsely with specks of yellow green cultivation, but containing the ruins of the two ancient capitals, and, on the east coast, the port of Trincomalee. The lower half of the island swells out in the Kandyan provinces into a mass of gneiss and granite mountains, with a margin of rich and luxuriant lower land; and here we find the best scenery and the chief centers of modern enterprise. Almost in the middle of the island is the capital, Kandy, connected by railway with Colombo on the west coast; and at the southwest corner is the former port of call, Point de Galle.

To the sea-trained eye of the voyager across the hot Indian Ocean from the east or west, Ceylon unfolds a scene of loveliness and grandeur unsurpassed by any land. It enjoys two monsoons in the year, and the abundant supply of moisture thus afforded clothes it with perpetual green. Its slopes are enameled with verdure, flowers of gorgeous hues deck its plains, palms of all descriptions abound, climbing plants rooted in the rocks hang down in huge festoons, and trees dip their foliage

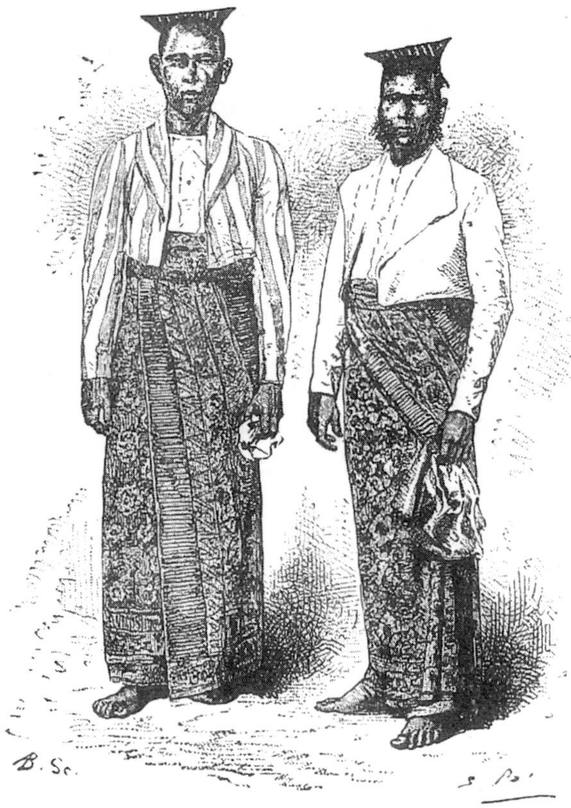

SINGALESE MEN OF THE COAST.

into the sea. By the Brahmans the island was called Lanka, "the resplendent"; by the Buddhists, "a pearl upon the brow of India"; by the Chinese, "the island of jewels"; by the Greeks, "the land of the hyacinth and the ruby." It has with reason been regarded as the country whither the ships of Solomon came for "gold and silver, ivory and apes, and peacocks" (1 Kings x. 11, 22), and the "almug trees, and precious stones in abundance from Ophir," are the most obvious productions of Ceylon. The very terms by which these things are designated in the Hebrew Bible are identical, Sir J. E. Tenant tells us, with the Tamil names by which some of them are still called. Fable contributes to the charm attaching to Ceylon. The tale of Sinbad in the *Arabian Nights* runs that in the Indian Ocean, near a mountainous island of loadstone, the ships fell asunder, and nails, and everything of iron flew to the loadstone; and hence native boats are put together without the use of iron nails. Bishop Heber's "spicy breezes" of poetry, are hardly in keeping with fact, because the cinnamon gives forth its odor only when crushed. Yet they bear witness to a fascinating charm belonging to the island, and Milton has immortalized them in his great epic where he says of Arabia:

> To those who sail
> Beyond the Cape of Hope, and now are past
> Mozambic, off at sea northeast winds blow
> Sabean odors from the spicy shore
> Of Araby the blest.

Ceylon is a little smaller than Ireland, and its population now, 1891, three millions. They are mainly of two races, the Tamils, of black complexion and slight-limbed, active and wiry, a mixed Dravidian race from South India, and the Singalese. The Singalese, again, are two types, the Kandyan type of highlanders, of robust frame, hairy chest, open countenance, yellow brown tint, and the coast

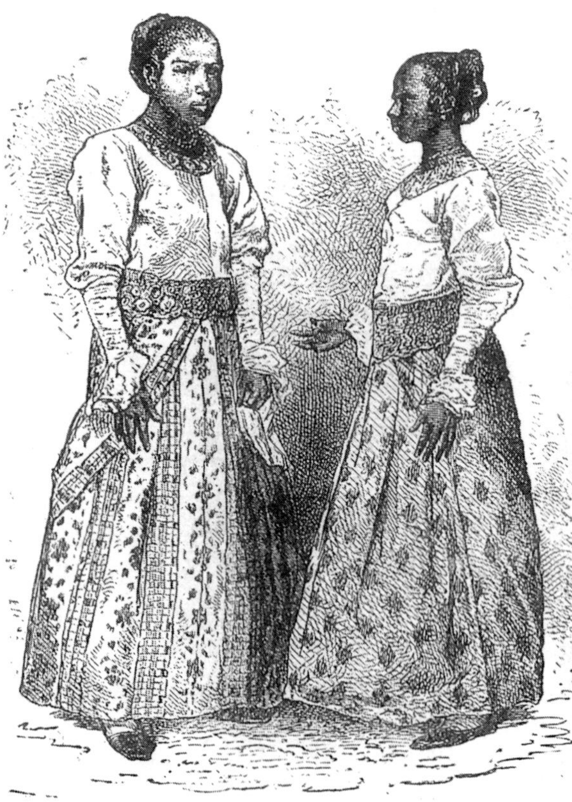

SINGALESE WOMEN OF THE COAST.

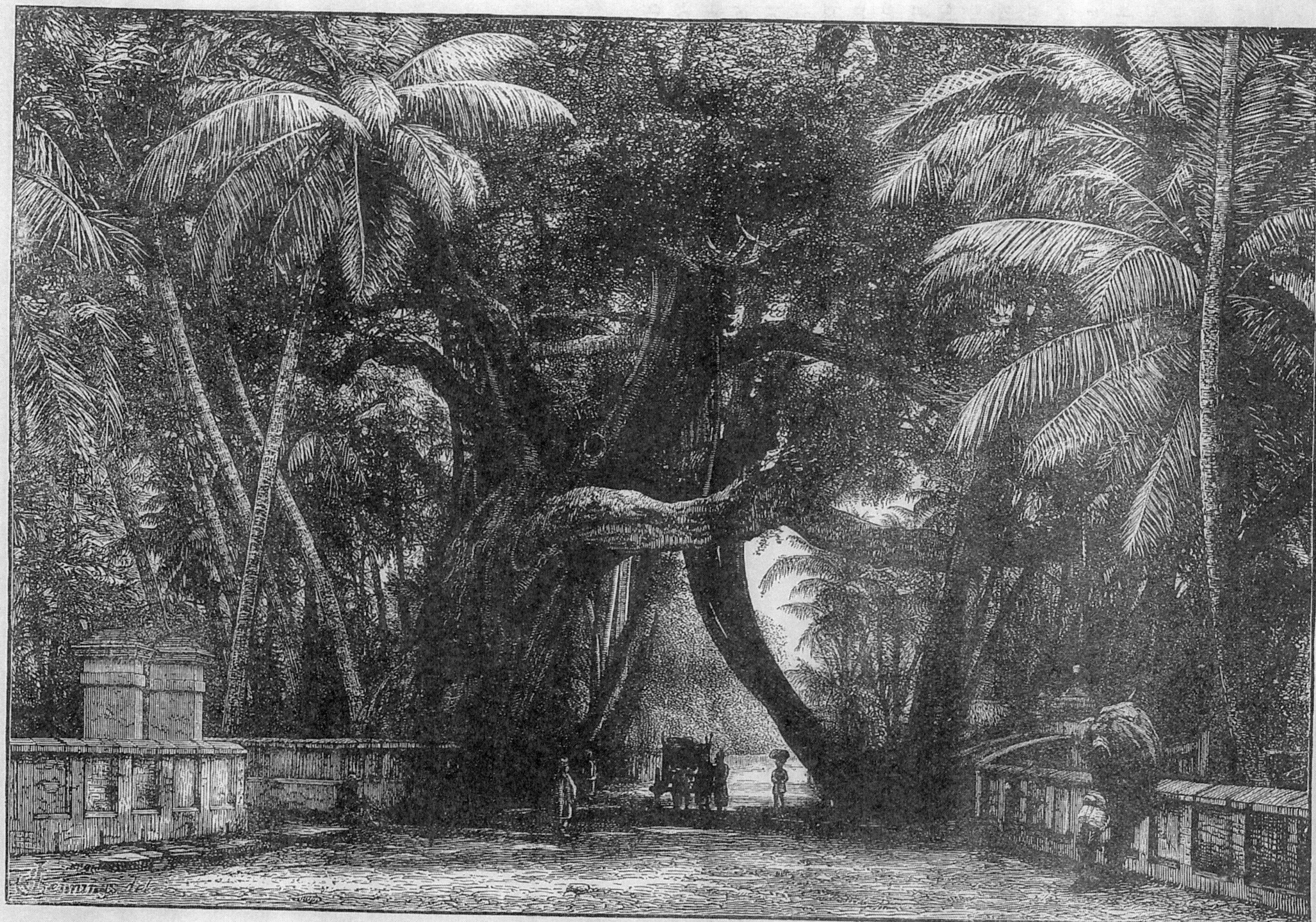

ON THE ROAD FROM GALLE TO COLOMBO.

Singalese, effeminate-looking, with little beard and long hair rolled into a lump at the back of the head and fastened by a tortoise-shell comb. The Tamils of the north are in religion Brahmans, the Singalese of the south are Buddhists. Buddhism was brought hither from India fully two centuries B. C. Its sacred books in Pali, written on *Olas, i. e.* Palmyra palm leaves, are called the *Pitakas*, the three baskets, treasuries, or collections, viz.: 1. Rules of the Order; 2. Doctrine; 3. Supplementary matter. Its temples are called *Dagabas*. A dagoba—from *dhatu*, a relic, and *gabbhan*, a shrine—is properly a monument raised to preserve one of the relics of Gautama Buddha. Fragments of his bones, locks of his hair, are inclosed in masses of masonry; a dome of brickwork resting on a square elevated platform covers the shrine, and is surmounted by a *tee* or pinnacle. The oldest of these shrines is that raised by King Tissa, B. C. 200, over the collar-bone of Buddha. The Dagoba of Anurajapura, built B. C. 89, was four hundred feet high—forty feet higher than St. Paul's. Besides Buddhism in the south, and Brahmanism chiefly in the north, there is Mohammedanism among the Moormen, who are in the main of Persian origin. Romanism, planted by the Portuguese, took its complexion from Buddhism, and in its rites conformed to the heathen customs of the people; indeed, the churches at Jaffna, in the north, were fitted up as theaters. The Parawas, or fishermen class, were the first to embrace Christianity.

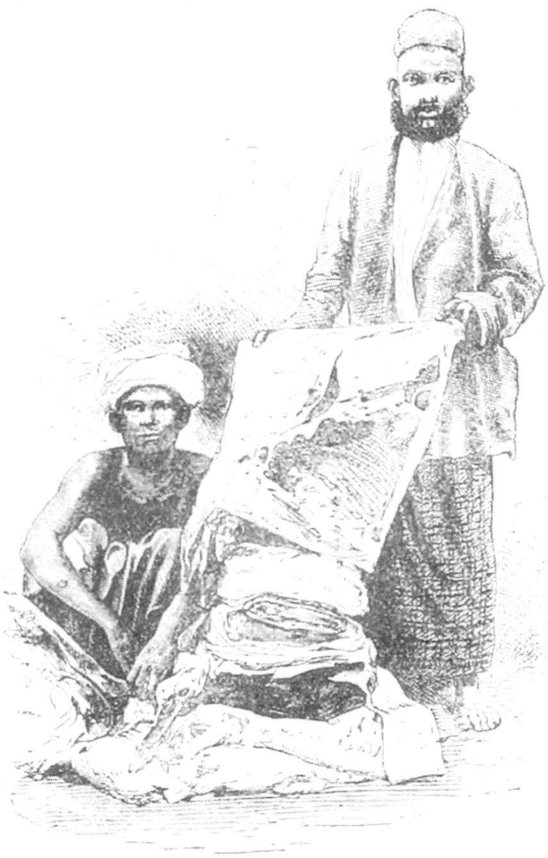

MOORMEN HAWKERS.

The *Dipawansa*, "island history," and the *Mahawansa*, "great history," contain the Chronicles of Ceylon. They tell us that for four hundred years, from the seventh to the eleventh century, the incursions and exploits of the Malabars harassed the island. What tended to civilize—as the huge reservoirs called "consecrated lakes" to water the paddy or rice lands still bear witness—was introduced by the northern rulers; and all that contributed to debase is traceable to the Malabars. The reign of Prakrama Bahu, A. D. 1150, stands out prominently as a time of prosperity and advance. Religion and agriculture went hand in hand, and huge tanks were constructed, called "seas of Prakram"; security of life and property was established, so that a girl decked with gold might traverse the island in safety. But it came to pass that in the year 1505 ships from Portugal arrived at Jaffna and Colombo. The Portuguese by degrees gained a footing along the coast, and they held territory there for a hundred and forty years. In 1602 the Dutch began to come, and by degrees overthrew and supplanted the Portuguese, occupying Galle in 1640. Theirs was a military tenure, and lasted also one hundred and forty years. In 1796 their settlements were in turn ceded to the British, who have borne rule ever since, and in 1815 won by conquest the Kandyan provinces.

Nearing Galle, but still some miles from land, we met several of the curiously constructed "double canoes" which the Singalese fishermen use. They are from twenty to thirty feet long, only twenty inches wide, three feet in depth, including the washboard, which is sewn to the gunwale, and are hollowed out of a single stem. The most striking feature about them is the balance-log, a solid, buoyant outrigger, the same length as the boat, and like a second canoe, fixed by two long curved bamboo poles projecting eighteen feet from one side and carrying a high sail hoisted on two poles. This outrigger is always kept to windward when sailing, the canoes having prows at both ends, and being steered with short flat paddles. In these boats the fishermen can sail ten knots an hour, and they venture out twenty miles to sea.

Conveyed from the steamer across the harbor within the old Dutch ramparts, the traveler soon finds himself in Galle, besieged by hawkers (chiefly Moormen) of precious stones, tortoise-shell, ebony, stuffs, and fancy work in wood and gold; but ridding himself of these he will gladly enjoy a stroll along the ramparts and by the lighthouse, and a drive to the Cinnamon Gardens and Wakwella. The cinnamon laurel grows to the height of six or eight feet, and is not barked before the ninth year. Peeling the bark begins in May and lasts till November. The beautiful shrubs are now growing wild, the cinnamon trade having long ago passed to other lands through the monopoly of the Dutch.

At the foot of one of Galle's wooded hills is a Buddhist temple, apparently modern and decorated in a very gaudy fashion. The paintings represent scenes in the history of kings and others. Within is a gigantic figure of Buddha, with images of Siva and Vishnu on either side. The Buddhist priests wear bright yellow garments hung on their dark, lanky forms. The usual worship consists mainly in the offering of flowers and fruits.

The railway from Galle to Colombo not being yet complete, we drove in her Majesty's mail—a wretched conveyance, shockingly horsed—along the lovely road of seventy miles which skirts the shore. It is an avenue of stately palms with a rich undergrowth of tropical trees and gorgeous orchids. Away on the right are the mountains, away to the left glitters the blue sea; the beach is fringed with verdure, and at the headlands the ripples kiss the overhanging leaves. The tides about Ceylon are very slight, the water falling only thirty inches. The white cottages of the natives, each with its garden of cocoa-nuts, nestle in the groves, and the fishermen's canoes skim along the sea. The natives whom we pass look clean and picturesque, but their mouths are invariably discolored with betel chewing. The leaves of the betel vine, together with lime and the sliced nuts of the areca palm, form a tonic, which from time immemorial it has been the national habit to chew, and the mixture imparts a blood-like color to the mouth. The betel is an intoxicating kind of pepper, and with the Singalese answers to the opium of the Chinese, and to the tobacco of other nations, but it is not considered so injurious.

The cocoa-nut trees about the dwellings of the natives along this road are countless; and they have a saying that the cocoa-nut, like the magpie and robin, will only flourish within the sound of the human voice. Like the Palmyra palm in the north of Ceylon, the cocoa-uut in the south yields most of the necessaries of life. Its fruit furnishes food, its shell drinking vessels, its juice palm wine and sugar, its stem materials for building, its leaves roofs, matting, baskets, and paper. The number of these trees in the island is estimated to be twenty millions. The natives climb them with great agility, partly with the help of bamboo ladders, and oftener with the help of a short band of cocoa-nut fiber between the feet or round the loins.

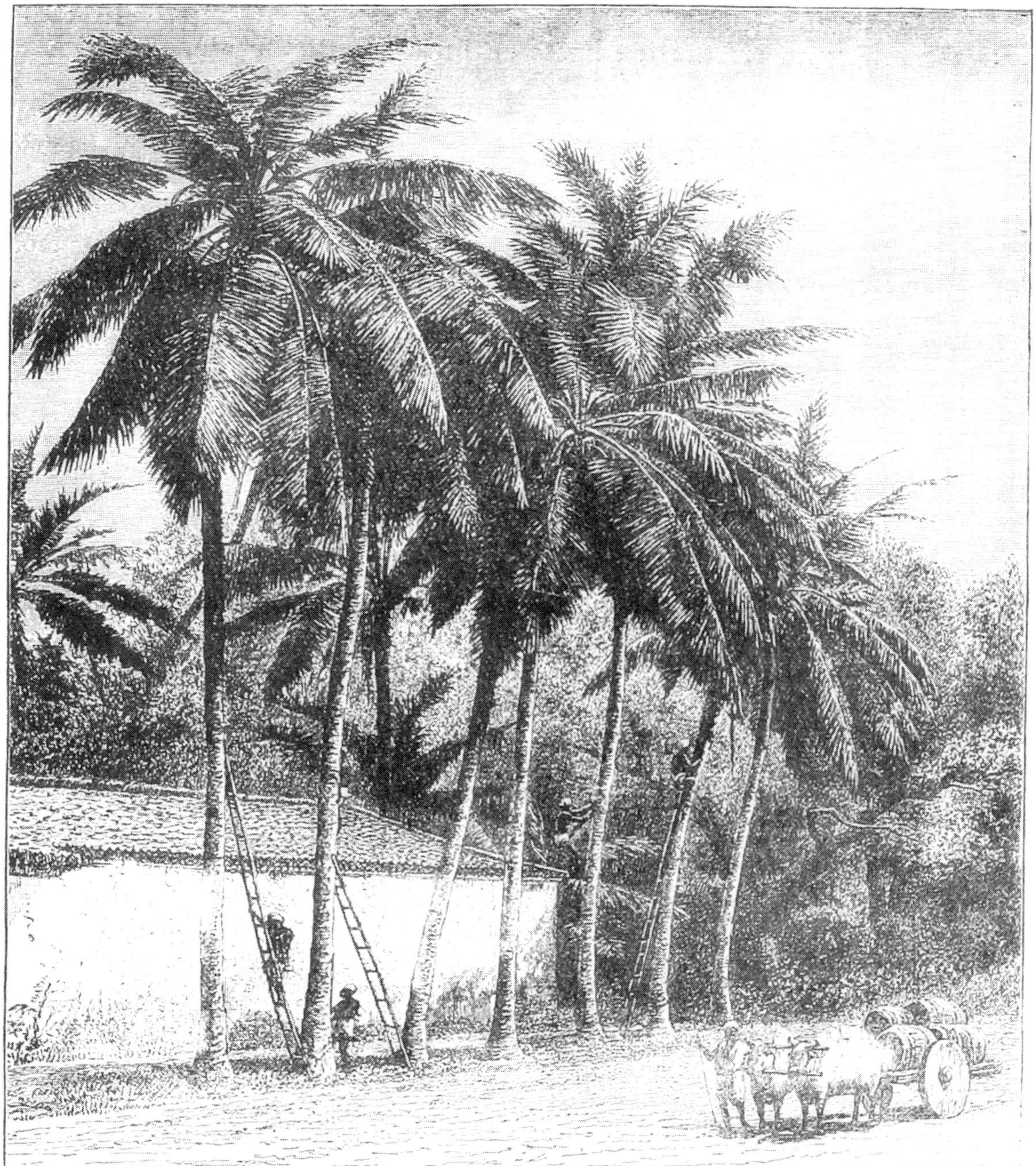

COCOA-NUT TREES AND CLIMBERS.

The city of Colombo, whose population now numbers one hundred and twenty thousand, presents but few features of interest to the tourist.[1] It extends about four

[1] Now that Colombo is the calling port for Oriental steamers, its harbor and streets present an attractive appearance. A great number of Europeans are here, for a longer or shorter time, enjoying its perpetual summer. The artificial harbor and the elaborate water works,—costing five million dollars,—the delightful drives about Colombo, the Lunatic Asylum, Leper Hospital, the Medical School, Wesley College, Wellewatta Industrial Home, and numerous mission stations will furnish ample materials of interest to the stranger. The ten days spent here by the writer were the most restful passed in India.—ED.

miles along the coast and two miles inland, and is divided, like most Indian cities, into the black, or native town, and the European quarter. The buildings in the latter are chiefly of Dutch origin—as the fort, the belfry and clock tower, the barracks, and the Wolfendahl Church. The old name Kalambu was altered by the Portuguese to Colombo in honor of Columbus. Here one sees the Singalese chiefly as servants, the Parsees as merchants, the Tamils as laborers, the Moors as retail dealers. The heat at mid-day is most oppressive, but the drive along the Galle Face by the sea at sunset is cool and refreshing. A favorite resort, seven miles south by railway, is Mount Lavinia, on the sea, once a governor's house, now a hotel, near which is a magnificent banyan tree. In Colombo there are two cathedrals, one Roman Catholic, the other English; and in the street of the dealers in rice is a grotesquely ornamented Hindu temple. In Colombo the raw coffee brought from the plantations undergoes the process of curing at several mills for the purpose. Here may be seen the drying of the beans; the removal of the skin by passing the beans under rollers; the picking out of the bad berries, done by women and children; the distribution of the different sizes by means of sieves; the process of packing in huge barrels for exportation. The Tamil women employed in these establishments present a neat, healthy, and happy appearance. We found the new Museum in the midst of the Cinnamon Gardens well worth a visit. Besides the natural and manufactured products of the island, there are archæological remains from ruined cities, and in particular a magnificent stone lion. The drive round the lake is lovely, and several miles in extent, but the moist heat was like a perpetual Turkish bath.

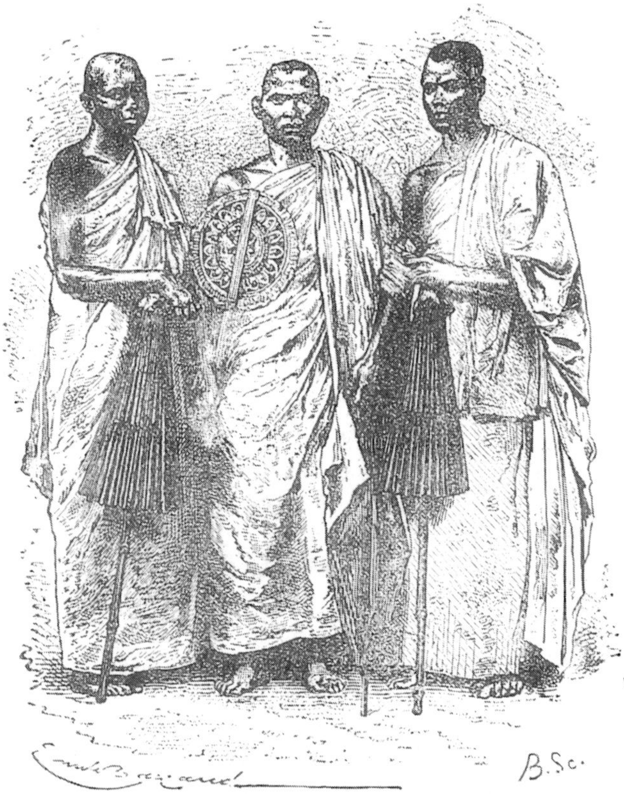

BUDDHIST PRIEST WITH NOVICES.

The distance from Colombo inland to Kandy is seventy-five miles, and the railway winds its way among the mountains, through scenery combining Alpine grandeur with tropical luxuriance. A huge, isolated hill, called the Bible Rock from its resemblance to a Bible open upon a cushion, stands out conspicuously in the distance on the right. The line winds and curves round beetling cliffs and overhanging precipices draped with luxuriant creepers. Coolies, *i. e.*, laborers, chiefly Tamils, are conveyed in gangs of not fewer than six at reduced rates, upon the certificate from their importer or estate manager. Children *under four feet in height* are charged half fare. The journey occupies four hours and a half. A branch line leads to Gampola, which is the station for Newera Ellia. Gampola, the last of the native capitals, was fifty years ago the cradle, and is still the gateway, of the great coffee plantations. Though the plant had before been brought to Ceylon, the Portuguese and Dutch did little or nothing for its cultivation. It was not until 1825, that by the removal of the heavy duty the plant rose to importance among the products of the island. Now, all round Gampola, for miles, the hills are covered with coffee plantations. The leaves are bright and smooth, like the laurel, but darker; the flowers are white, and of sweet odor; the berries are crimson, like cherries. It is calculated that two hundred thousand natives are employed on the plantations, which cover over one hundred thousand acres.[1]

A coach runs daily from Gampola, winding up the mountains through Pussilawa, "valley of flower," to Ramboddie in four hours, and the views are majestic and charming. In the magnificent glen of Ramboddie we reach a barrier of mountains seemingly impassable. Waterfalls on every hand come tumbling over precipices, and

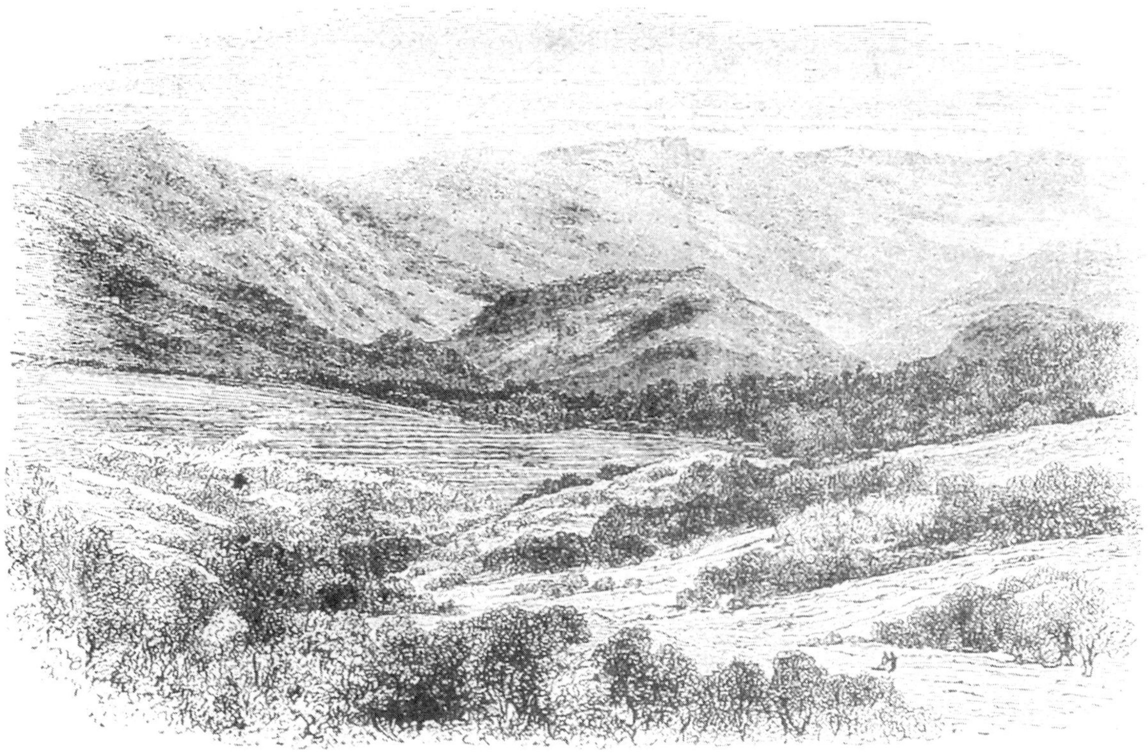

THE PEDRO-TALLA-GALLA RANGE.

roaring through deep ravines mantled with palms and orchids, yellow gamboge trees, and white-flowered daturas. From this point the road climbs the mountain gorge in terraces—cut in many places out of the rock—through a wild forest to the height of six thousand feet; and from the summit of the pass a view of Newera Ellia is obtained. At this height, the coffee plantations give place to those of tea, lately introduced, and found to grow well at this altitude. Several acres of forest have been cleared for tea plantations. From this point you rapidly descend into the far-famed valley of Newera Ellia; and taking up your quarters at one of the homely and comfortable lodging-houses, after the heat of Colombo and the railway, you now feel cold enough to be glad of a fire.

[1] Since the blight on coffee, here and elsewhere, attention is given to the raising of Ceylon tea. While I was there a dealer remarked that thirty-five million pounds of tea had been exported during the previous year. The jobbing price was twenty-four cents, higher than that of Chinese exporters. The quality is the best in the world, and Chinamen are coming to Ceylon to learn, as this is the only machine-made tea in the market. There are two hundred thousand acres under cultivation, and three hundred thousand persons employed at an average of thirteen cents a day, of which amount they save one-half. Ceylon tea sells in New York for one dollar a pound.—ED.

NEWERA ELLIA, the Buxton of Ceylon, its great sanatorium, whither the jaded European, overdone with the heat of Galle or Colombo, resorts for refreshment and rest, is a widespreading valley, green and grassy, watered by crystal streams, high up among the mountains at the foot of Pedro-talla-galla, the highest mountain in Ceylon. Here one seems to get into England again; English-looking cottages, with gardens full of English flowers, fruit trees, and vegetables; oaks and firs, green fields and

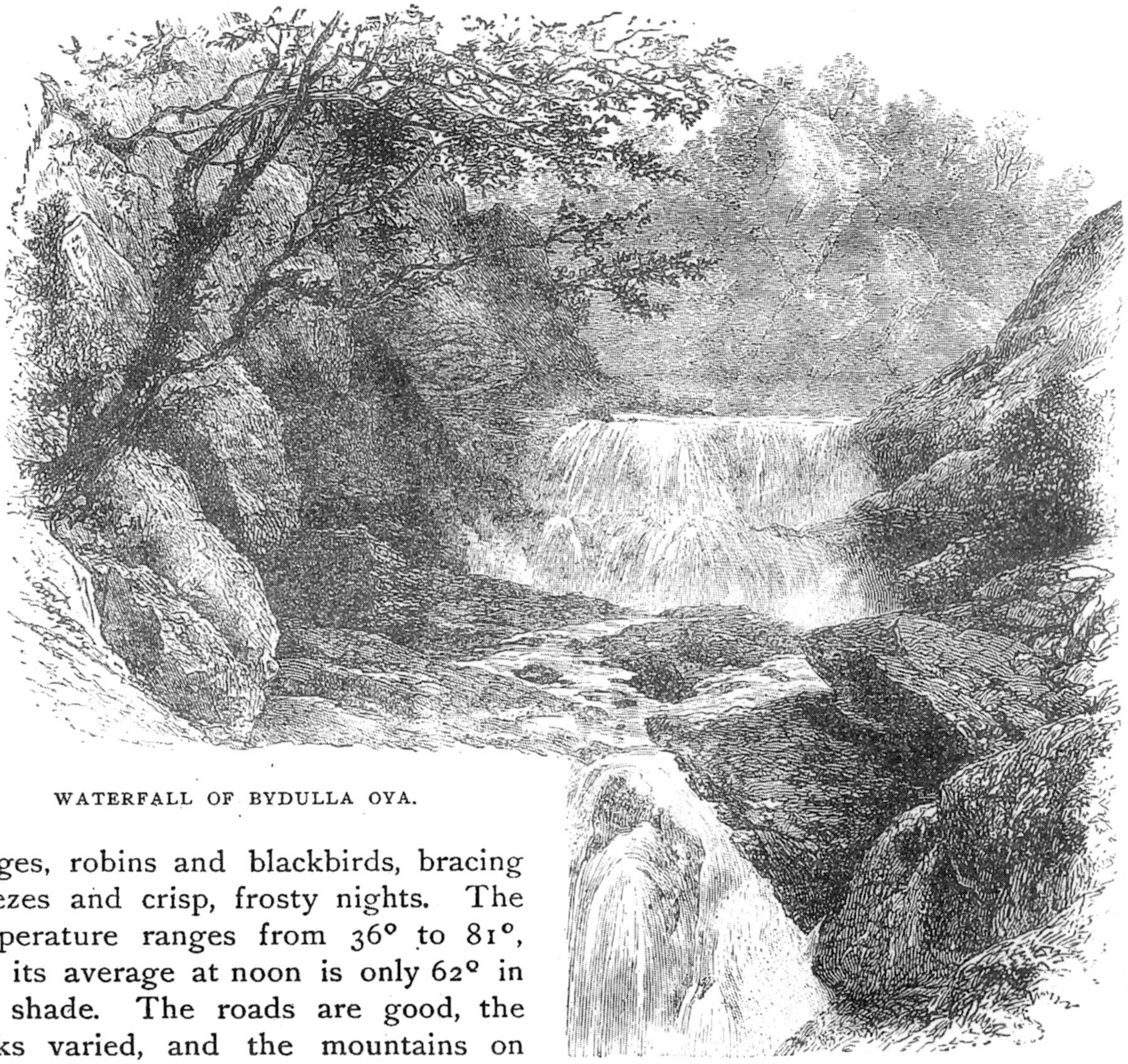

WATERFALL OF BYDULLA OYA.

hedges, robins and blackbirds, bracing breezes and crisp, frosty nights. The temperature ranges from 36° to 81°, and its average at noon is only 62° in the shade. The roads are good, the walks varied, and the mountains on every side invite to a sturdy climb.

A well-kept bridle-path, cut through the forest in zigzags, leads to the summit of Pedro-talla-galla, which is eight thousand three hundred and forty feet above the sea, or nine hundred and forty higher than Adam's Peak. Here one soon gets into the lonely jungle, where in the early morning nature teems with life and motion, and the air is melodious with the voice of birds. We started at 6 A. M. and reached the top of the mountain in two hours and a half. At the height of about seven thousand five hundred feet we came upon a large antlered elk quietly grazing; he gave a deep bark, and scampered off. The Ceylon elk is a large animal, four feet high, of a dark brown color, rough mane, heavy antlers, and body five feet long. Almost to the summit there is brushwood, and the rhododendrons were in full bloom. The

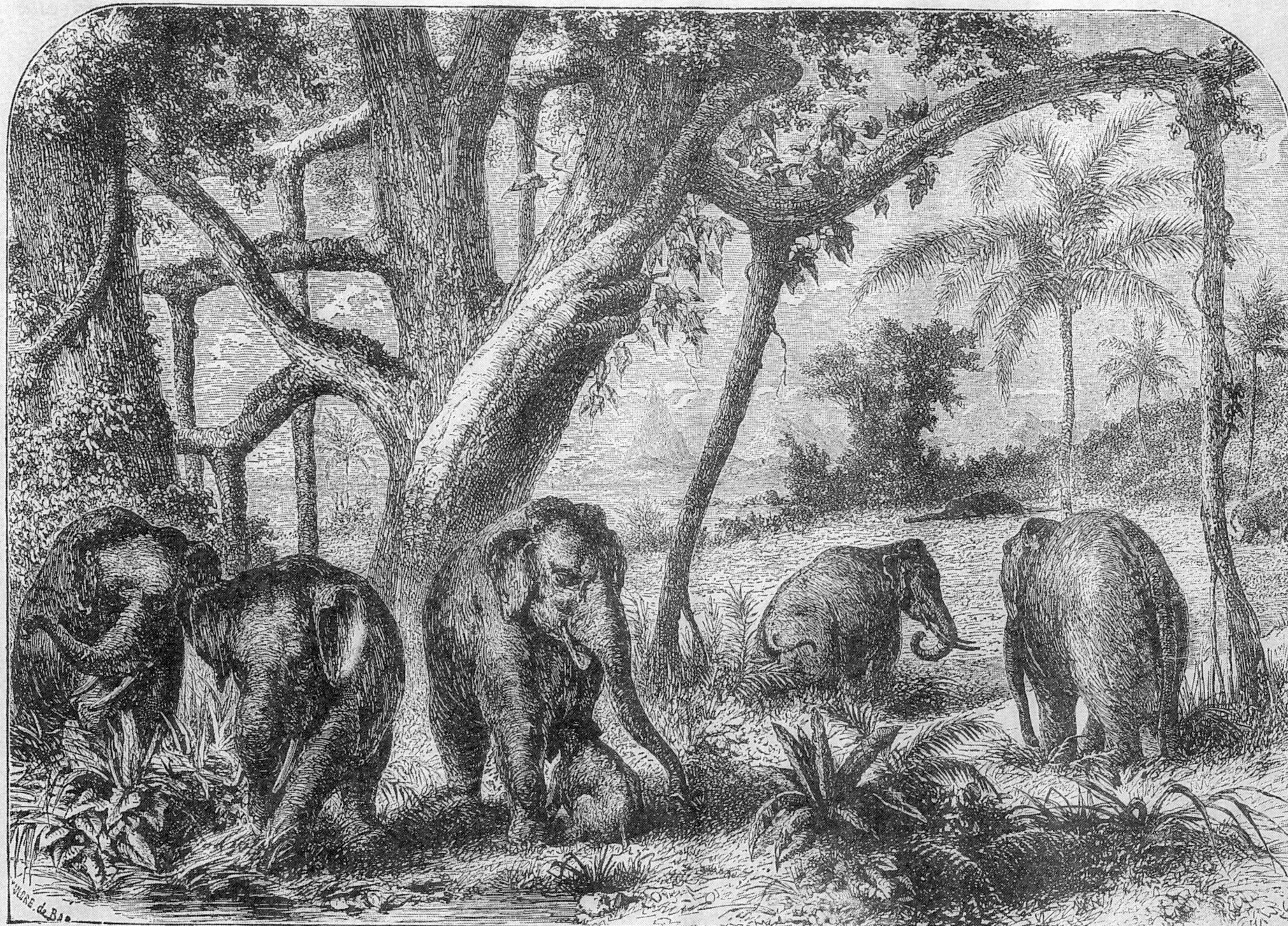

CEYLON ELEPHANTS.

morning was beautifully fine, and the prospect was most extensive and delightful. The sea was visible in the distance toward the west and south, Adam's Peak to the west, the hills of Kandy to the north, and those of Badulla to the east. From Newera Ellia to Badulla the road descends three thousand feet in forty miles, and commands splendid views. No scene in nature can be more peaceful and lovely than the valley of the Badulla Oya. At Ella the river forces its way through a wild ravine in a series of falls. There are no lakes, properly speaking, in Ceylon, but from these mountain ranges one sees what look like lakes, the immense tanks, relics of a former civilization, formed by means of artificial dams drawn across valleys

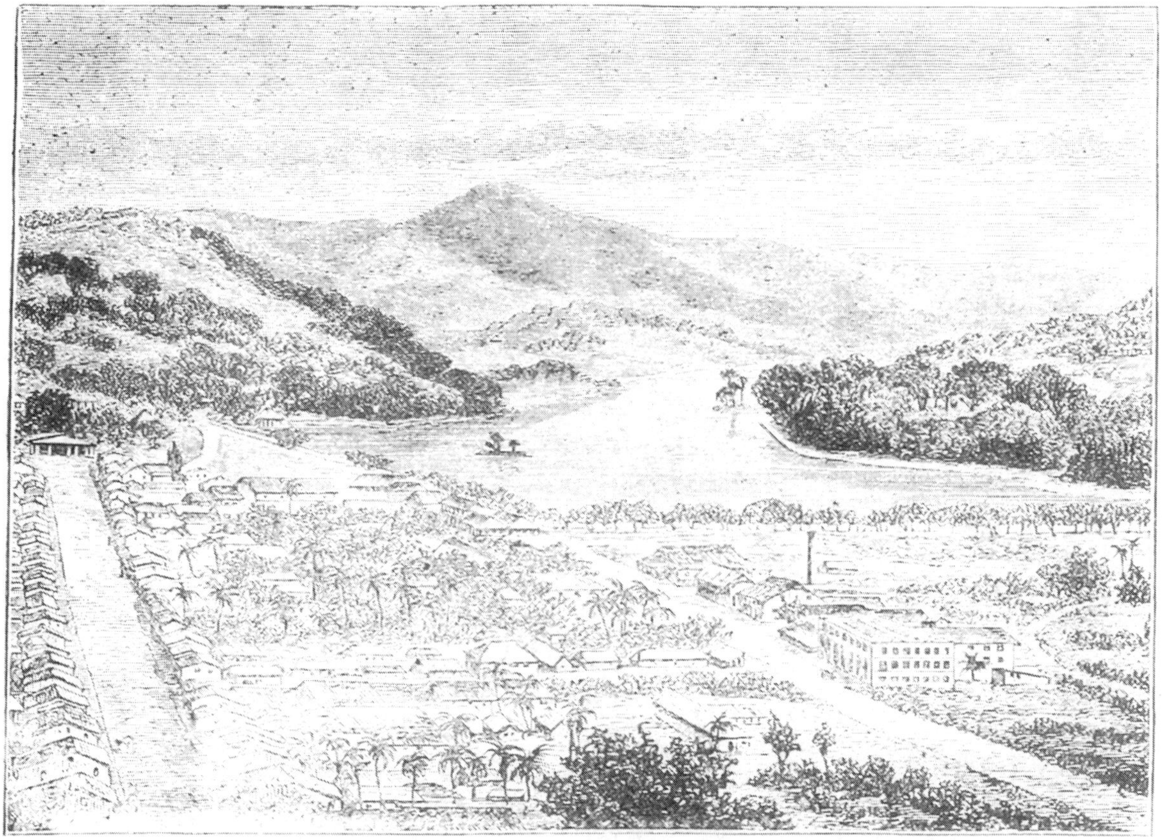

KANDY.

shut in by hills, and making sheets of water six, eight, or ten miles long, by two or three wide. The embankments are from sixty to seventy feet high, and two hundred feet broad at the base; they consist of earthwork, faced in some cases with stone. The design of these immense reservoirs was to supply water for the paddy lands in the districts lying north of the mountains. Every village northward was provided with a tank, and canals conveyed the water to the fields. They date from the seventh century downward.

Descending from Pedro-talla-galla, I came upon the track of a wild elephant. The jungle was freshly trodden down, soil disturbed, and trees uprooted. It is an Eastern saying that the last word can never be said about an elephant. When the British first came elephants were numerous, but now they are rare. Very few Ceylon elephants have tusks. They are smaller than the African; twice the circumference of the foot gives the animal's height, which is usually eight or nine feet. They are said to live seventy years, and it is a trite saying, "A dead elephant is never seen." The elephant has marvelous facility in ascending and descending mountains, the joints of the hind legs bending inward, and enabling them to kneel like a man, and in this posture to slide down, the forelegs being kept straight out. At the approach of the white man they retire; they possess defective sight but powerful scent. A story is told of a wild elephant at Goa which had got loose in the market-place, and was destroying all before it; but recognizing in the crowd the child of a woman

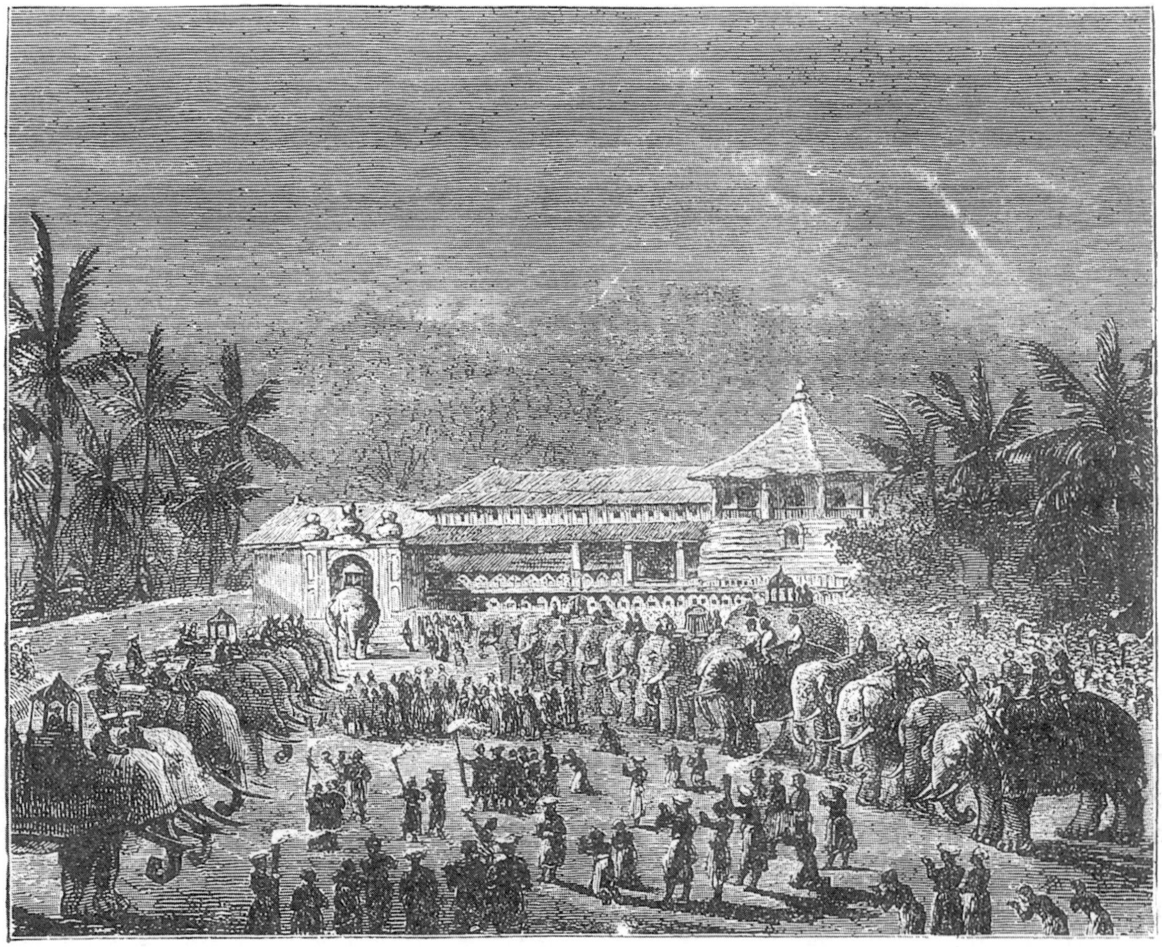

TEMPLE OF THE DALADA.

who had been in the habit of feeding him when passing her shop, he took it up in his trunk and carried it safely home. Elephants have been exported from Ceylon to India ever since the First Punic War. Of late their numbers have been considerably reduced. They cannot lift the head above the level of the shoulder, and they show timidity and shyness at the sight of man. They like the mountains and the shady thickets. They go in herds, and a solitary elephant is usually a thief.

The famous Adam's Peak may be ascended either from Newera Ellia or the Maskeliya side, where the climb is comparatively easy, or from Ratnapura, on the south side, which is reached by coach from Colombo. The rocky cone which forms its summit is climbed with the help of chains fastened in the rock. A fearful ladder, forty feet high, lands us on the top, where is a small temple, and beneath a sheltered space beside is the *Sri pada*, or footprint, a natural indentation in the rock, artificially made to assume the shape of a man's left foot, five feet long by two and a half broad. The Brahmans call it the footstep of Siva, the Buddhists that of Buddha, the Chinese that of Fo, *i. e.*, Buddha, and afterward the Mohammedans called it the footprint of Adam. Adam, it was fabled, when driven from Paradise took refuge in Ceylon, and spent years of exile on this mountain before his reunion with Eve on Mount Arafath near Mecca. Hence the name Adam's Peak. Between Adam's Peak and the sea, quantities of precious stones have been found ; indeed, this is the

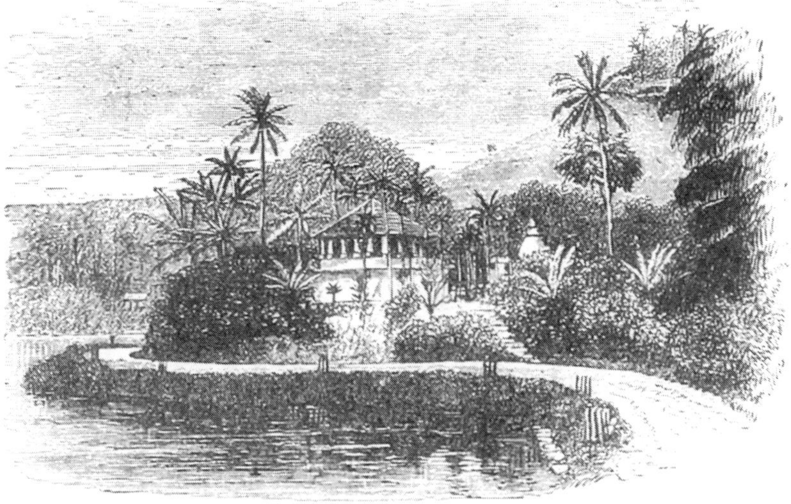

BUDDHIST TEMPLE, LAKE OF KANDY.

region where still they are sought—sapphires, amethysts, topazes, rubies. Ratnapura means "the city of rubies," and the sands of the rivers still abound with small particles of tiny gems. Lapidaries use it to polish softer stones. The cat's eye, a green translucent quartz, is specially appreciated by the Singalese. The precarious occupation of gem-hunting is chiefly carried on at Saffragam. The chief polishers and sellers of gems are Moormen.

The tourist in these mountain districts is almost sure to find something he does not want, in the form of leeches, whose presence is first discovered by the chill feeling of the creature hanging heavily on the skin when full and distended. They are about an inch in length, and only one-eighth of an inch in thickness, but they swell into more than twice that length and size. They make their way through the finest stocking. They live not in pools, but in rank and damp herbage. In moving, they plant one extremity on the ground and advance by semicircular strides. You may often see them hanging like tassels round the ankles of the palanquin bearers, and dogs and horses are tormented by them. Crocodiles too, are occasionally seen across one's path in dry weather when the tanks are low, making their way in search of water. They are very tenacious of life, indeed it is almost impossible to kill them.

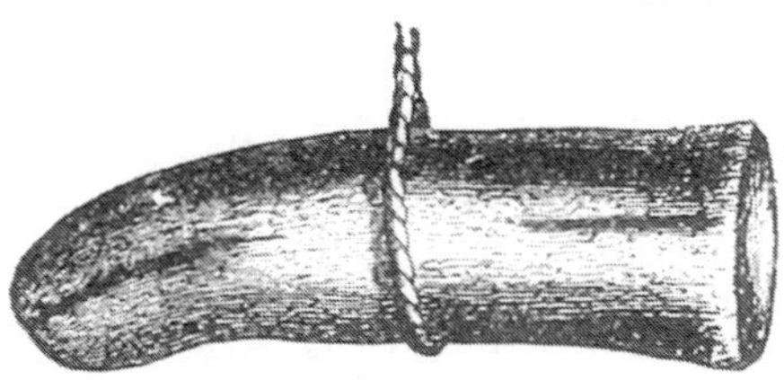

BUDDHA'S TOOTH.

Kandy, the ancient capital of the Highland Singalese, is a beautifully situated little city, of about ten thousand inhabitants, in a nest of hills, itself fifteen hundred feet above the sea; and the thickly wooded hills around it are fully two thousand feet high. At the foot of its main street, which slopes down a hill, is a long artificial lake, made in 1807 by the then King of Kandy; and this sheet of water adds much to the loveliness of the scene. Here, for centuries, the Kandyan kings lived secure, as if in their mountain fastnesses; but upon the conquest of the place by the British in 1815, a road was constructed through the mountains to the coast, which even still presents wonders of engineering skill; and now a railway sends two trains daily to and from Colombo in a four hours' journey. The climate is delightful and the scenery charming. From the fourteenth century downward, the place has been dis-

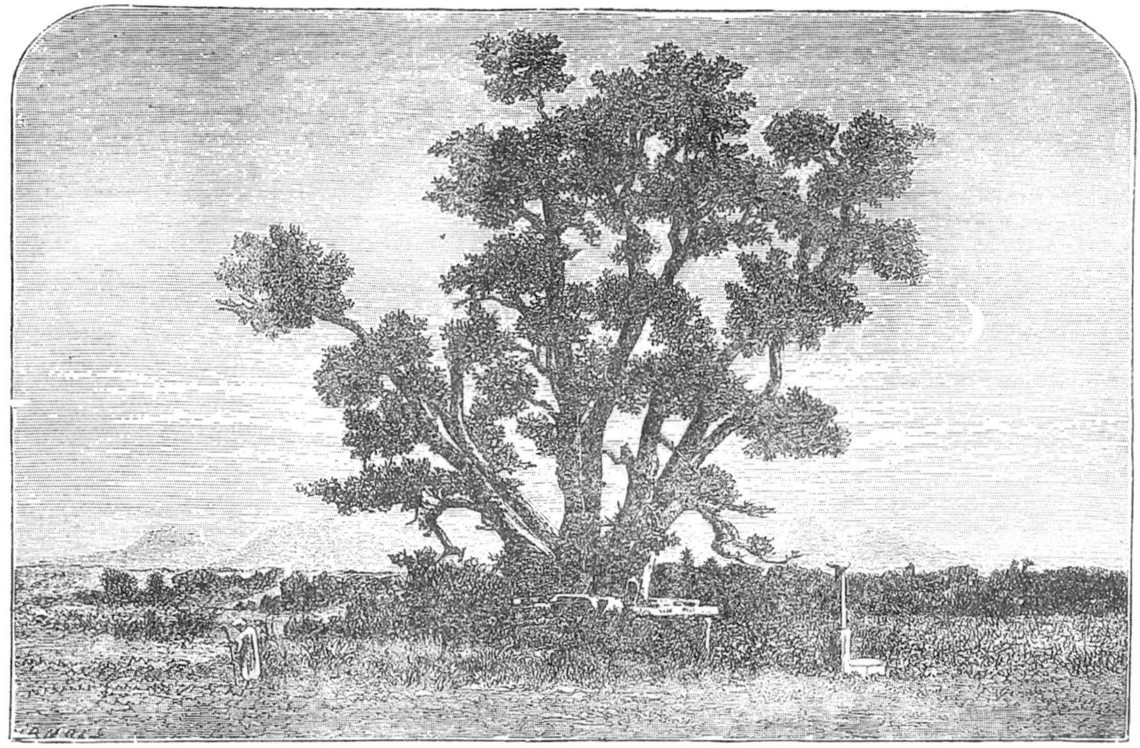

SACRED BO TREE, ANURAJAPURA, 2100 YEARS OLD.

tinguished as the headquarters of Buddhism, finding its center in the Temple of the Dalada, the shrine of Buddha's tooth, round which the Buddhist hierarchy gather. This, with the adjoining palace, is the most interesting building in Ceylon. There is an octagonal stone edifice of two stories, in the upper part of which is an Oriental library, containing several valuable Pali manuscripts, and the Buddhist scriptures written on wood and sumptuously bound. A balcony runs outside, on which the kings of Kandy were wont in former times to appear before the people, and to witness performances on the green below.

The relic of the left eye-tooth of Gautama Buddha, here said to be enshrined, has a curious history. Rescued from his funeral pile, B. C. 543, it was preserved for eight centuries at Dantapura in South India, and brought to Ceylon A. D. 310. The Malabars afterward captured it, and took it back to India, but the great Prakrama recovered it. The Portuguese missionaries got possession of it in the sixteenth century, carried it away to Goa, and after refusing a large ransom offered for it by the Singalese, reduced it to powder and destroyed it at Goa in the presence of witnesses.

The account of this destruction of the tooth is most circumstantial in the Portuguese records. Nevertheless, the Buddhist priests at Kandy produced another tooth, which they affirmed to be the real relic, that taken by the Portuguese being a counterfeit, and they conducted this to the shrine with great pomp and ceremonial. This is the relic now treasured with such care and reverence. It is probably not a human tooth at all, being, as those who have seen it affirm, much too large (two inches long) ever to have belonged to man. When the British got possession of it in 1815, there was great excitement, the relic being regarded as a sort of national palladium. They allowed it, however, to be restored to its shrine amid great festivities. The sanctuary in which it reposes is a small chamber, without a ray of light, in which the air is stifling, hot and heavy with the perfume of flowers, situated in the

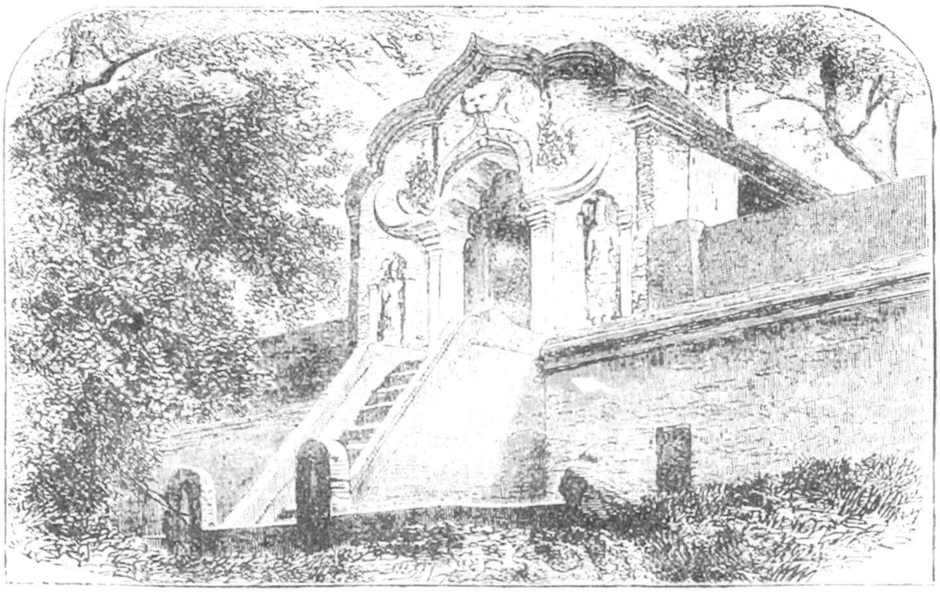

GATEWAY LEADING TO THE SACRED TREE, ANURAJAPURA.

inmost recesses of the temple. The frames of the doors of this chamber are inlaid with carved ivory, and on a massive silver table stands the bell-shaped shrine, jeweled and hung round with chains, and consisting of six cases of silver gilt, inlaid with rubies. On removing the innermost one, about one foot in height, a golden lotus is disclosed, on which reposes the sacred relic. In front of the silver altar is a table upon which worshipers deposit their gifts.

The hills round Kandy command charming views of the city and the outlying district. Gregory's Drive is a new road that winds up the hill above the miniature lake, with bungalows looking out on lovely scenery; and a path through the opposite woods, called Lady Horton's Walk, leads up to a point commanding a panoramic view of the Vale of Dumbera and the Knuckles range of hills, the river Mahawelli-ganga flowing rapidly below. The Peridenia Botanical Garden, covering one hundred and fifty acres, is about three miles from the town, and is rich in all varieties of palms and other tropical plants. A fine avenue of india rubber trees leads to a noble group of palms—the palmyra, the talipat, the areca, the date palm, the cocoa-nut, and a huge Kew Palm House in the open air, with a river overhung with bamboos flowing through. The sacred *Bo tree* of the Singalese, to which they, as Buddhists, attach symbolically the same importance as Christians do to the cross, is found close to every dagoba. Buddha himself is said to have made frequent allusions to the growth of this tree as an emblem of the rapid propagation of his faith. It differs from the

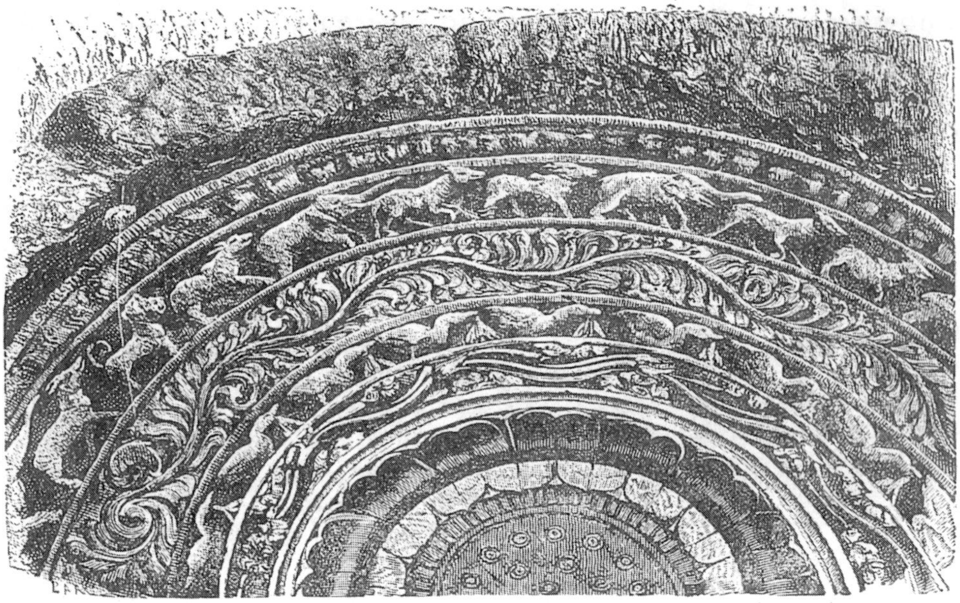

CARVED STONE AT ANURAJAPURA.

banyan by sending down no roots from its branches, but its heart-shaped leaves are attached to the stem by so slender a stalk that they appear to be ever in motion, and thus, like the leaves of the aspen, of which the cross was thought to be made, whose

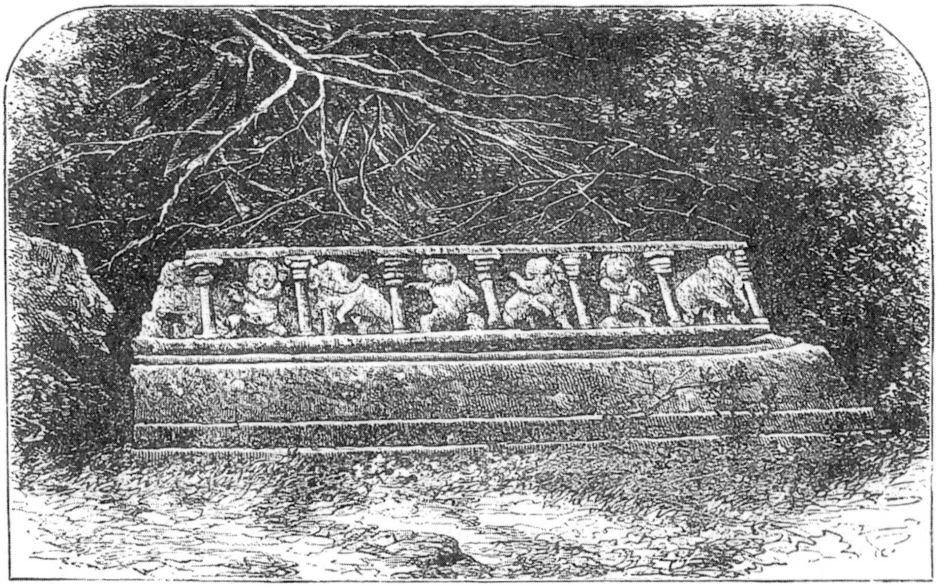

CARVED STONE AT ANURAJAPURA.

leaves are said to tremble in recollection of the crucifixion, those of the Bo tree are supposed by the Buddhists to tremble in remembrance of the sacred scene of which they were the witnesses. It was while reclining under the shade of this tree at Budh

Gaya in Magadha or Bihar that Gautama received Buddhahood. The first Bo tree in Ceylon is said to have been sent by Asoka, king of Magadha, a branch from the parent-tree at Uruwela, B. C. 245, and to have been planted at the old capital Anurajapura. It is still pointed out as the oldest tree in the world, and is said to be the parent-tree from which all other Bo trees in the island have been propagated. A wall is now built round it, and a flight of stone steps leads to the sacred inclosure. Pilgrims come to visit it from China, and even from Japan. The solitary column on the

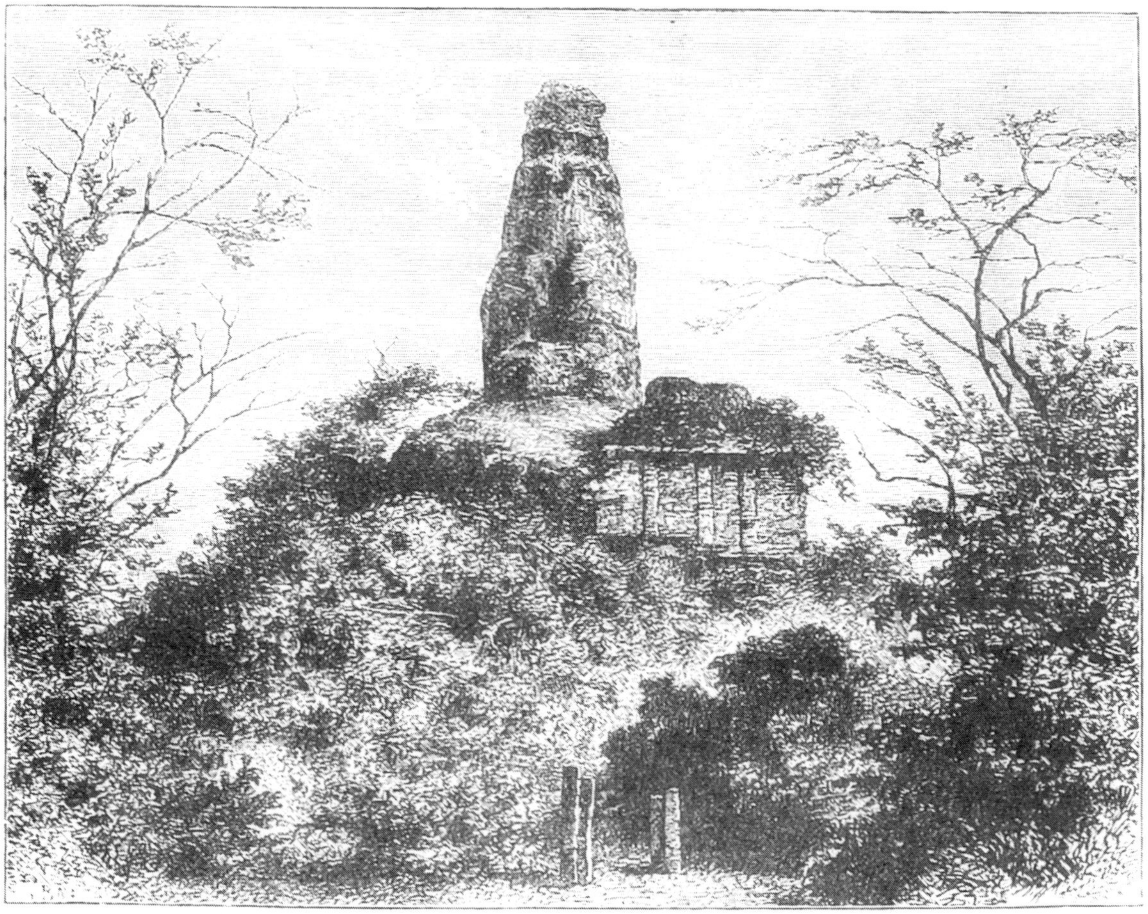

JETAWAN-ARAMA DAGOBA.

right marks the place where Elala, a Malabar invader, who reigned with justice and moderation, fell (B. C. 160). It was erected by his rival in admiration of his bravery, and it is still regarded with veneration. Among the neighboring ruins is a beautifully carved stone of great antiquity, now forming a doorstep, and representing the lotus flower in the center, a procession of wild animals on the outside, and in the intermediate circle the *hanza*, or sacred goose, an object of veneration formerly in all parts of India.

Pollonarua and Anurajapura, the two ancient and long ruined capitals of Ceylon, lie to the northeast and north of Kandy. The tourist starts by the road to Trincomalee as far as Matale, sixteen miles. Three miles off is a cave temple, called the *Alu Wihare*, curiously built, amid loose and tumbled masses of rock. The place is specially interesting as the spot where, as the Mahawanso says, the books of Buddhism were first compiled, and its precepts reduced to writing. The statement runs: "The wise monks of former days handed down the text of the Three Pitakas by word of mouth. But seeing the destruction of men, the monks of this time assembled, and, that the Faith might last, wrote them in books." Leaving Matale, we make our way through Nalande, fourteen miles, to Dambulla,[1] fifteen miles, where is one of the oldest rock temples in Ceylon. The rock is five hundred feet high, and is visible from afar. The temple is reached by hewn steps, and upon climbing these, we behold a noble gateway adorned with carvings. The building was known as "the cave of the golden rock," darkness being the characteristic of the interior of all Buddhist temples. Indeed, the word Wihara or Vihara, now denoting any Buddhist temple or monastery, literally signifies "a residence." In the forest stretching south of Dam-

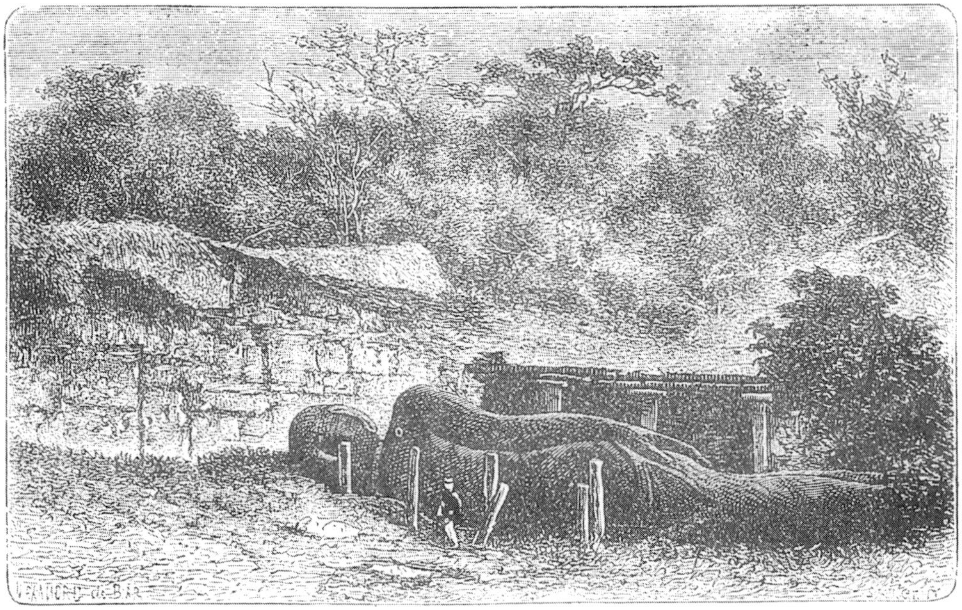

GAL-WIHARA, PULASTIPURA; IMAGE OF BUDDHA RECUMBENT.

bulla there stands a colossal statue of Buddha carved in a mass of rock. It is upward of fifty feet high, and reminds one of the Daibutz of Japan. It would appear that in early times this statue was roofed over. It is called the Aukana Wihara.

The road leads on through jungle by the great tank of Topare to POLLONARUA, or Pulastipura, where are the ruins of a city built by the famous King Prakrama Bahu, which continued to be the capital of the Kandyan monarchs till the fourteenth century. The remains are extensive and display beauty of design and excellence of execution. The forest abounds with them, but perhaps the most striking is the Jayata-wanarama, a huge Buddhist temple, containing, between two octagonal towers forming the main entrance, a statue of Buddha fifty feet high, formed of brick covered with polished *chunam* or cement. The side view gives a good idea of the elaborate carving and extensive range of this building.

Another still more curious building at Pulastipura is the Gal-wihara, a rock temple, which has in front four richly-carved columns, a raised altar, with a statue of Buddha seated, a statue of Buddha standing, and a statue of the same famous saint forty-five feet in length, representing the state of Nirvana.

North of Matale, about sixty miles, is another, and still more ancient ruined city, called ANURAJAPURA. According to the narrative of the Mahawanso, this city was founded four hundred years B. C. When King Asoka sent his son Mahinda to introduce Buddhism to Ceylon, the reigning monarch was Tissa (250–230 B. C.), who received him with favor and espoused the new religion. He built the famous temple called the Thuparama Dagoba, of bell-shaped outline, the most elegant in Ceylon, which still rises sixty-three feet from the ground, and stands on a platform fifty

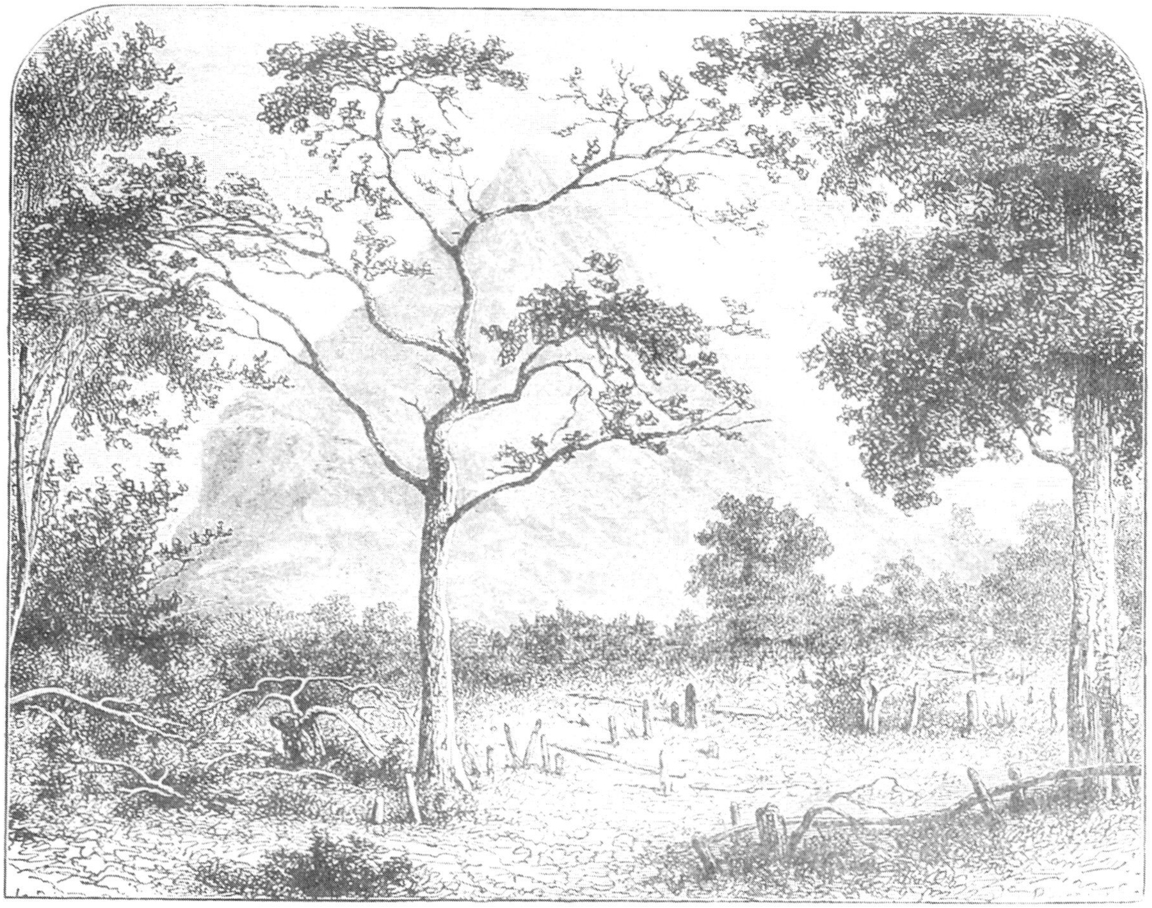

RUANVELLY DAGOBA, ANURAJAPURA.

yards square, with three rows of monolith pillars twenty-six feet high, one hundred and fifty in all. He erected it as a shrine for the right collar-bone of Buddha. The pillars are supposed to represent and answer to the stone rail surrounding the topes in India. They were probably connected with each other by beams of wood and frames of canvas covered with paintings. Paintings, as distinct from sculptures, are characteristic of Ceylon temples.

A precipitous rocky hill, a thousand feet high, eight miles to the east, connected with the city by a long street, was chosen as an appropriate site for another huge temple of brick, under which was deposited another relic of Buddha—a hair which grew on the mole between his eyebrows. Regarding this hill, the hill of Mihintale, a visitor to it thus writes : " It was on this hill, the three peaks of which, each now surmounted by a dagoba, form so striking an object from the central trunk road which runs along its side, that the famous missionary Mahinda spent most of his after years. Here, on the precipitous western side of the hill, under a large mass of granite rock, at a spot which, completely shut out from the world, affords a magnificent view of the plains below, he had his study hollowed out, and steps cut in the rock over which alone it could be reached. The great rock effectually protects the cave from the heat of the sun, in whose warm light the valley below lies basking; not a sound reaches it from the plain, now a far-reaching forest, then full of busy homesteads; there is only heard that hum of insects which never ceases, and the rustling of the leaves of the trees which cling to the sides of the precpice. I shall not easily forget the day when I first entered that lonely, cool, and quiet chamber, so simple and yet so beautiful, where more than two thousand years ago the great teacher of Ceylon had sat and thought and worked through long years of his peaceful and useful life. On that hill he afterward died, and his ashes still rest under the dagoba, which is the principal object of the reverence and care of the few monks who still reside in the Mahintale Wihare."[1]

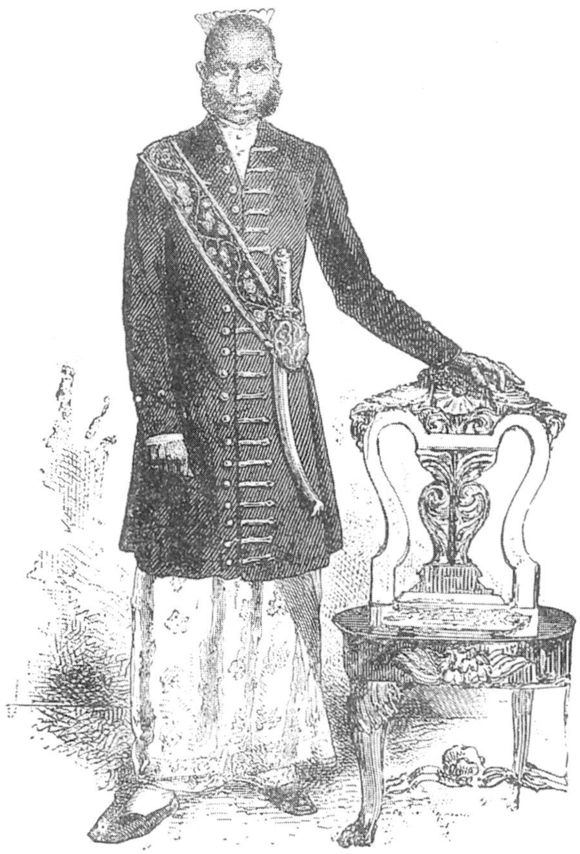

MUDALIYAR OR HEADMAN.

The square of the entire city of Anurajapura, including tanks, was walled in about B. C. 48, by Queen Anula, and each side is said to have been sixteen miles long. The entire distance from Anurajapura to Colombo by way of Kandy is one hundred and sixty miles.

Conjectures have been eagerly made concerning traces of Christianity in Ceylon in the early centuries; but if in those days there were any Christians in Ceylon, they must have been sojourners only from among the Syrian Christians on the Coromandel Coast. "Its light appears," says Sir J. E. Tennent, "to have been transiently kindled, and to have speedily become extinguished." Cosmas, A. D. 535, speaks of Christians here, with a priest and deacon ordained in Persia. These were probably Nestorians. The two Mohammedan travelers of the ninth century, whose narratives have been translated, are silent as to the existence of any form of Christianity, and Março Polo, A. D. 1290, declares that the inhabitants were idolaters. The Portuguese in the sixteenth century brought with them Romanism, and Xavier was invited in 1544 to come to Jaffna; but though many were baptized, he has recorded his disappointment at the inward unsoundness of all he had outwardly achieved. Many natives, both in the north and in the south, became Roman Catholics; but in the charges officially brought against the Jesuits, it was alleged to be doubtful whether by affecting idolatry, and tolerating it among their proselytes, they had not them-

[1] *Buddhism*, by T. W. Rhys Davids. Society for Promoting Christian Knowledge.

selves become converts to Hinduism rather than made Hindus converts to Christianity. They assumed the character of Brahmans of a superior caste, and even composed a pretended Veda. They conducted images of the Virgin in triumphal procession, imitated from the orgies of Juggernaut. Among their most distinguished preachers has been Joseph Vaz (died at Kandy, 1711), who added to the Church

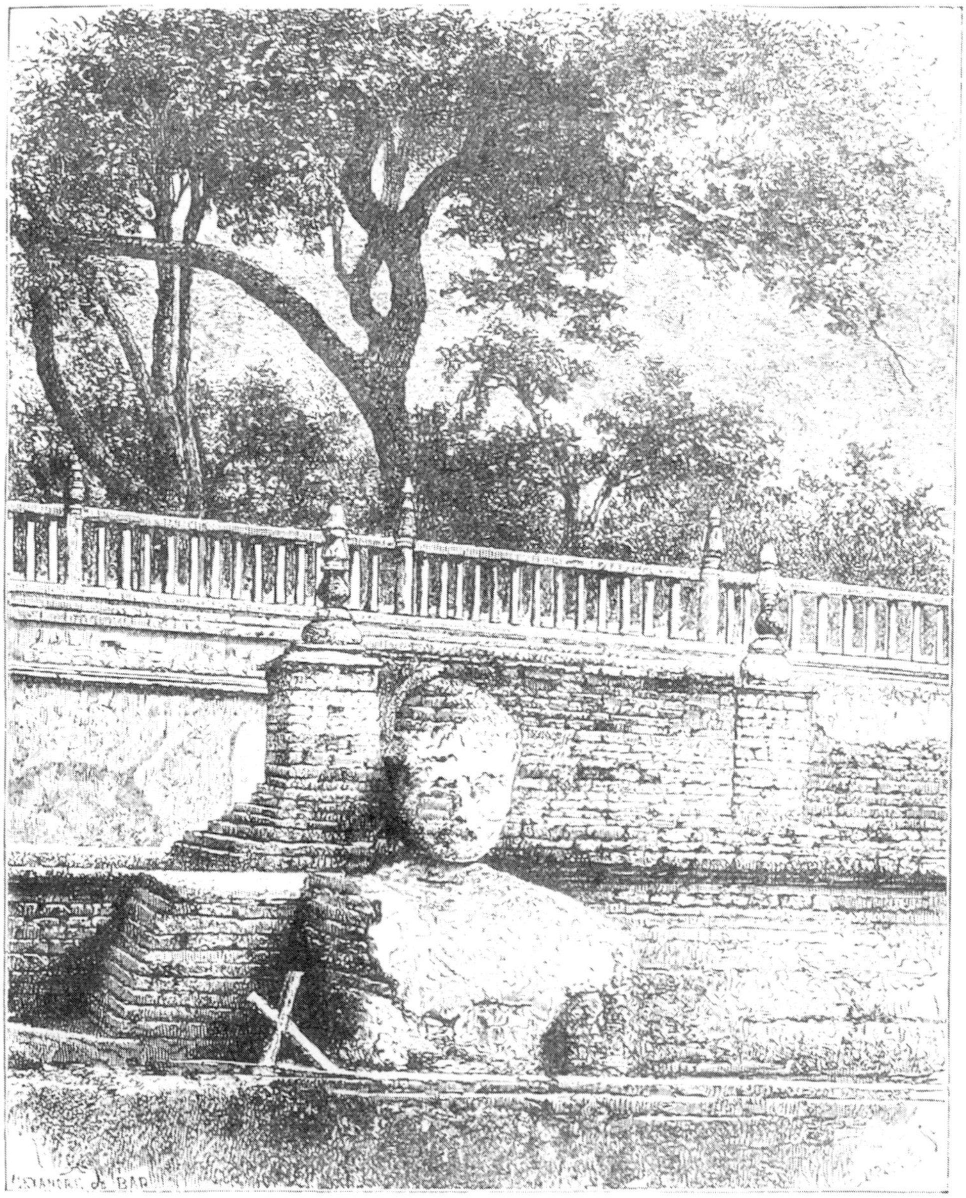

COLOSSAL IMAGE OF BUDDHA.

thirty thousand converts from the heathen. The Dutch on their coming established the Reformed Church of Holland as the religion of the colony, and the first Presbyterian clergyman began his ministrations in 1642. In 1658 they forbade the presence of Roman Catholic priests. They pulled down and broke the Romanist images, and in Jaffna took possession of the churches. But in spite of all this severity, Romanism kept its ground, and the Dutch missionaries did not succeed. Since the British rule began, this coercive policy has ceased, and the Gospel has been preached in a Christian spirit. In 1816 Ceylon was made an archdeaconry under the see of Calcutta.

It was made a bishopric in 1845. Protestant missions, set on foot by the American Board in 1816, have been uninterruptedly efficient. Upward of six hundred students have been under instruction from time to time in the American seminary at Batticotta; and of these more than half have openly professed Christianity, and all have been more or less imbued with its spirit. The majority are filling situations of credit and responsibility in the island. The Wesleyans[1] also have been and are still extensively at work with churches, colleges, and schools in North and South Ceylon. The Baptists have useful missions at Ratnapura, at the foot of Adam's Peak and among the pilgrims thither, at Colombo, and at Kandy. Lastly, the Church Missionary Society has been successful in several stations, though of late years unfortunate hindrances have sprung up through Ritualistic tendencies and claims of the newly appointed bishop. Out of the taxes levied upon the native population the sum of sixty thousand dollars is annually paid by the government in support of this episcopate and other religious establishments in the island. The Kandy Collegiate School educates a large number of boys and young men. Nevertheless, Brahmanism has still a strong hold upon the Tamils of the north, and Buddhism, with its flower-offering and devil worship, is still vigorous among the Singalese. Books, too, in favor of Buddhism, with extracts from English writers who extol its early literature, are published and circulated. Evangelical Christianity is, however, gaining ground, and the present census will probably show the number of Protestants to be upward of seventy thousand. A scheme of disendowment is proposed, to take effect in five years.[2]

[1] They report, August, 1890, 70 ministers, 155 lay preachers, 4,644 church members, 20,000 in the congregations,—to which sermons in four different languages are preached,—and 21,435 day and Sunday-school pupils.

[2] Entire freedom from state patronage and control is now granted to all religions. The proportion of Christians, including Romanists, is ten per cent. higher in Ceylon than in India. *Vide*, "Ceylon in the Jubilee Year," James Fergusson, Colombo, 1887.

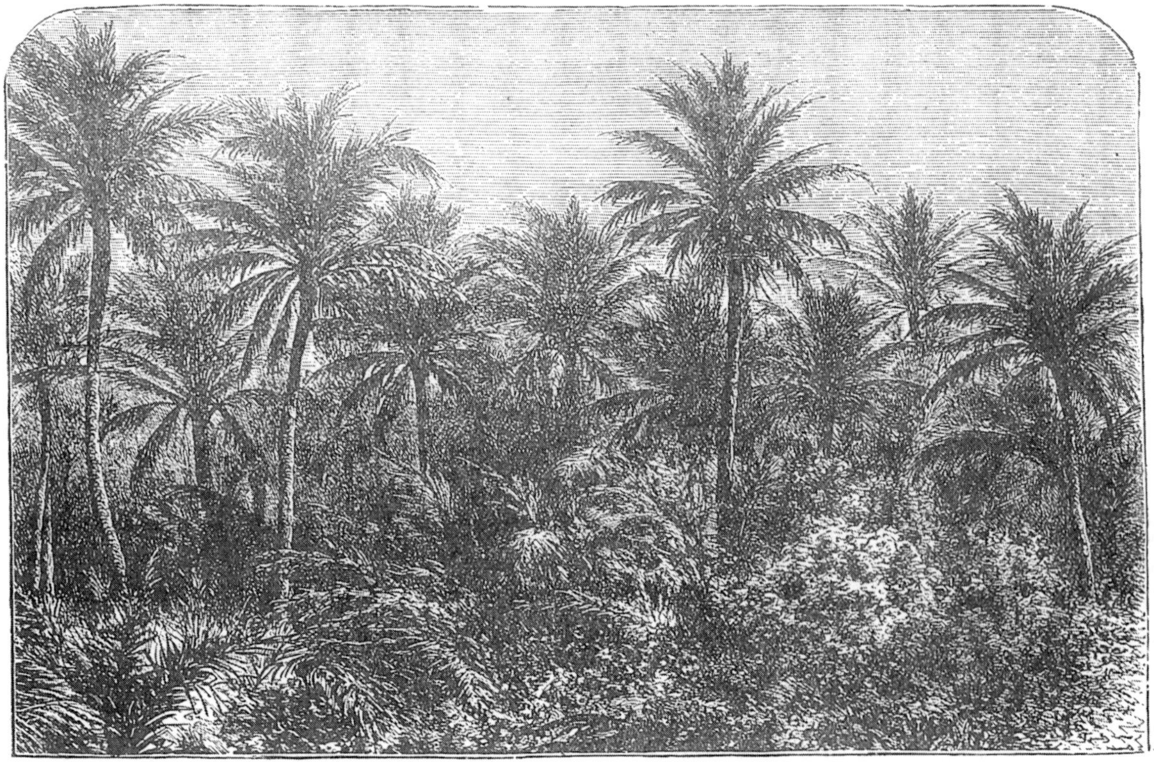

COCOA-NUT PALMS AND JUNGLE.

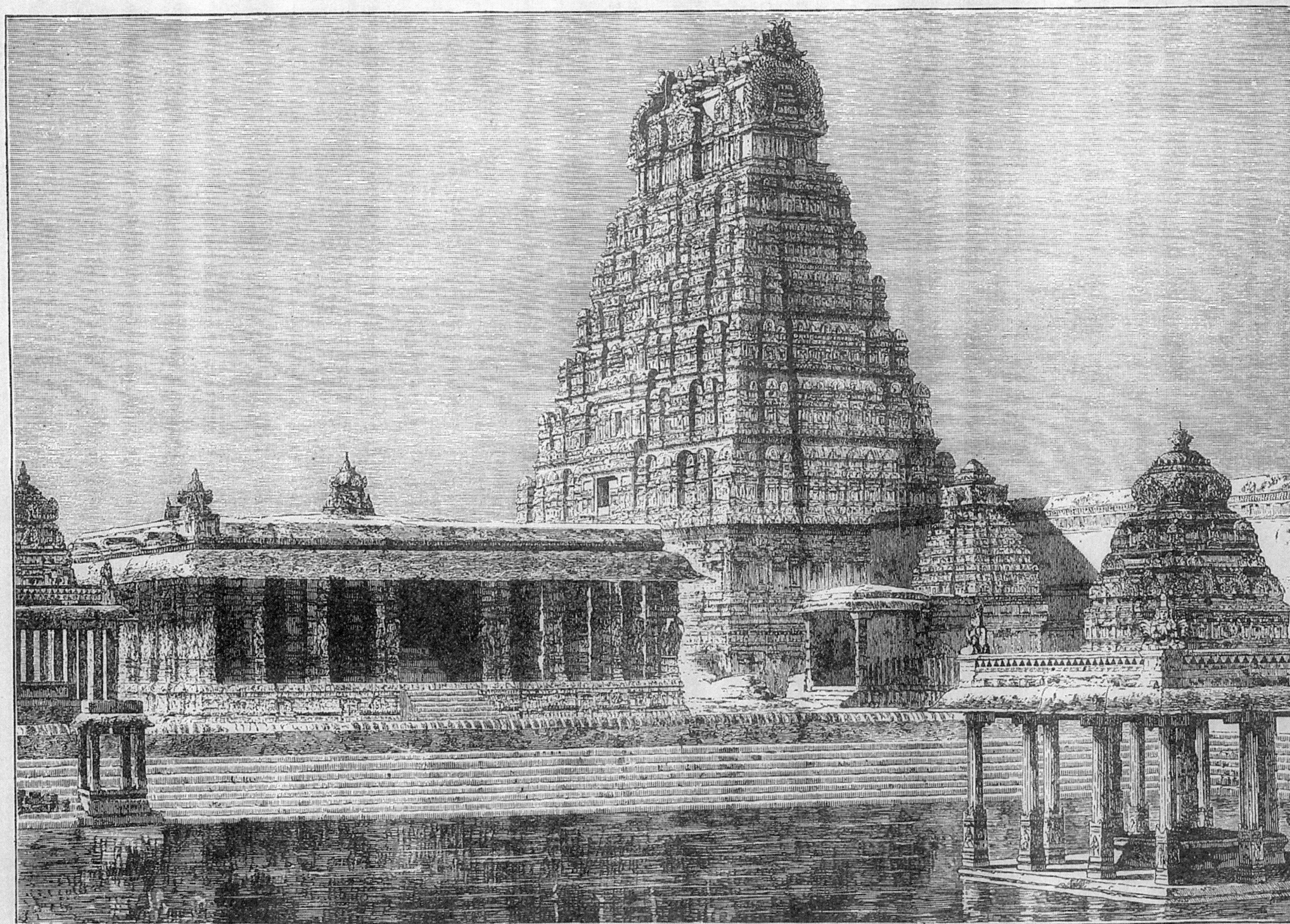

GRAND PAGODA, CONJEVERAM; GOPURA AND SACRED TANK.

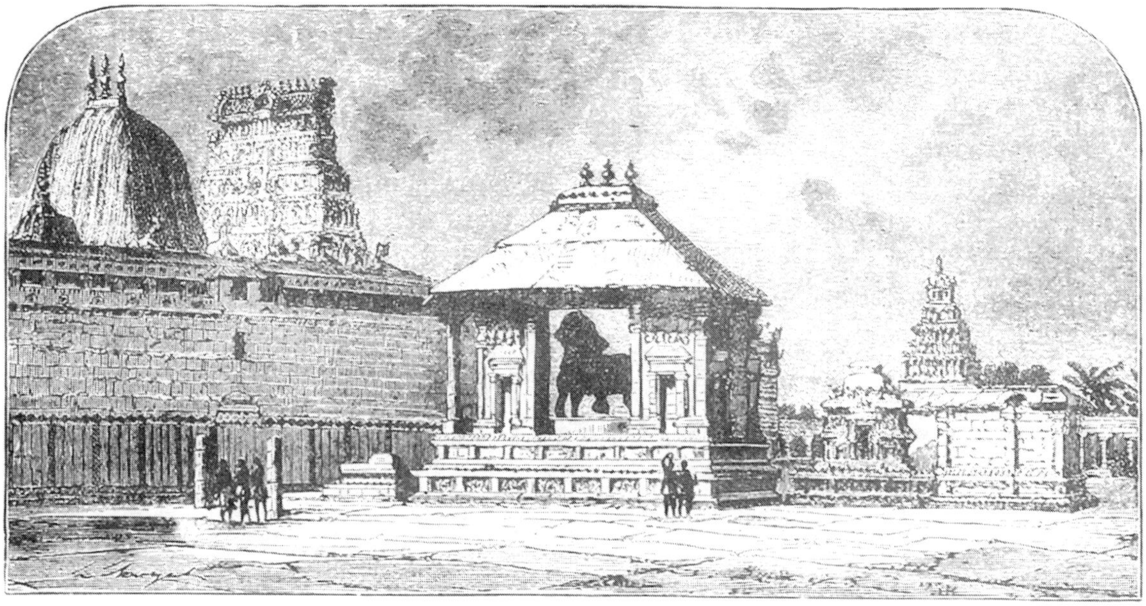

CHAPEL OF THE SACRED BULL, CHILLAMBARAM.

MADRAS PRESIDENCY.

TINNEVELLY AND TRAVANCORE—THE DRAVIDIAN TEMPLES—MADURA—TRICHINOPOLY—TANJORE—MADRAS—THE COAST VOYAGE NORTHWARD.

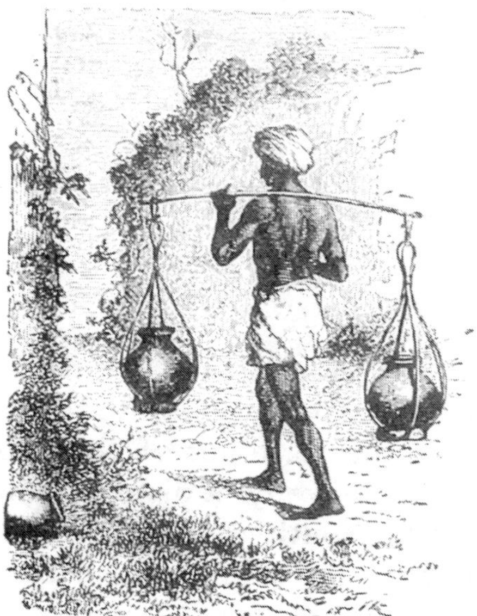

CEYLON is linked on to India not only naturally and politically, but by a continual transfer of population. The Tamils, who are the chief work-people on the coffee plantations of Ceylon, come from the Madras Presidency, and they do not generally settle permanently in the island. There is a continual stream of comers and goers. There are six ports on the western coast of Ceylon, to and from which vessels run to the Coromandel Coast, as the eastern side of Southern India is called. Of these six ports the chief are Pesalai and Vankalai in the north, and Colombo on the west. In 1874, for example, there arrived in Ceylon one hundred and twenty-five thousand of these Indian coolies,[1] and the departures numbered ninety thousand. A great exodus always follows the gathering of the crop; in the steamer in which we crossed from Colombo to Tuticorin, one hundred and fifty miles, there were about five hundred Tamils, men, women, and children, on board, returning to their native land.

[1] In 1887 there were 206,495 employed on Ceylon estates, nearly all Tamil immigrants.—Ed.

Many of them crowded the deck all night, and, in spite of much roughness from the sailors and boatmen, seemed patient and light-hearted. The noise and jabbering as the boats conveying them from shore swarmed round the steamer was amusing, and almost deafening. After a calm starlight night we found our vessel anchored off the flat, sandy coast of India, about six miles from shore. The steamer could not be brought nearer on account of the shallows. Though the sea was calm the billows of a heavy swell chased each other over the sand banks with a long lazy sweep toward the land. A fleet of heavy native sail-boats came out to take the

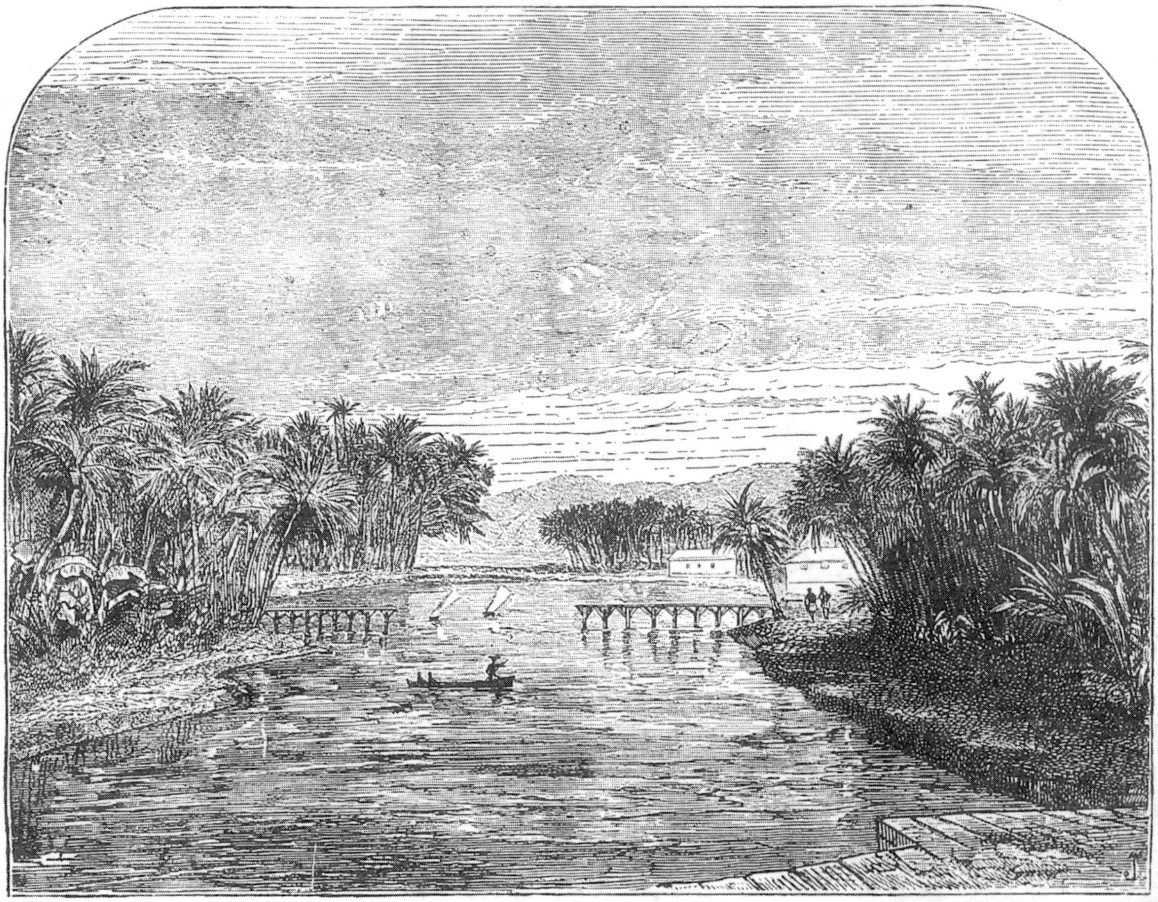

MAHÉ, MALABAR COAST.

passengers ashore; and in a four-oared boat, after passing Hare Island, we reached the landing stage of Tuticorin in an hour. Tuticorin was once celebrated for its pearl fishery, and is now a town rising in importance as the terminus of the South Indian Railway. It is the main port of the District of Tinnevelly, a district which, together with the Native State of Travancore, forms the southern part of India. Cape Comorin itself is within the boundary of Travancore, but Tinnevelly occupies two-thirds of the breadth of the peninsula. These two provinces are separated by the range of Western Ghauts, which run north and south along the western coast, rising to the height of seven thousand feet, and are the highest mountains to be met with till we come to the Himâlayas. Tinnevelly has a population of a million and a half. Northward, the country is well cultivated, and of a green, fertile aspect, paddy lands extending for miles on either side the railway; but southward there stretches

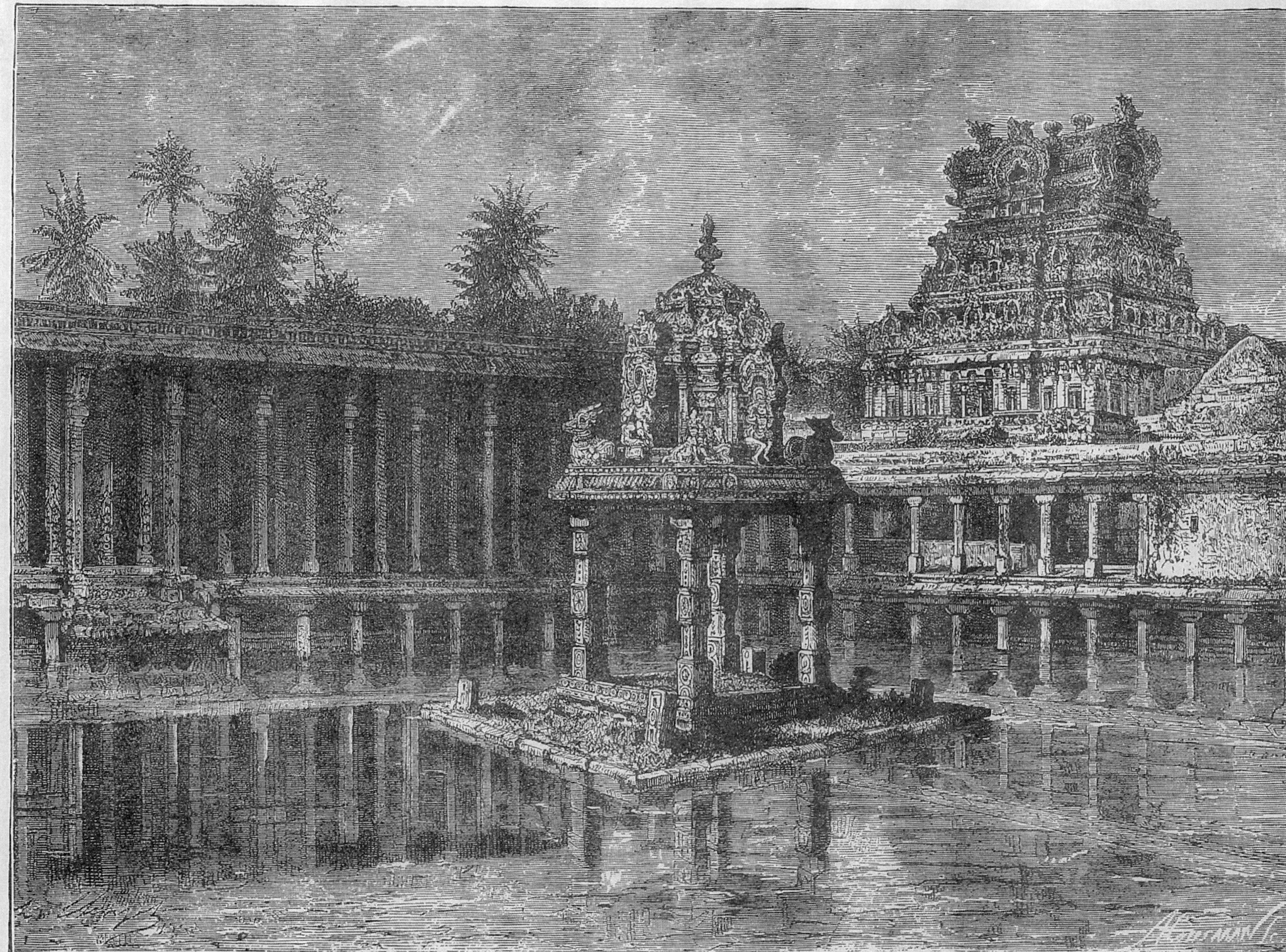

PAGODA, TINNEVELLY.

a vast sandy plain of a fiery red color, dotted over by groves of tall, majestic Palmyra palms. While all around is parched and arid, this tree strikes its roots forty feet below the surface, gathers up the moisture, and daily gives forth quantities of sap

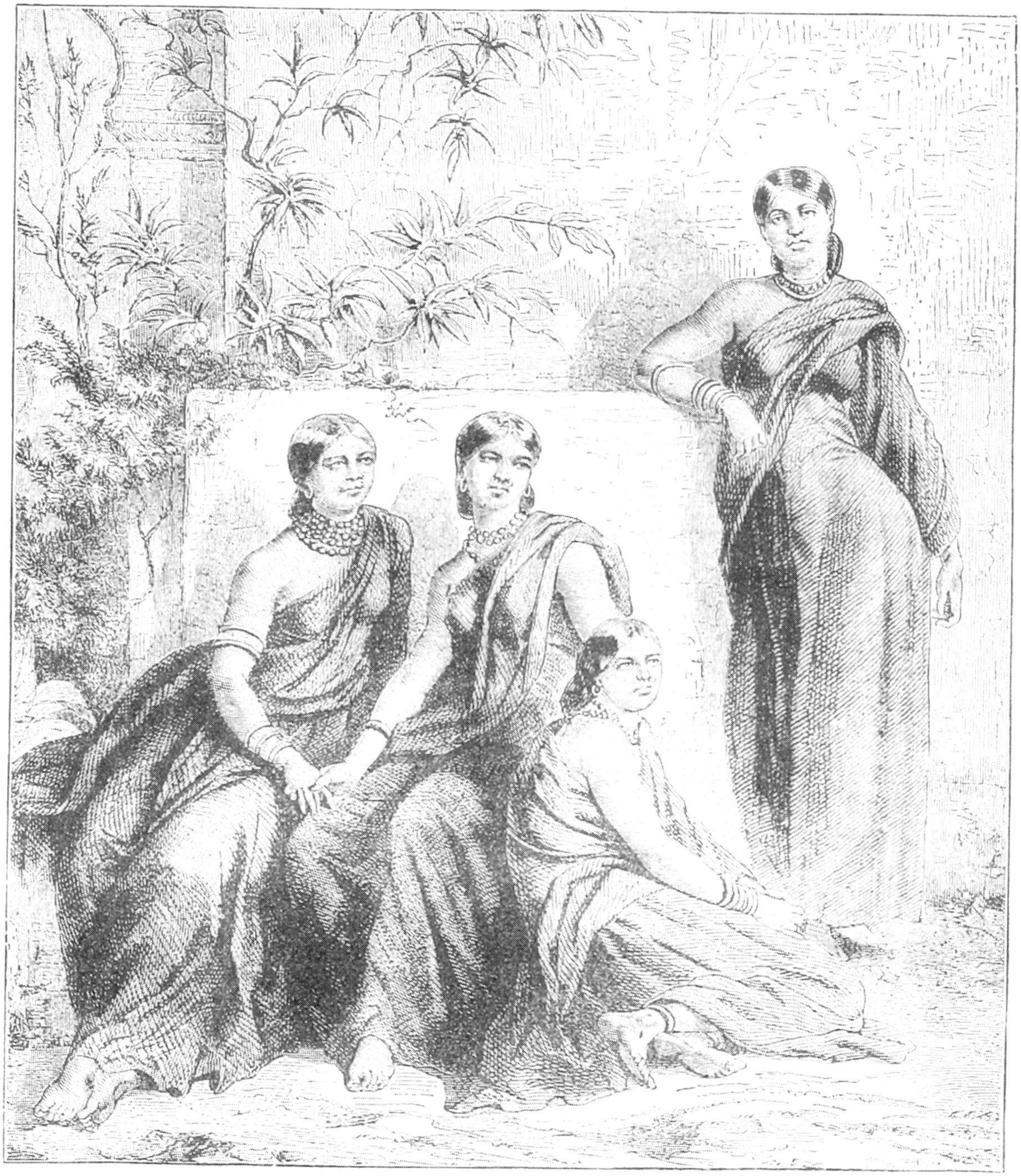

CHRISTIAN NATIVE GIRLS.

called "toddy," which is collected in small earthen vessels attached to the tree, and is largely manufactured into sugar. The Shanar laborer climbs thirty or forty trees seventy feet high twice every day to collect the sap. The Hindus call the Palmyra "the tree of life," and dedicate it to Ganesh. It gives three quarts of "toddy" daily, its wood is hard and durable, and its leaves thatch the native houses, are woven into mats and baskets, or, smoothed by pressure, they serve for books and parchments. In a word, the Palmyra palm in South India as well as in the northeast of Ceylon supplies shelter, furniture, food, drink, oil, and fuel for the people, with forage for their cattle and utensils for their farms.

It is an interesting fact that Tinnevelly and Travancore, more than any other part of India, have been brought under the influence of Christianity, and this from the earliest times. The Christians of St. Thomas, as they are called, early in the third century, it is supposed, occupied portions of the Coromandel Coast on the east, and of the Malabar Coast on the west. Indeed, the Syrian Churches here claim to have sprung from the preaching of the Apostle Thomas himself;[2] however this may

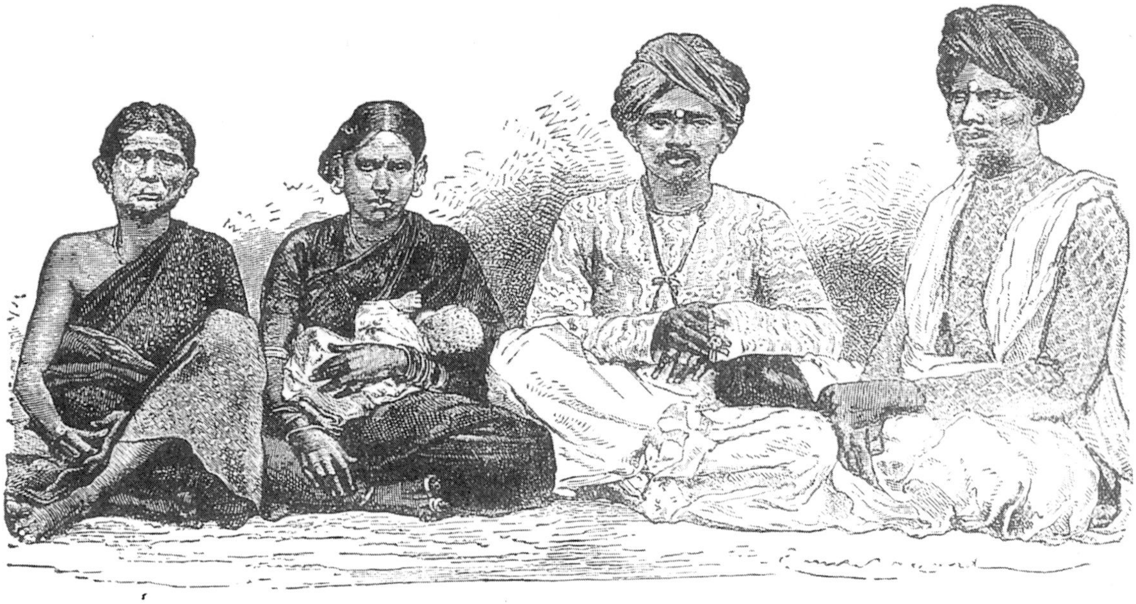

TAMILS OF SOUTH INDIA.

be, a Syriac MS. of theBible, brought from this district, now at Cambridge, is said to date from the eighth century. And in modern times Christian missions have been more successful here than anywhere else in India. Travancore, unlike Tinnevelly, is a mountainous country, full of diversified scenery. In its northern part, the Malayâlam language is spoken. The view from the Peak of Agastya, seven thousand feet high, which is usually ascended from Trivanderum, is said to be the finest in Southern India. As on the east the Palmyra, so on the west of these mountains the cocoa-nut palm flourishes. Here there is a group of missions. The population of Travancore numbers upward of two millions, of whom one-fifth is Christian. The London Missionary Society takes the lead, and the census report witnesses that "by the indefatigable labors and self-denying earnestness of the learned body of the missionaries in the country, the large community of Native Christians are rapidly advancing in their moral, intellectual, and material condition." Travancore is perhaps one of the best governed and most enlightened native states in India. North of it, on the west coast, is Cochin, near to which is the old Hebrew colony known as "the Black Jews of Malabar." Their religious knowledge is much narrower than that of the "White Jews," who have been settled there since the destruction of

[2] It is declared by modern scholars that there is no evidence that he ever came to India at all, but that the myth is of the same spurious origin as that of Peter's visit at Rome.—ED.

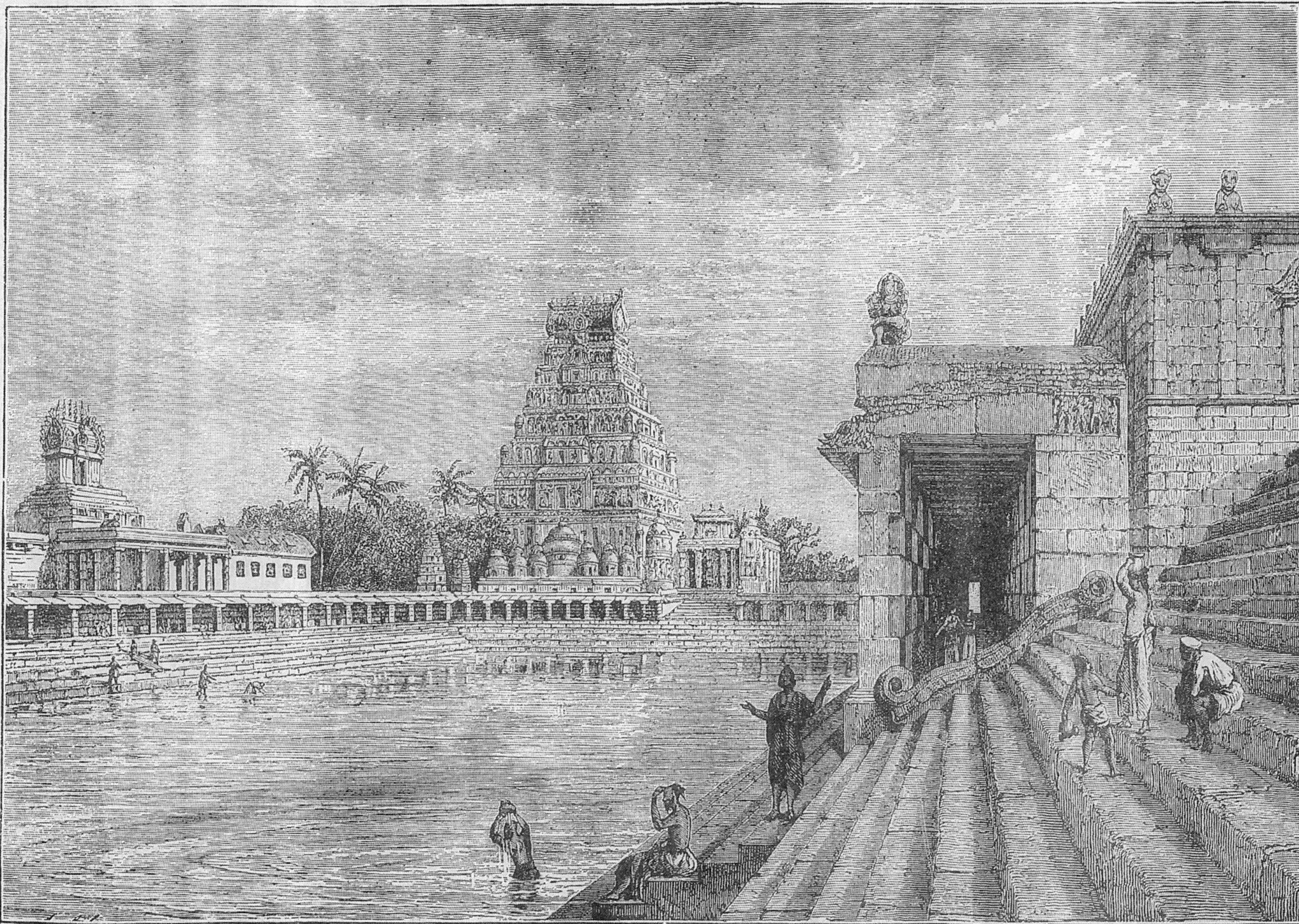

PAGODA OF CHILLAMBARAM.

Jerusalem. The Black Jews are supposed to have come thither upon the conquest of the Ten Tribes, and perhaps through Afghanistan.

Taking the train which runs through Maniachi Junction, a branch line brought

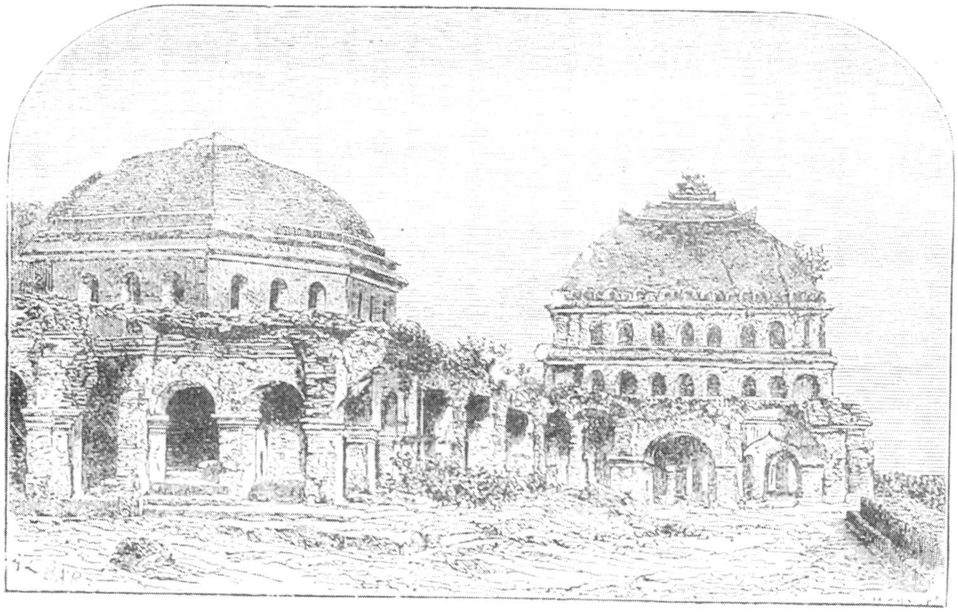

RUINED PERUMAL PAGODA.

us in three hours to Tinnevelly. The railway terminus here is half way between the town of Tinnevelly and the celebrated settlement of Palimcotta. Tambiravarni, "the copper-colored river," rising in the Ghauts, waters the plain and gives it a

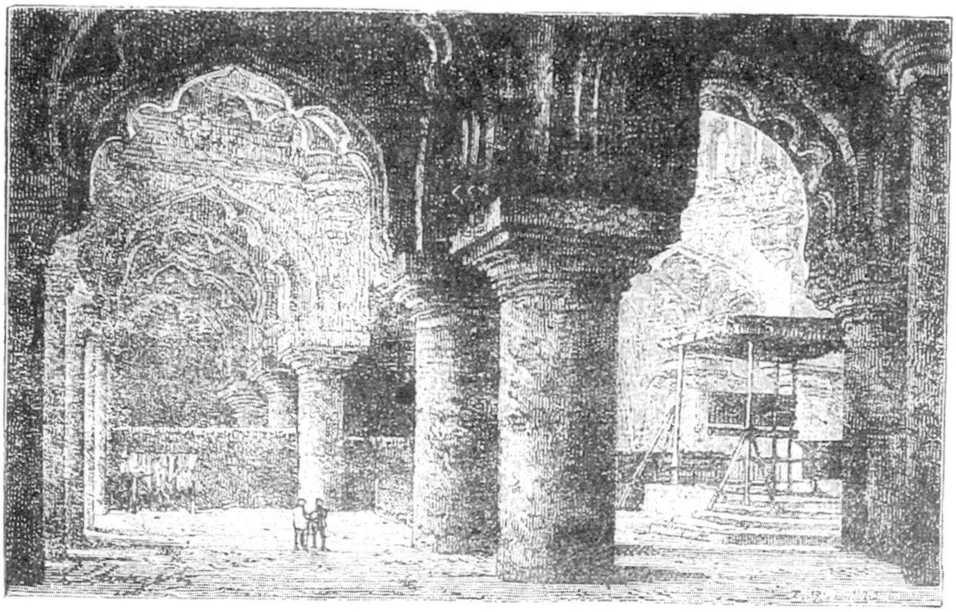

GREAT HALL OR AUDIENCE CHAMBER IN THE PALACE OF TIRUMALA, MADURA.

most fertile aspect. The country is covered with cotton and rice fields. Tinnevelly, the native city, with its Temple of Siva, lies to the west, and Palimcotta, fifty-seven miles from Cape Comorin, the English station, to the east. Nothing can be more strange and pleasant to the eye of a Christian than to see the spire of a Christian church, with the surroundings of a missionary compound, rising amid the emblems of decaying heathendom in that far-off land. Hearing the church bell on the quiet Sunday morning, and seeing the schools and the people wending their way to worship, one might almost fancy one's self in some neat English village, were it not for the dark faces of the villagers and the strange tower of an old heathen temple looming above the trees. The mission here was begun by the Danish missionaries in 1771, and Schwartz himself visited Palimcotta twice. The Christians of the

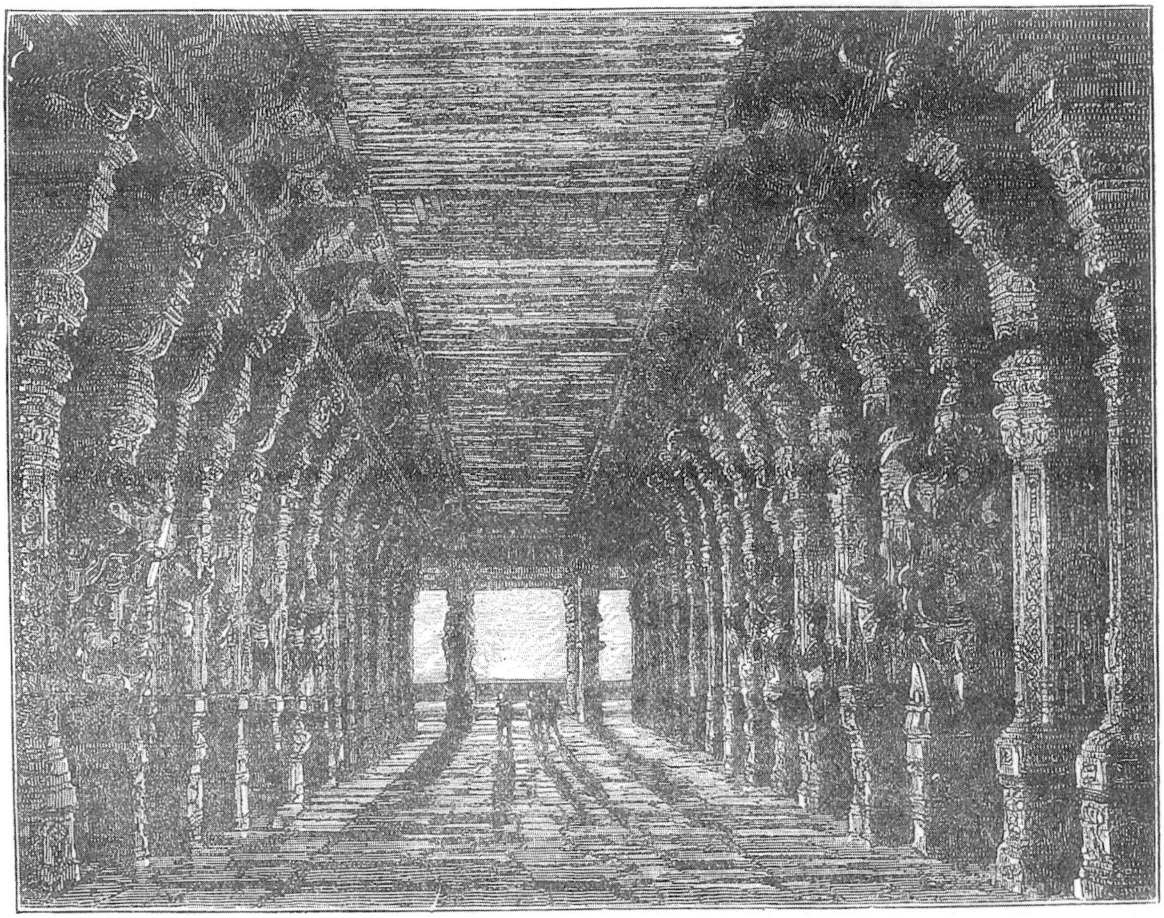

TIRUMALA'S CHOULTRY, MADURA.

district now constitute one-fifth of the population, but they are for the most part from among the lowest castes. Large numbers of natives are putting themselves under Christian instruction, in the hope of protection from oppression. Many more have joined the Christians in their gratitude for relief given in time of famine. But, whatever the motive, they hear the Gospel message, and are instructed in Christian truth ; they become intelligent, progressive, promising.

Bishop Sargent had at table one day a young native who had passed the Indian Civil Service examination—a gigantic achievement for any man, especially for a Hindu—and who had thoroughly mastered the English language, and literature also. To test his knowledge, each one at table quoted some familiar lines from an English poet ; and thereupon the young Tamil not only recited each quotation, but named the work it was from, gave the connection, and the author's name. "Your quotation," he began, "was from such a play of Shakespeare, and this is the connection." Again, a native missionary was once asked when preaching, "How do you explain the differences among you? Here are Church Missionary and Propagation Society missionaries, Baptist missionaries, Presbyterian and London Society missionaries.

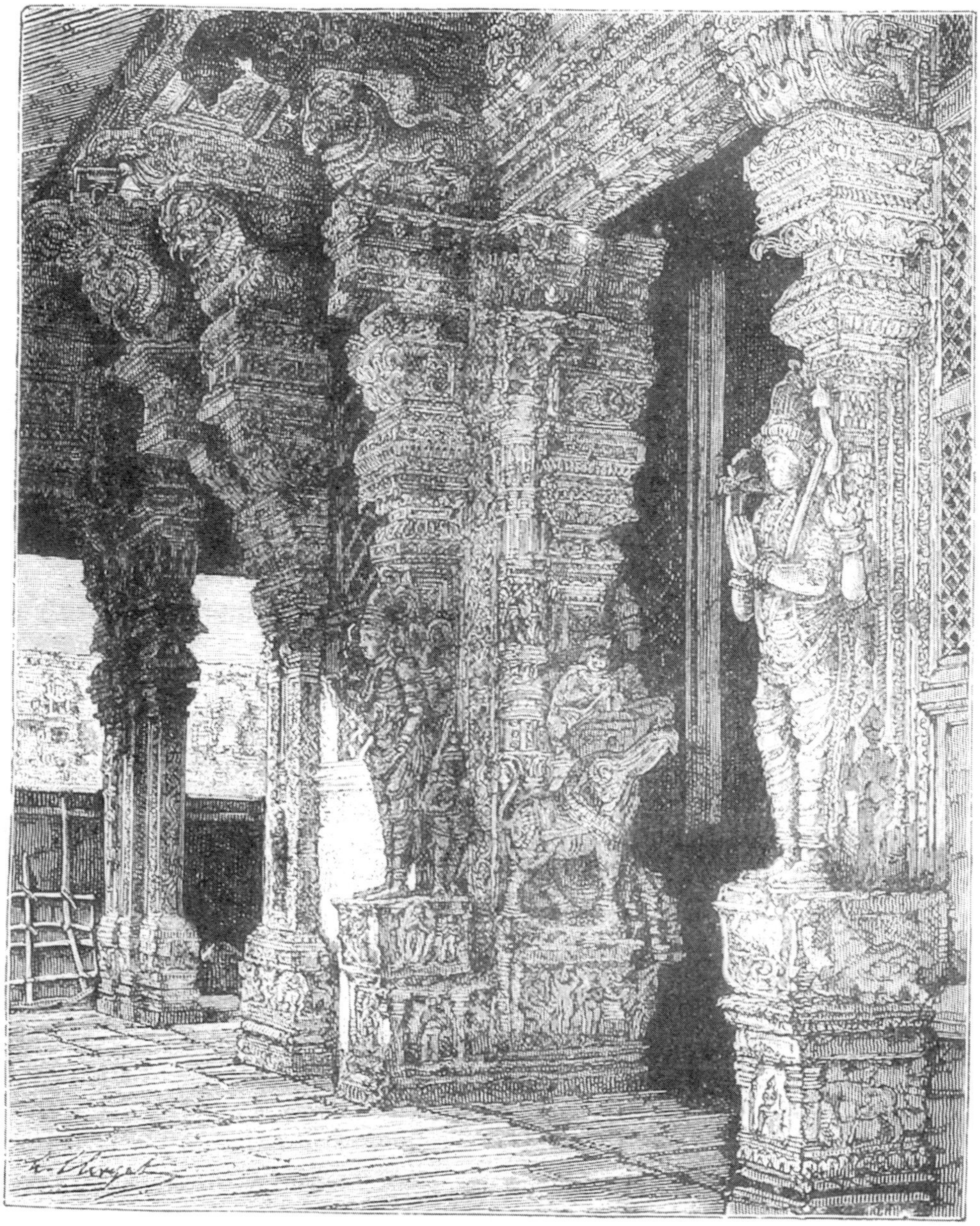

ENTRANCE TO THE PUTHA MANDAPAM, MADURA.

How are we to tell which is right?" The native preacher replied: "There was once a dispute among the fingers of the hand, which should have the pre-eminence. The thumb said, 'I ought to have the pre-eminence, for it is plain, you can none of you do anything without me.' 'Ah,' said the first finger, 'what is more important than pointing out the way? This is my office; I ought to have the pre-eminence.' 'I,' said the second finger, 'rest my claim on mathematical principles. When you hold the hand upright, which finger is the tallest? I am; therefore I ought to have the pre-eminence.' 'No,' said the third finger, 'for though it is something to point out the way, and mathematics too are strong, there is one thing stronger, and that is love. And when you put the symbol of love upon the hand it is the third finger that you choose; therefore the supremacy is mine.' 'Hear me, too,' said the little finger; 'true, indeed, I am small and you are large, mathematics are strong, and love is stronger, but there is one thing higher than all, and that is worship; and when you approach the god, I am the finger that you choose to present nearest in your prayer, for you press your hands together, lift them up, and hold them thus. Therefore I should have the pre-eminence.' Now," continued the native pastor, "each finger has something to say for itself, each is important in its way; and so with the various Christian Societies. But all derive their life and strength from a common source, and all working harmoniously, under the guidance of a common Will, become mighty for the accomplishment of Christ's work in the world." These examples show how the Hindu may become competent both for the Indian Civil Service and for missionary work in India.

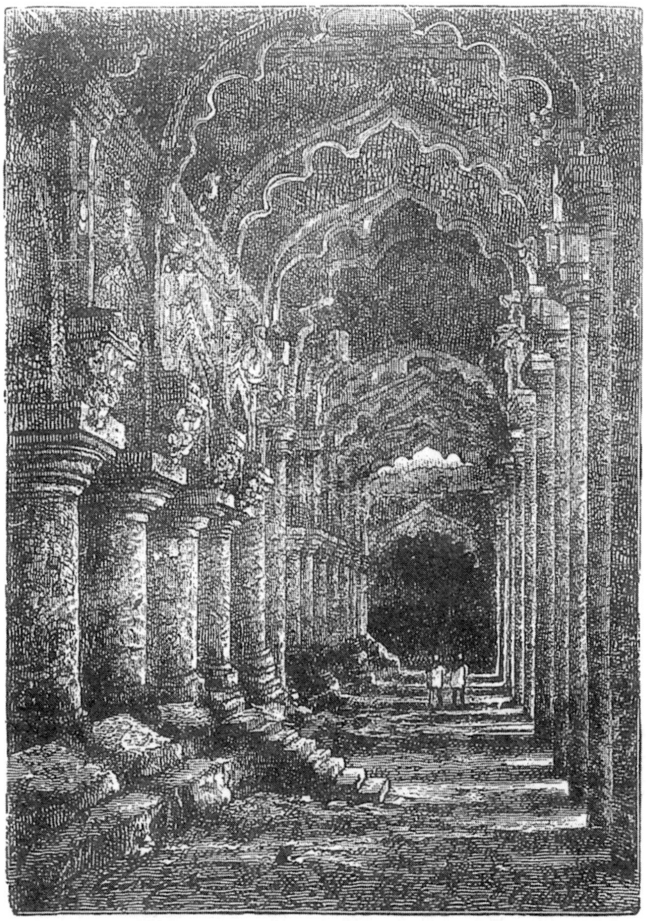

ENTRANCE TO THE GREAT HALL, PALACE OF TIRUMALA, MADURA.

The whole of that part of Southern India that lies between the eighth and the sixteenth parallels of latitude used to be called the Carnatic or Black Country, and is peopled by the Dravidian race; not the aborigines of the country, but, like the Aryans of the north, early immigrants who came in successive waves from some part of Central Asia, and settled chiefly in the southern portion of the great peninsula. They are quite distinct from the Aryans; their skin is darker, and their language different. They form one-fifth of the whole population of India. They are active, hard-working, docile, and enduring. They are more sober, self-denying and less brutish in their habits than Europeans. They show greater respect for animal life, they have more natural courtesy of manner, and, as servants, attach themselves to those who treat them well with far greater affection than English servants. The Dravidian tongue embraces four groups of languages: Tamil, Telugu, Canarese, and Malayâlam.

The railway from Tinnevelly runs north, about a hundred miles, through a flat productive country, in about seven hours to Madura, the ancient capital of the large district which bears that name. Madura was for centuries before the Mohammedan

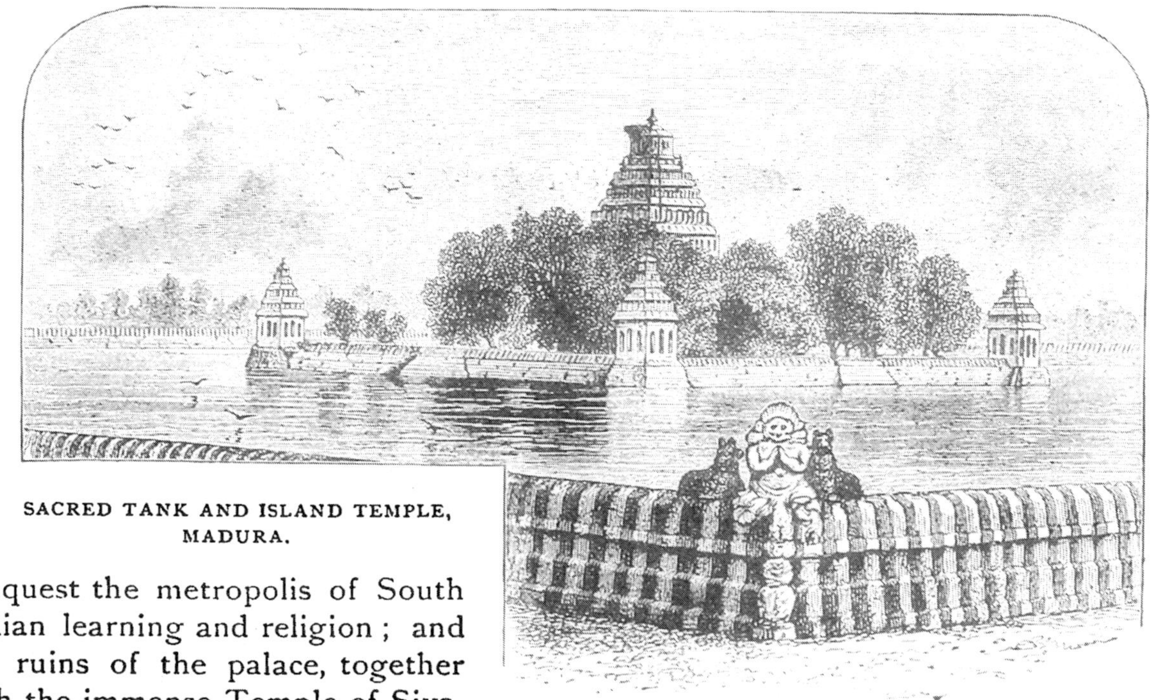

SACRED TANK AND ISLAND TEMPLE, MADURA.

conquest the metropolis of South Indian learning and religion; and the ruins of the palace, together with the immense Temple of Siva, covering twenty acres, are standing memorials of its early greatness. Here we come face to face with the masterpieces of Dravidian architecture for which the Madras Presidency is famous, and which in their number, vastness, and elaborateness almost bewilder the Christian tourist. The Dravidians of Southern India offered their labor to their gods. Their temples are divided into the following parts:

I. The Vimana or Adytum, square, and surmounted by a pyramidal roof overlaid with gold. Here, in a dark cubical cell, the altar and idol are immured, and a lamp is kept burning dimly night and day.

II. Around the Vimana, and leading up to it usually from the four points of the compass, are the Mantapas, huge stone porches richly carved.

III. The Gopuras, or gate pyramids, the most obvious features from the outside, towering two hundred feet high, and elaborately carved with most grotesque figures in stone, raised tier upon tier in diminishing stories, of which there are from ten to fourteen, terminating in a dome.

IV. The pillared halls, or Choultries, ten to twenty feet high, with a thousand stone pillars elaborately carved from base to capital, and supporting a flat stone roof.

V. Sacred Tanks, surrounded with corridors, and with flights of steps descending into the water. All these, leading to a common center, form the widespreading temple of South India called the PAGODA. This has nine towers, one of which we ascended by a narrow staircase leading from story to story to the highest. Each small chamber has pigeon-holes in its walls, opening north and south; but the peeps thus gained, being very limited, hardly repay the fatigue of the climb. This temple dates from the third century B. C.; it was destroyed in A. D. 1324, and restored in the seventeenth century. It is kept in good repair, and many masons were still at work upon it. It is dedicated partly to Minakshi, the fish-eyed goddess, and partly to Siva.

Passing through the corridors used as bazaars, we came to the dark flat-roofed hall of a thousand pillars, some of black granite, all carved more or less elaborately, and representing male and female deities dancing. One of the figures represents the devil, and boys are allowed to spit in his face. One pillar is subdivided into twenty-four smaller ones. The sacred tank is about fifty yards square, and full of dark green water, in which some Brahmans were bathing. The corridors around this tank are covered internally with fresco paintings, some astronomical, others of a gross

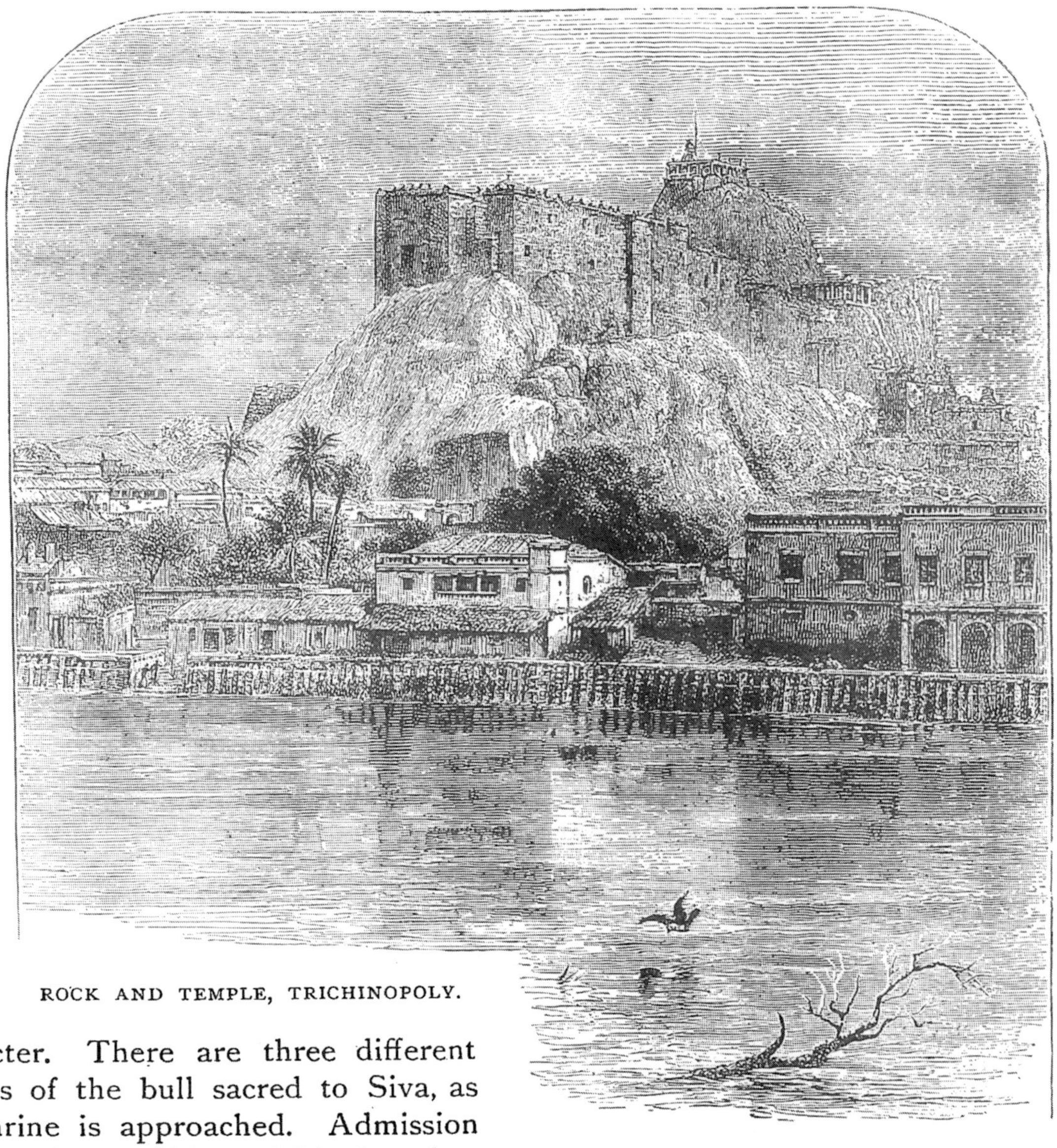

ROCK AND TEMPLE, TRICHINOPOLY.

character. There are three different statues of the bull sacred to Siva, as the shrine is approached. Admission to the shrine itself is prohibited, and as you look up the aisle within, all is darkness and stillness, save in the distance the glimmer of the lamp before the idol. The favorite idols are plastered with oil and red ochre ; and there is a general greasiness about the precincts by no means fragrant or cleanly. Outside the great pagoda, in the street, stands the car in which the idol is taken round the city in pomp on festive occasions. Grandeur and abomination, massiveness and uncleanness, are in this temple strangely combined.

Another celebrated building in Madura, now in great part ruined, is the Palace of Tirumala, one of the greatest of the rulers of the province, built by him in 1623. The hall is a quadrangle, two hundred and fifty by one hundred and fifty feet, and

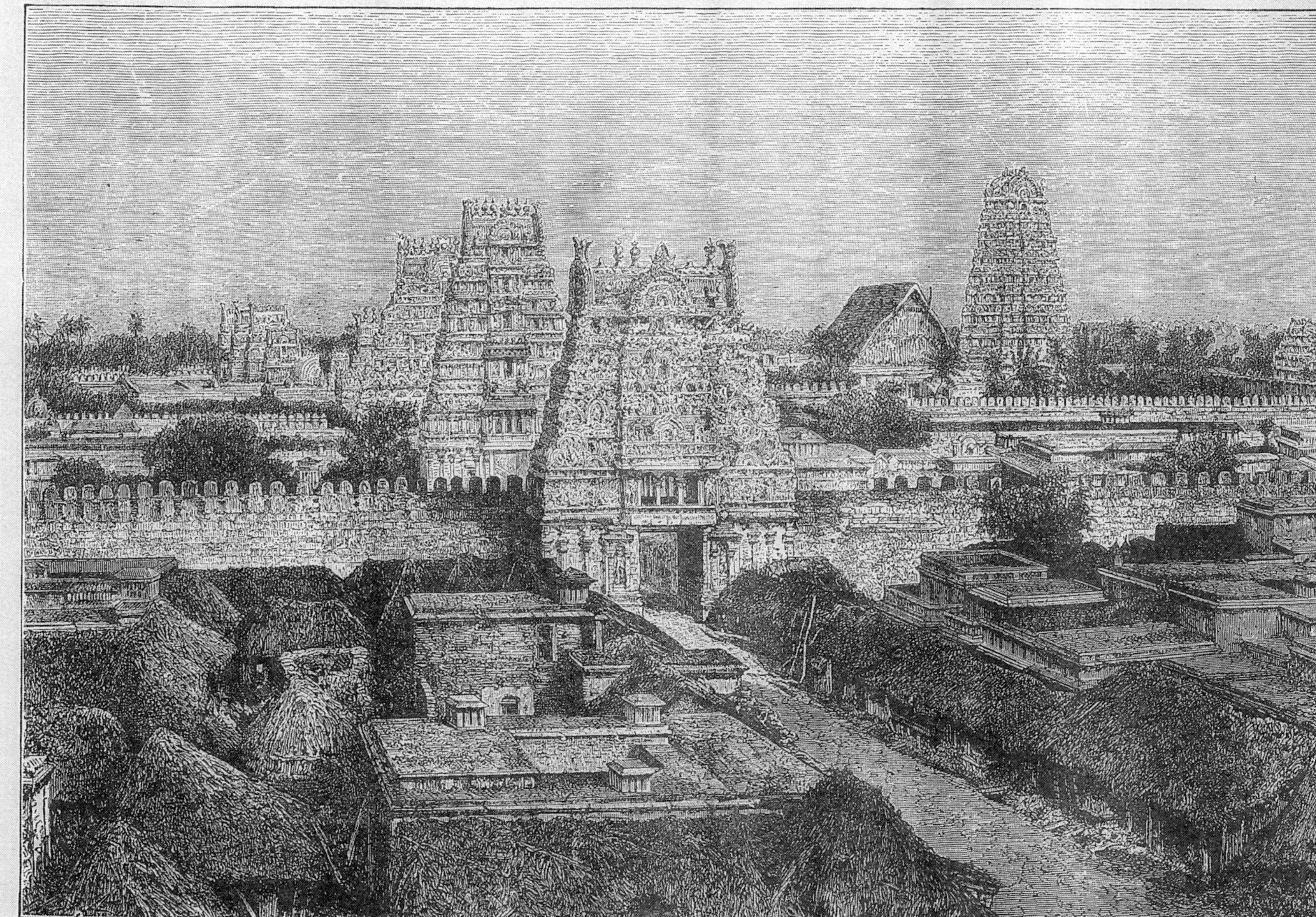

 SERINGHAM.

with an elaborate corridor, and one hundred and twenty-eight massive granite pillars ornamented with stucco, made from *chunam*, or shell lime, which is a characteristic of the Madras Presidency. The British Government is now restoring it, and using it for legislative purposes.

On the other side of the town there is a lovely drive leading to a large sacred tank, the Teppu-kulam, with an island and temple in the center. The road is arched over and shaded with banyan trees; and a very fine specimen of this tree is to be seen in the garden of the Collector. The COLLECTOR in India is, of course, the Civil

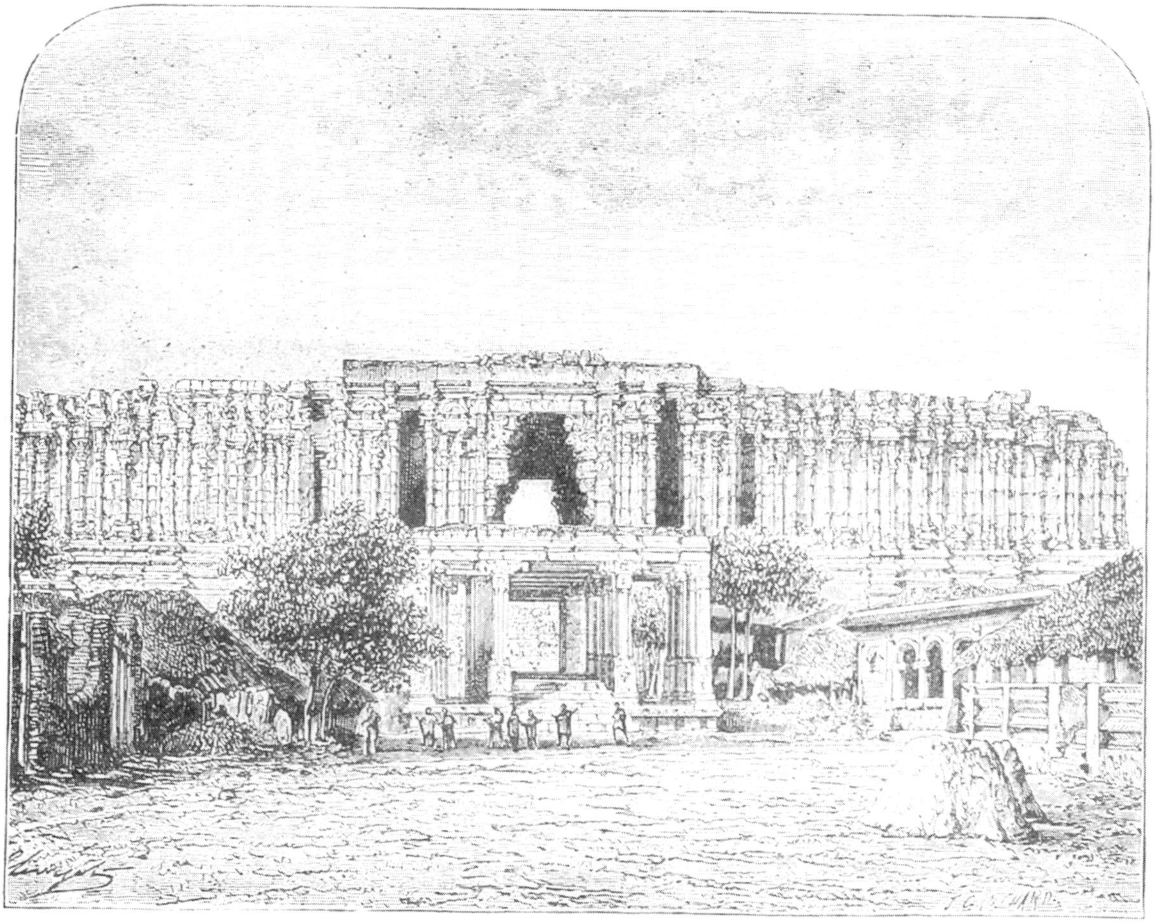

THE RAJAH-GOPURA, SERINGHAM.

Servant, a prince in his way, who represents government in the District. Under the Collector in a Zillah District there are usually four Assistant Collectors, and on a level with him one District Judge, with two Assistant Judges, one Superintendent of Police, with an assistant, and one Medical Officer. The Collector and his English staff hardly ever know the vernacular. By the natives they are regarded with awe, not affection. A Zillah District is in extent somewhat like an English county, and usually contains an area of two or three thousand square miles, and a population of one or two millions. "The Collector is separated by an impassable gulf from the people of the country," says Sir J. B. Phear; and he adds, "To the eyes of a native, the English official is an incomprehensible being, inaccessible, selfish, overbearing, irresistible." This statement is made with reference to the Bengal Presidency, and it applies in its full force to that of Madras. The Collector is paid from the taxes ten or fifteen thousand dollars a year, and retires with an annual pension of five thousand dollars.

At Madura the American Board has a very efficient mission, with valuable schools. It was founded in 1834; since which time it has covered the entire province with a network of stations. It includes one hundred and thirty-eight congregations, a hundred native missionaries, and a hundred native teachers. The institution of boarding-schools, peculiar to missions in Southern India, was introduced by

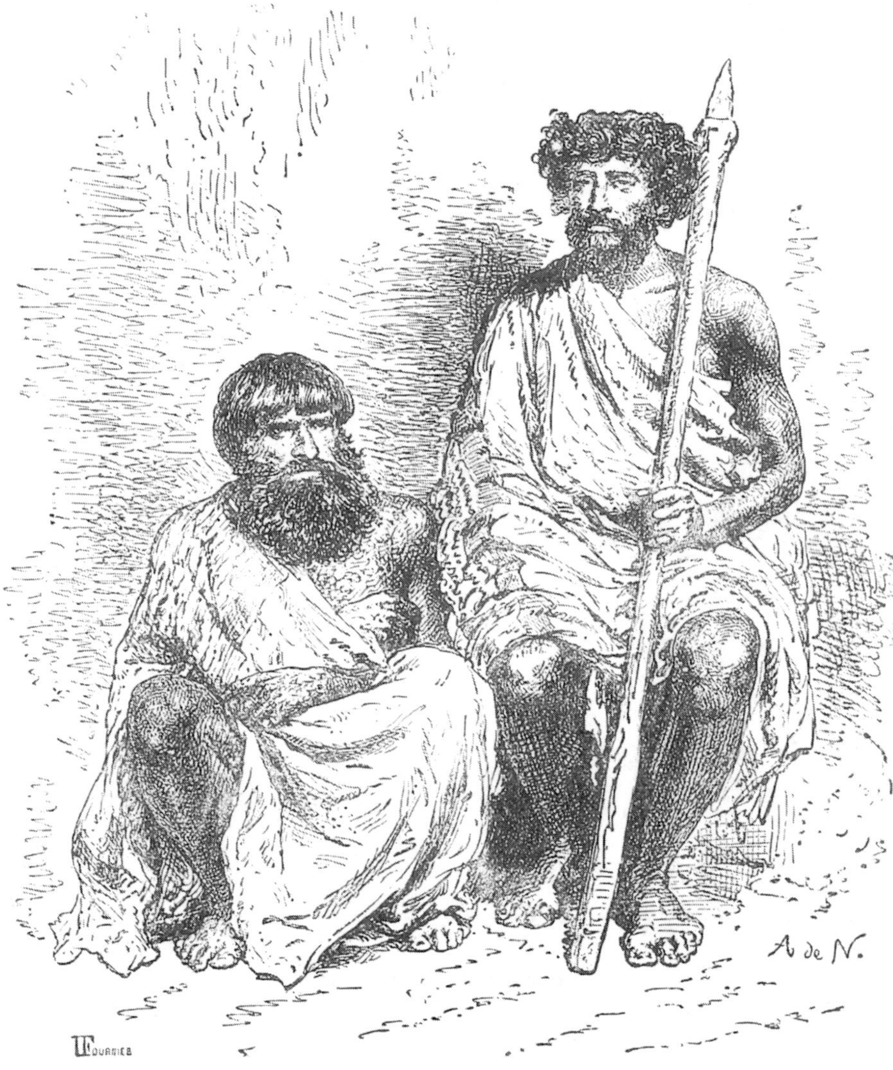

TUDAS IN THE NILGIRIS.

the American Board, and there are in the Madura province one hundred and eighteen schools and training colleges.

In India, even in the coolest season, if you want coolness, you must rise early. It was New Year's morning, and the bright stars of the Southern Cross were still shining, when we drove in the missionary's conveyance to the railway station and took the early train one hundred miles northward for Trichinopoly, a city often taken and retaken in the wars between the French and English in the last century. The sun rose in a clear sky at 6.30, and hills sweeping up from the plain were kindled by his beams. The peasants were already at work like dark skeletons upon the land,

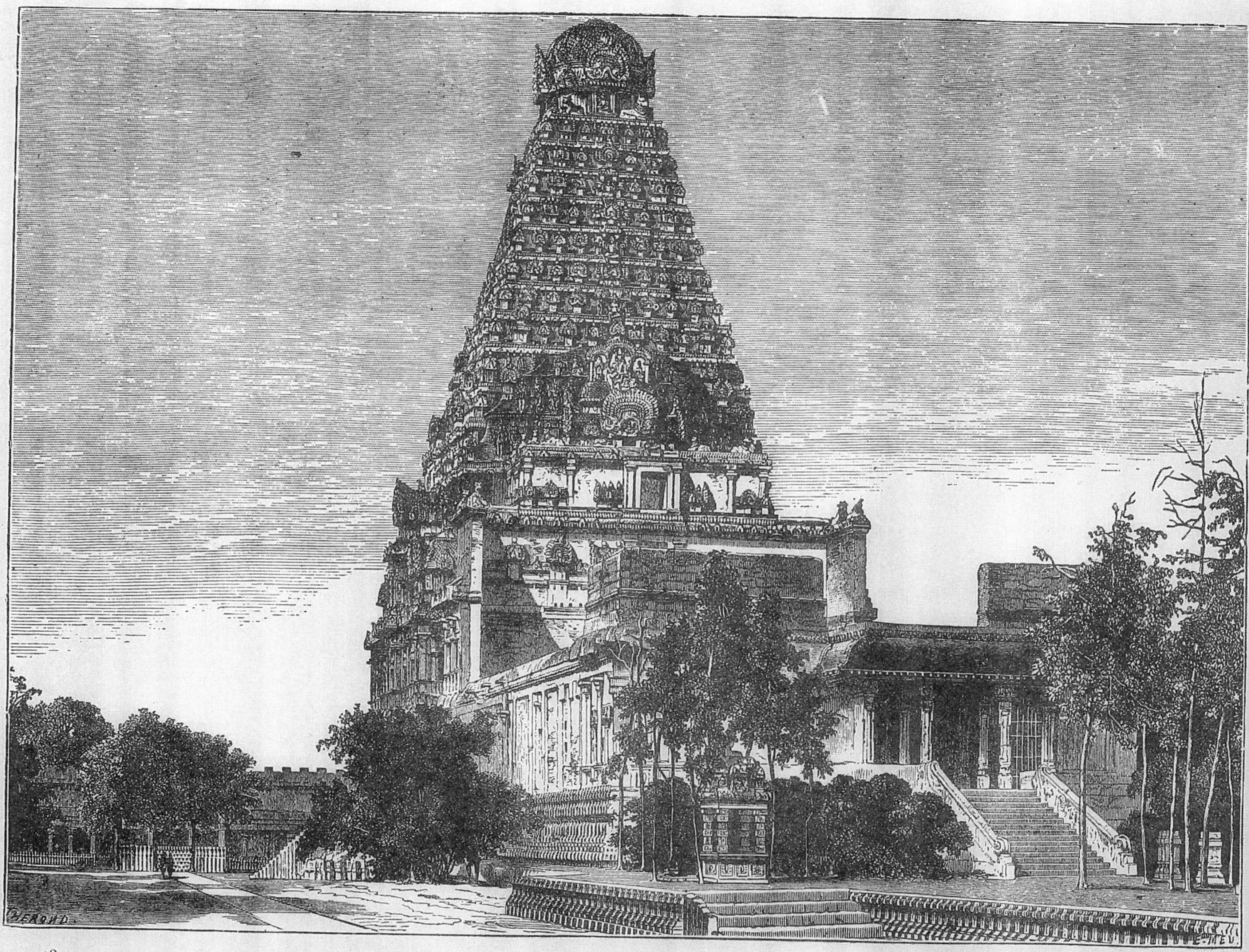

TANJORE.

employed chiefly in lifting water from wells and tanks by means of long bamboo levers, and pouring it into trenches cut through the rice fields. Long before we arrived the famous rock of TRICHINOPOLY was in view before us, and we reached the city in the heat of the day, after a seven hours' journey.

The main feature of Trichinopoly is its noble rock of syenite, rising abruptly five hundred feet above the sea, and towering two hundred and fifty feet over the town. Half way up is a temple to Siva, cut in the rock and built against it. We climbed stair after stair, and up the last dangerous flight of steps cut in the bare precipitous rock, without banister or rail, to the Mandepam or pavilion on the summit, a temple to the god Ganesh. Here there presents itself a clear and extensive view in every direction over the wide-spreading plain, northward over Seringham, east to Tanjore, south and west over the town, where the streets were all alive with

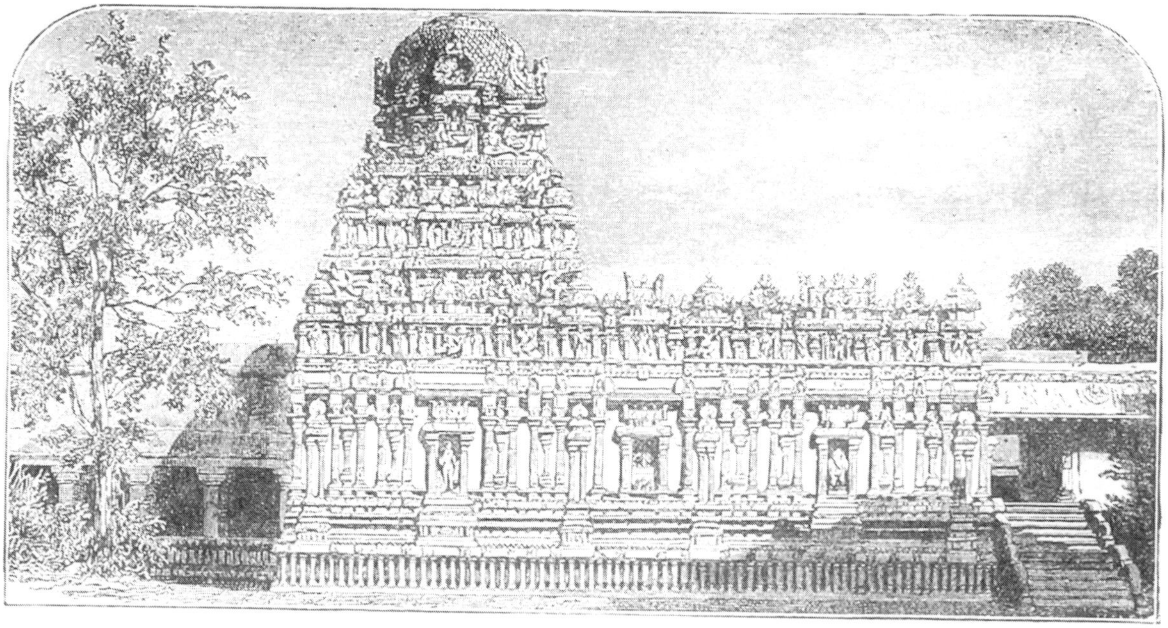

TEMPLE OF SOUBRAMANYA, TANJORE.

a Mohammedan procession and the beating of drums. Outside the town to the southwest lay the military cantonments, where about five thousand troops are kept; and to the west are the chapels, monasteries, and nunneries of the Roman Catholics. Almost all the Tamil servants are said to be Romanists. The Lutherans too have missions here, called the Leipzig Mission, and the new Lutheran church is a conspicuous object. They recognize the laws of caste among their converts. Immediately at the foot of the rock is the chapel in which the well-known missionary, C. F. Schwartz, preached. The old pulpit from which he so often proclaimed the message of Christ to the natives is still there. His influence with the native population was irresistible. In their transactions with the English they would treat only through him. He was born in Germany, on the 26th of October, 1726, and died at Tanjore on the 14th of February, 1789, "revered," as the tablet in his church there says, "by Christian, Mohammedan, and Hindu alike." He left three thousand converts to Christianity behind him, in Tanjore alone. The remains of another famous Indian missionary, Bishop Heber, lie here in St. John's Church. He died suddenly at Trichinopoly, in 1826, when taking a cold bath, in the forty-third year of his age.

A three miles' drive northward brings you to the famous Dravidian temples of SERINGHAM, the largest in all India. Seringham is a river island. The Great Pagoda is seven miles in circumference, and includes many bazaars and streets of Brahmans' houses, so that it is more like a walled town than a temple. The sight of the fourteen magnificent gate towers from the outside is very impressive. Each has huge monoliths of granite on either side, the portico about forty feet high; and above the majestic gateways are pyramids of elaborate stone carving towering up to the height of two hundred feet. You drive through a succession of these towers,

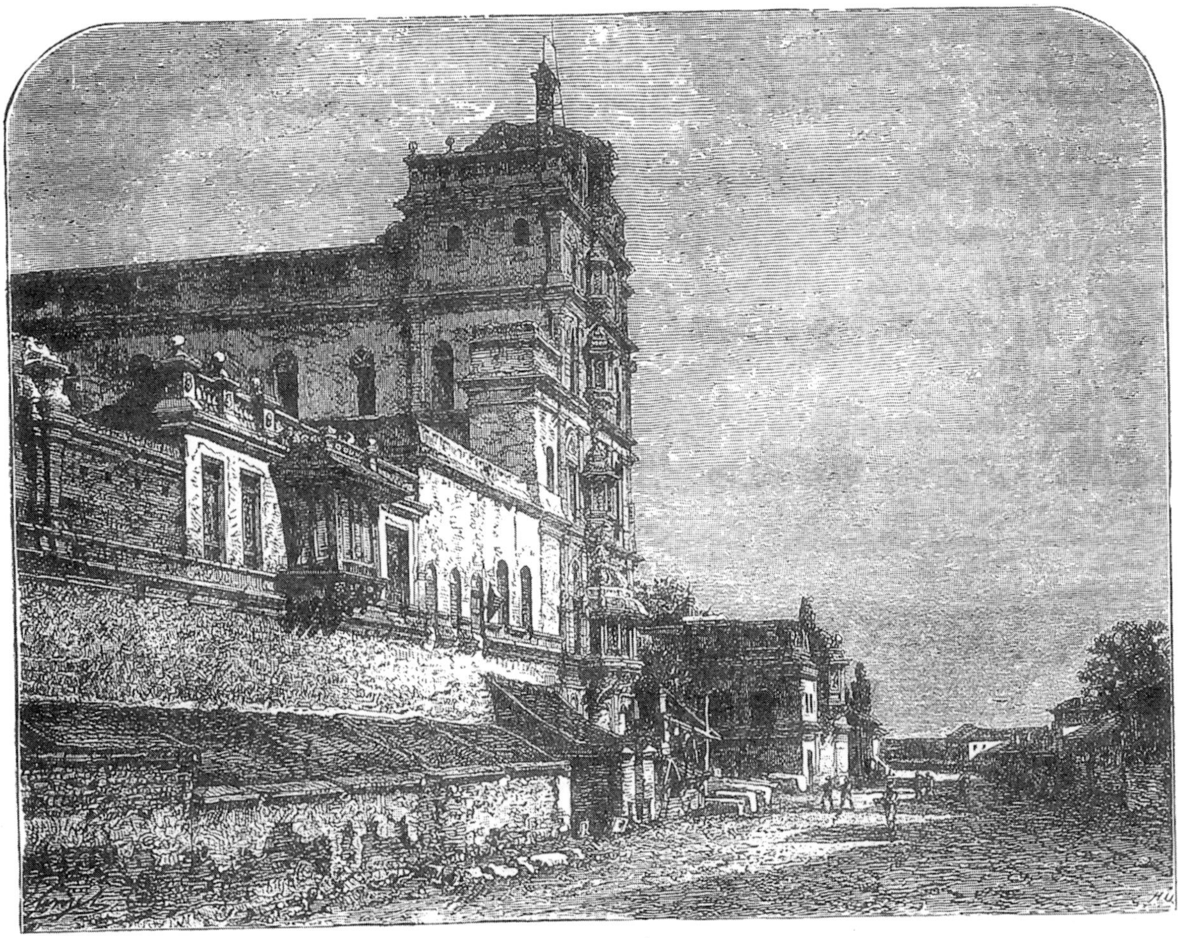

PALACE OF THE RAJAHS AT TANJORE.

and, alighting, you enter on foot a great pillared hall. Its flat stone roof, fifteen feet high, is supported by one thousand columns, each a single block of granite, and all carved into grotesque figures of men mounted upon rearing horses, and spearing tigers, and the like. Beyond is the central shrine, dark and dismal, but surmounted by a golden dome. Near to this four sacred elephants are stabled, and a staircase leads up to the flat stone roof which covers all these acres. The highest tower was ascended by the Prince of Wales during his tour through India in 1875, and he left a gift of five hundred rupees to the temple. The contrast between the vastness, majesty, and grandeur of the temple precincts, embodying the skill and toil of thousands of laborers and lapidaries for years, and the hideous, dirty, greasy little idol before the dimly burning lamp in the center, is striking. The most laborious and elaborate architecture in the world has been raised in honor of hideous idols, and for the most degraded idolatry.

A mile distant is another, smaller but older, pagoda, in decay, but a very compact specimen of Dravidian architecture. As the large temple of Seringham is dedicated to Vishnu, this is raised to Siva, and its name denotes him as "Lord of the rose-apple," or "Lord of India."

Looking westward from Trichinopoly, one sees the noble range of the Nilgiri hills, a group of granite mountains shaped like a triangle, and about forty miles

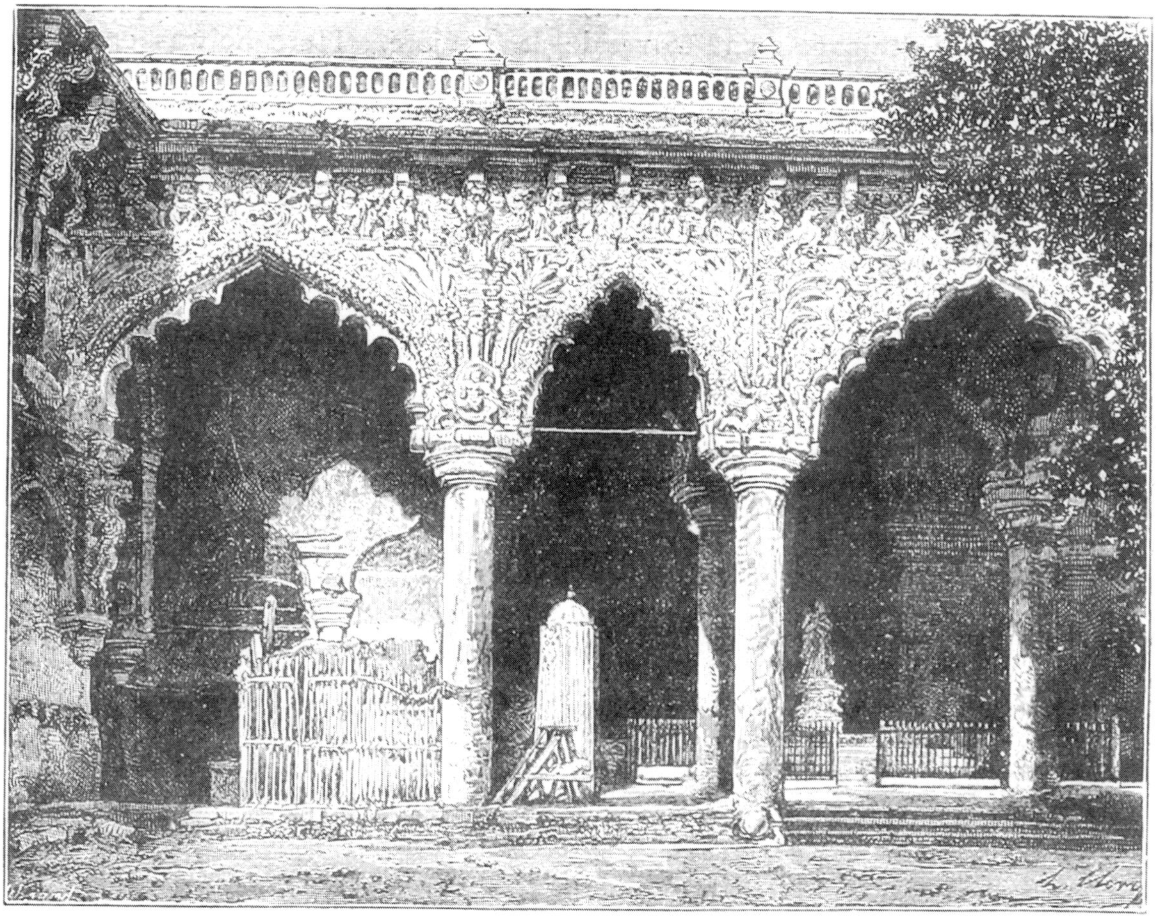

COURT IN PALACE OF THE RAJAH, TANJORE.

in length. Owing to their great elevation of seven thousand feet, they have a delightful climate and are much resorted to. A branch line of railway runs from Coimbatore, northward to Mettapollium ; and thus this healthy and delightful resort is brought within a sixteen hours' journey of Madras itself. Utakamund is the summer seat of the Madras Government. The hills, covered with dark soil and grass, possess a vegetation of the temperate zone, with a mean temperature of 58°. Here live the tribe of Tudas, numbering about two thousand, a handsome race, theists in religion, but with no idols. Three miles from Coimbatore is the Pagoda of Perur, not of very ancient date, but containing interesting details of architecture, and elaborate compound pillars. The subjects of the carving show that degradation which is justly described as "the fatal characteristic of art in India." The excursion to the Anamalai or elephant hills is healthy and exhilarating. There are now extensive coffee plantations on the slopes of the Nilgiri hills. Here is a small but singular tribe of people called TUDAS. They are a handsome race, tall and athletic, with Roman noses, beautiful teeth, and large, full, expressive eyes. They never wear any head covering, but let the hair grow six or seven inches, so that it forms a thick bushy mass of curls all round. They are honest, brave, inoffensive, and live as herdmen, but are somewhat indolent. Polyandry prevails among them, the brothers of a family having often only one wife among them. Their language is peculiar, but Dravidian. They have no idols, but they have a temple dedicated to *Truth.* They regard the Brahmans with contempt. They are considered to be the aborigines of these hills. They only number a few hundred, and are gradually decreasing. The Badaga tribe is more numerous and more accessible to Christian influences.

TANJORE is two hours' journey by railway from Trichinopoly; and crowds of

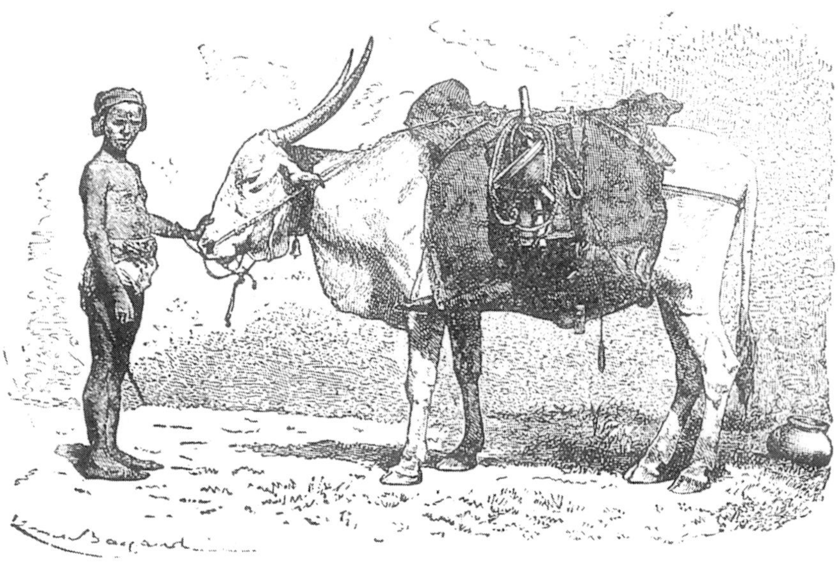

BHISTI, OR WATER-CARRIER.

natives, with the varying symbols of their caste painted on their foreheads, filled the stations and thronged the carriages. There are first, the Brahmans, or priests, sprung from the mouth of Brahma, distinguished by the sacred cord around their bodies; secondly, the Kshuttries, or warriors, sprung from his arms; third, the Vaisyas, from his thighs, the merchants, men of commerce, industry, and agriculture; and fourth, the Sudras, the cultivators of the soil, laborers, and servants, sprung from the feet of Brahma. Below these are those of no caste, the Pariahs or outcasts. One sees men of all these several castes, crowded together, jostling one another on the railway platform and crowding into the same carriage; for though there are four classes of carriages on Indian railways, many of the highest castes are the poorest, and have to travel fourth class, and you will see the Brahman sitting side by side with the Pariah. The railway is the great antagonist to caste in India.[1]

Tanjore is a large city of a hundred thousand inhabitants. In former times it was the seat of Brahminical learning, and it contains several pagodas in large, green areas or gardens, and two large walled forts. As you approach the city, the Great Pagoda, with its lofty tower, is a conspicuous object, impressive and graceful. Its

[1] The Institutes of Menu provide that if Sudras, comprising three-fourths of the Hindus, dare to sit with their superiors, they shall be gashed on the buttocks or suffer exile. For sitting with a Brahman the penalty was maiming for life.—ED.

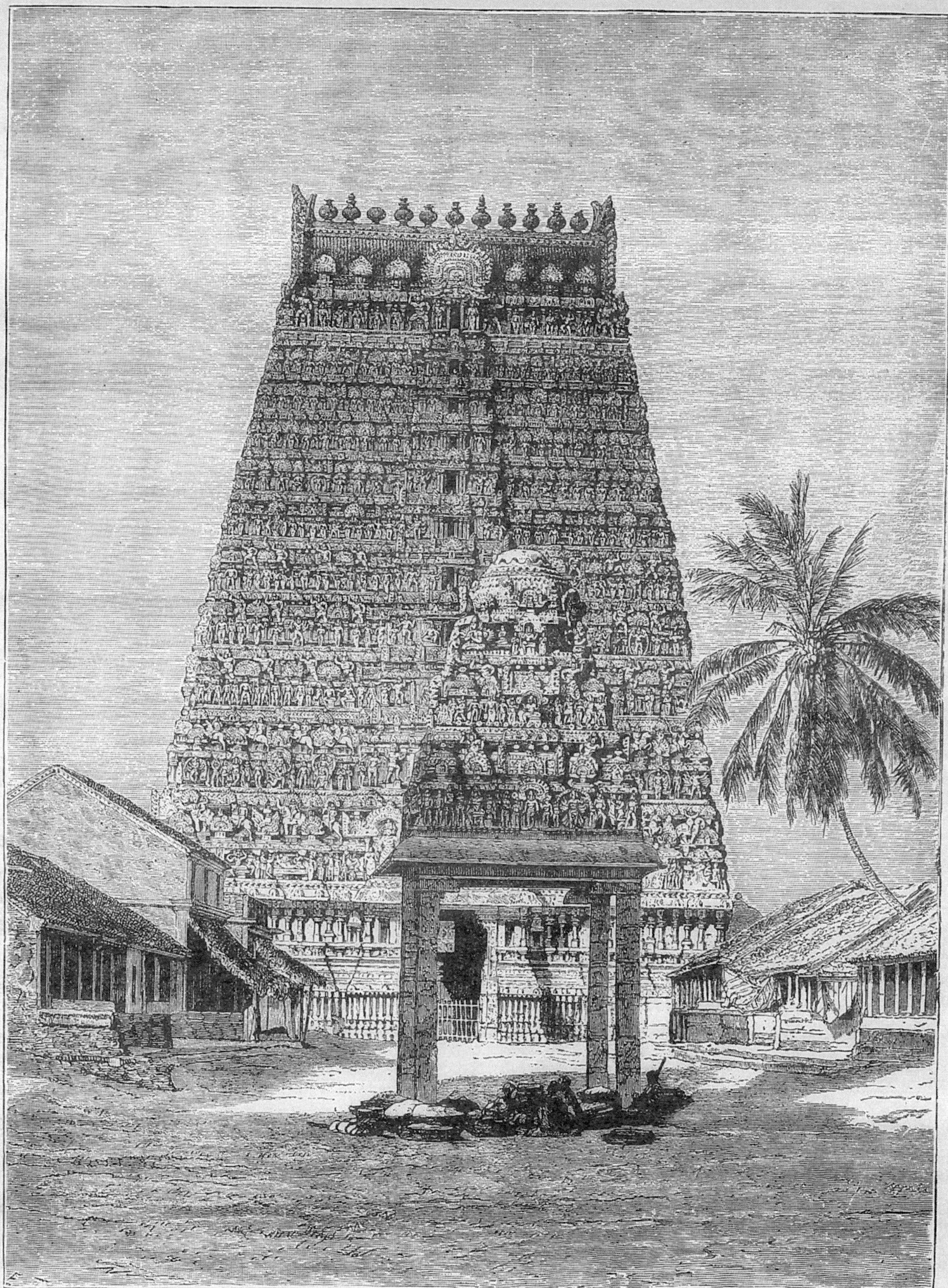

GOPURA AT COMBACONUM.

base measures eighty feet square, and the pyramid rises fourteen stories to the height of two hundred feet. The top-stone is a huge monolith, beautifully carved and weighing eighty tons. The courts are not covered over as at Madura, but are open to light and air, and within the precincts is a large open square six hundred feet by

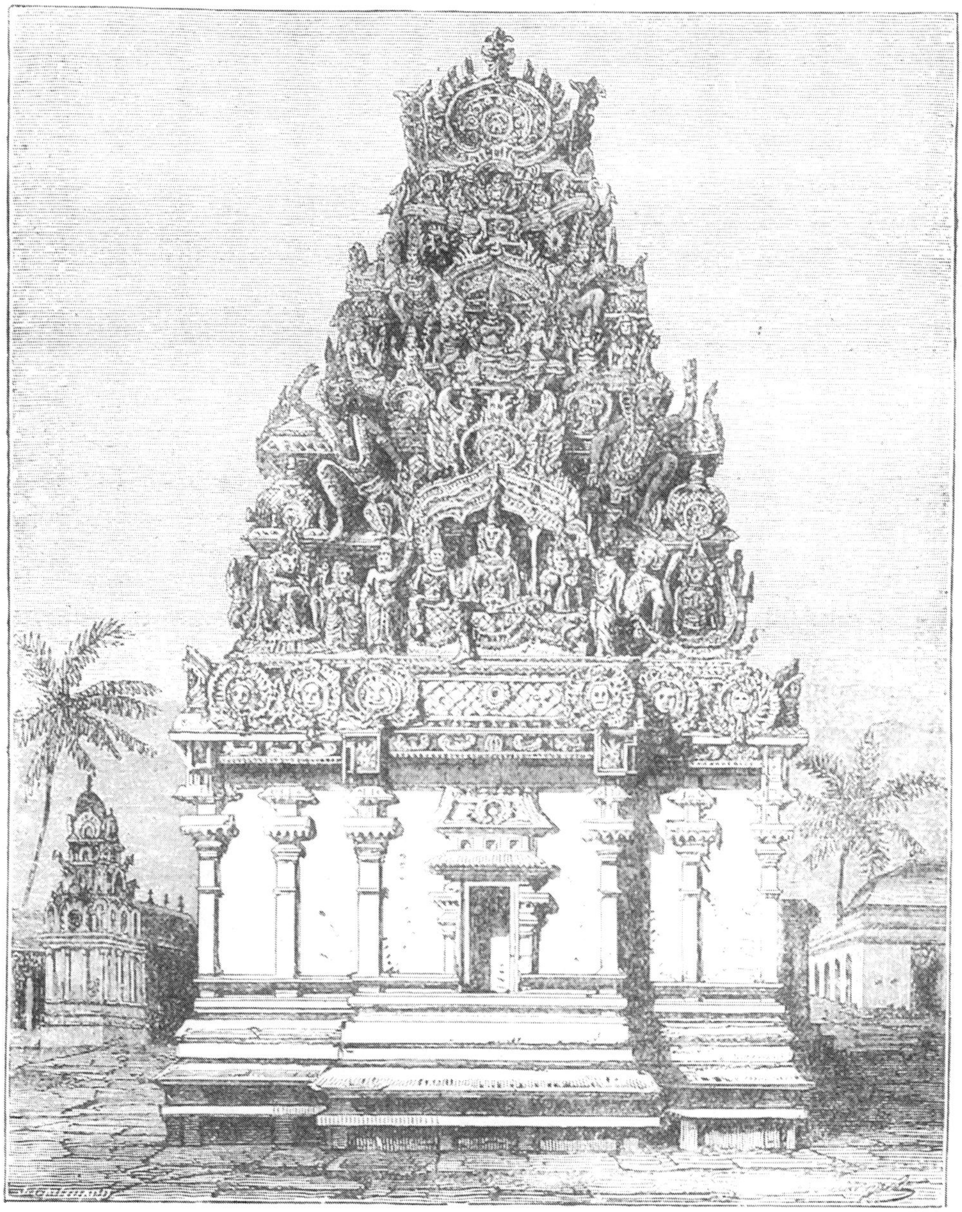

PAGODA AT PONDICHERRY.

two hundred. Here is the colossal stone bull Nundi, fifteen feet long and twelve feet high, in a couching posture. It rests upon a platform which you ascend by twelve steps, and has over it a large canopy supported by granite pillars. This bull, sacred to Siva, faces the magnificent temple, an oblong building of red sandstone, with the huge tower rising nobly over the shrine. Farther on to the left, but within the inclosure, is another but much smaller shrine, of beautifully carved stone, and cloisters surround the court, covered with coarse pictures of heroes. To the right, within the court, is the Temple of Soubramanya, "as exquisite a piece of decorative architecture," says Mr. Fergusson, "as is to be found in the south of India." The steps up to its entrance are supported by small carved elephants with men, in singular attitudes, sitting on or falling from their trunks. The palace of the Princess of Tanjore contains an open court, with singular figures in stone, and a statue in white marble of the late Rajah. In the Protestant mission church, built by Schwartz, the remains of this German missionary lie. A slab behind the pulpit, with an inscription, marks the spot. The country about Tanjore looked peculiarly rich and fertile. The great river Kâveri here opens out into a delta, and irrigation works of considerable extent distribute its fertilizing waters.

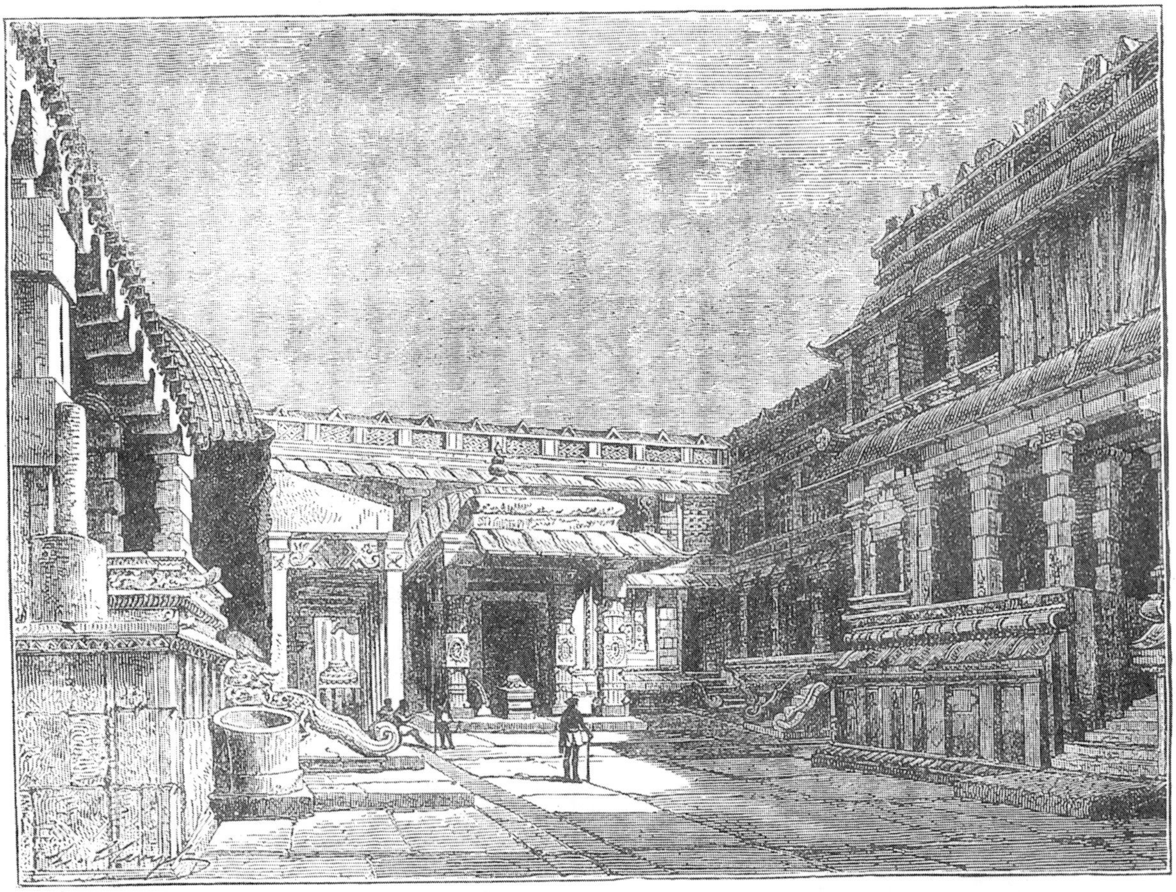

PAGODA OF CHILLAMBARAM: INTERIOR COURT.

The Danes were the first among Protestant nations to send the Gospel to India, for in the year 1705 Ziegenbalg came to Tranquebar on the east coast, and made his way to Tanjore dressed in native costume. The Rajah at first objected, but afterward sanctioned the mission. Ziegenbalg, having translated the New Testament into Tamil, died in 1719, and his work was resumed by Schultze, and several congregations of Christians grew up in the kingdom of Tanjore. Then followed the war between France and England which ended in the conquests of the latter under Clive, and the chaplaincy of the garrison of Trichinopoly by the equally eminent soldier, although of the Prince of Peace, the well-known Schwartz, whom the Rajah requested to remove from Trichinopoly and to reside at Tanjore. Here he was employed upon several occasions to treat with the native princes. "Let them send the Christian," said they; "he will not deceive us." On two occasions, when the Fort of Tanjore was threatened with famine, and the Rajah was powerless to obtain supplies, Schwartz, at his earnest request, undertook to relieve it, and succeeded in saving its inmates from starvation. A few hours before his death the Rajah requested Schwartz to act as a guardian to his infant son. Schwartz, in fact, was revered as a father by the people as well as by the Rajah of Tanjore. The Tanjore mission was his chief work, and he continued its guiding spirit to the end. At his death in 1798, after forty-eight years spent in the country, a long and bitter cry of lamentation arose from multitudes, and the Rajah shed a flood of tears over his body, and covered it with a gold cloth. The Christian Knowledge Society sustained the mission after Schwartz's death, and the Leipzig missionaries commended their Christianity to the Hindus by the adoption of caste, a step which has made the prosecution of Christian work very difficult. But the Propagation Society has nine central missions in the provinces of Tanjore and Trichinopoly.

The new railway between Tanjore and Madras was not yet complete, the bridges over the Peravanur not being built. In the middle of the night we were conveyed in bullock wagons inland and across this estuary, thus giving us an idea of what traveling must have been in the country before railways were made.[1]

The line runs along the tract of country long known as the Coromandel Coast, which stretches for about four hundred miles north from Adam's Bridge. Throughout its whole extent this coast does not afford any secure port or harbor. A heavy surf rolls in upon the flat, sandy shore. The soil near the coast is a mixture of sea-sand and loam, often in dry weather covered with salt. Farther inland low hills commence, and the soil, when irrigated, is fertile, but the upper part of the hills is sterile.

This coast, though destitute of harbors, has been the favorite country for European settlements. Here is PONDICHERRY, still belonging to the French, divided into two portions: the white town orderly, neat, with beautiful boulevards, the black, or native town, with a large pagoda. Its lower part is quite plain, but from its cornice upward there are large and fantastic figures, those in the center somewhat resembling Buddha, and indicating the influence of his system, even in South India. The summit seems to represent the Buddhist trinity.

Pondicherry is a town of fifty thousand inhabitants, including about a thousand Europeans. The *Missions étrangères de France* have a settlement here. They are successful among the natives; but they conform in great part to their idolatrous customs and caste prejudices. The priests have assumed the character of Brahmans of a superior caste from the Western world. In fact, at one time they were wont to wear the *cavy*, or orange robe, peculiar to the most venerated Brahmans, and carried on their foreheads the sacred spot of sandal-wood powder. "If," says Abbé Dubois, "any mode of Christian worship is calculated to gain ground in India, it is no doubt the Catholic form, which Protestants consider idolatry. Its external pomp and show are well suited to the genius of the natives. It has a *pooja*, or sacrifice, viz., the mass; processions, images, and statues; *tirtan*, or holy water; feasts, fasts, and prayers for the dead; invocation of saints and other practices which bear more or less resemblance to that of the Hindus."

Here, too, is Cuddalore, now a handsome town of forty thousand inhabitants, formerly belonging to the French, but yielded by treaty in 1795, and Tranquebar,

[1] The custom of reckoning time from midnight is now introduced on some Indian railways. Midnight is zero, noon, 12; 1 P.M. is 13, and so on to 23.59, one minute before the next midnight.

once a Danish settlement. The entire district abounds in specimens of Dravidian architecture. Far south by Paumban Passage is the great Pagoda of Ramessveram, exhibiting all the beauties of the Dravidian style, with four stone towers and corridors with columns elaborately carved.

On the railway, twenty-four miles northeast from Tanjore, we pass Combaconum, a town of forty-five thousand inhabitants, one of the old capitals of the native Chola kingdom. It was once called the Oxford of Southern India, on account of its learning. It has a richly ornamented tower, twelve stories, and is one hundred and fifty feet high. The Chola kingdom was one of that triarchy of kingdoms which existed in South India in the time of Asoka, and down to the Mohammedan conquests, the other two being the Chêra and the Pândya. The large pagoda here is dedicated to Vishnu, another indication of Buddhist influence, for Siva is the favorite deity of the south, and Vishnuism, Mr. Fergusson observes, is a bad and corrupt form of Buddhism. The great tower can be ascended, but the stone steps are old and broken, and there is no hand-rail ; the floors are of stone, and shake alarmingly to the tread. Near the temple is a large sacred tank into which it is said that the Ganges flows every year. So vast is the concourse of people who descend into the water to bathe at one time, that the surface rises some inches. This confirms their belief in the miracle. The idol cars are drawn through the streets, as at Puri, and every year persons are accidentally crushed beneath their wheels. The tank is surrounded by a number of small pagodas, each containing a *lingam*.

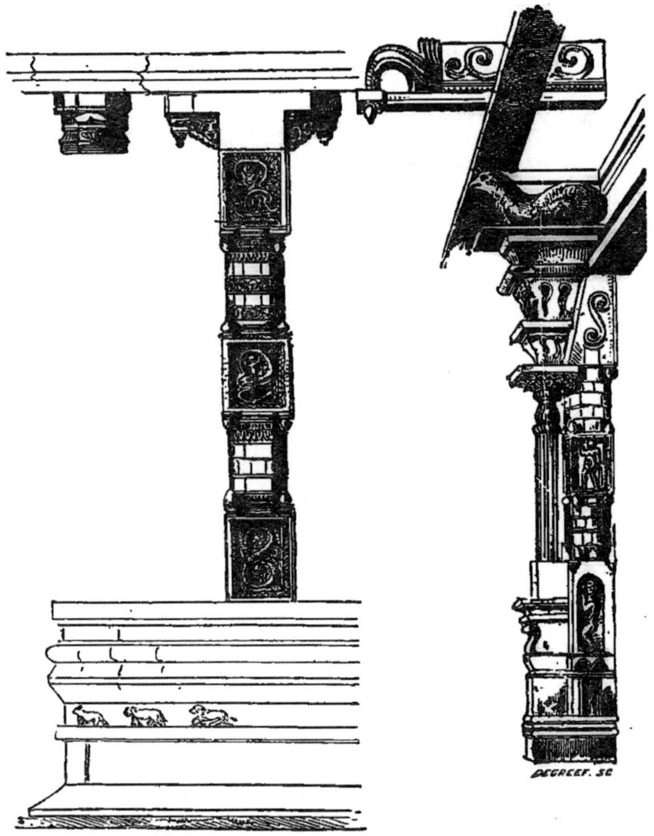

SPECIMENS OF SCULPTURE ON PILLARS, IN THE GRAND GALLERY, CHILLAMBARAM.

The Beauchamp College at Combaconum is one of the best educational institutions in South India, and there is a very good school for girls, with upward of a hundred scholars. Farther north is Chillambaram, with a very large tank, and at the four cardinal points four vast towers, together with the usual hall of a thousand pillars. On the west of the tank is the Temple of Parvati, sixty-eight feet high, and on the south the Temple of Siva, containing the sacred image of the dancing Siva. The roof is covered with plates of copper gilt. This temple is reputed to be one of the most ancient of the Dravidian pagodas. It is highly venerated by the people, who believe it to be the work of a king in the sixth century whose name signifies "golden-colored emperor." The tradition is that he was a leper, but miraculously recovered by bathing in the sacred waters of the tank at Chillambaram. In gratitude he rebuilt the temple. The outer wall is six hundred yards by five hundred, and in the center lies the celebrated tank around which the buildings cluster. The four points of the compass are marked by four large gopuras or towers. In the sixteenth century the kings of the triarchy made many donations to the fane. The oldest thing now existing is, in Mr. Fergusson's judgment, a little shrine in the inmost inclosure with a little porch of two pillars, more graceful and more elegantly executed than any other of their class. A chain cut out of solid stone connects two similar and corresponding pillars, upon which dancing figures are engraved in honor of Venna, the god of dancing, of Kashmir, with whom a legend has connected the building. A double gallery with plain and chaste columns runs along the interior inclosure wall. But the most elegant workmanship is found in the porch of the Temple of Parvati, the central aisle of which is seven yards wide. Here the architect has put forth all his power. The temple is an aggregate of buildings of different styles of architecture. Portions could not have been raised till after the Mohammedans had settled in the south and taught the Hindus their methods. It is of granite, and now covers thirty-nine acres of ground.

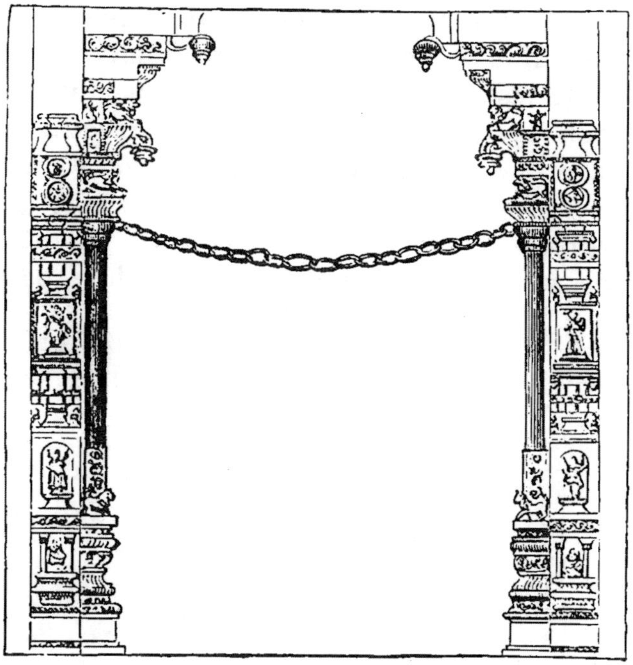

CHAIN CUT OUT OF A SINGLE STONE; PILLARS 27 FEET APART, CHILLAMBARAM.

At CONJEVERAM, one of the seven holy cities of India, and the Benares of the south, once a city of the Hindu kingdom of Chola, there are two groups of temples, with commanding gopuras nearly two hundred feet high. A symbol like a horseshoe on the wall of the inner inclosure is said to be the first letter of the word Vishnu, and there has been hard fighting for nearly a century about the form of this symbol; indeed, the Tamils are still at law about it. The one party contend that the mark or symbol—made with a kind of white paint on the forehead—should be made with a plain line, while the other party make it with a little boss at the bottom, extending half-way down the nose! These are the two sects of the Vishnuvites. The usual mark worn by the Vishnu worshipers is two *perpendicular* strokes meeting below in a curve; that of the Siva worshipers is quite different, consisting of three *horizontal* lines, usually white. The town of Conjeveram is full of fine trees and low houses. Fantastic figures in wood in the thousand-pillared hall are carried in procession on festival occasions. A large number of *nautch* girls are kept in this

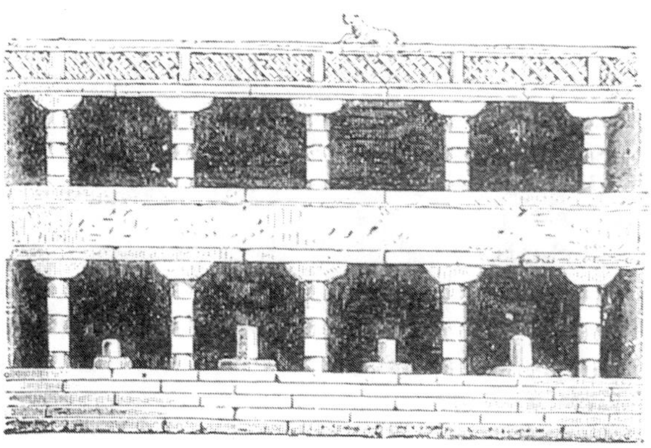

DOUBLE GALLERY, CHILLAMBARAM.

temple. The gopuras are full of chambers, but all unoccupied. This is strange, for their great height must conduce to airiness and coolness. But when asked, the Brahmans said they dared not sleep there, for fear of being attacked by evil spirits, ghosts of Brahmans turned into devils ; and they used both the Sanscrit and English word explaining the forms as high-caste devils.

About three hours before reaching Madras forty miles south, on the coast, are the ruins of an extensive town cut in rock, and called Mahavalipur, or the Seven Pagodas. Here are many curious excavations and carvings in the rock—groups of monkeys ; the boar's temple, representing Vishnu as a boar ; the tiger's cave, a cave surrounded with tiger's heads carved in the rock. Another singularly sculptured rock, forty feet high and twice as long presents a hundred strange figures of men, women, monkeys, and elephants. The shore temple is washed by the waves, and the legend tells of many similar buildings partially submerged.

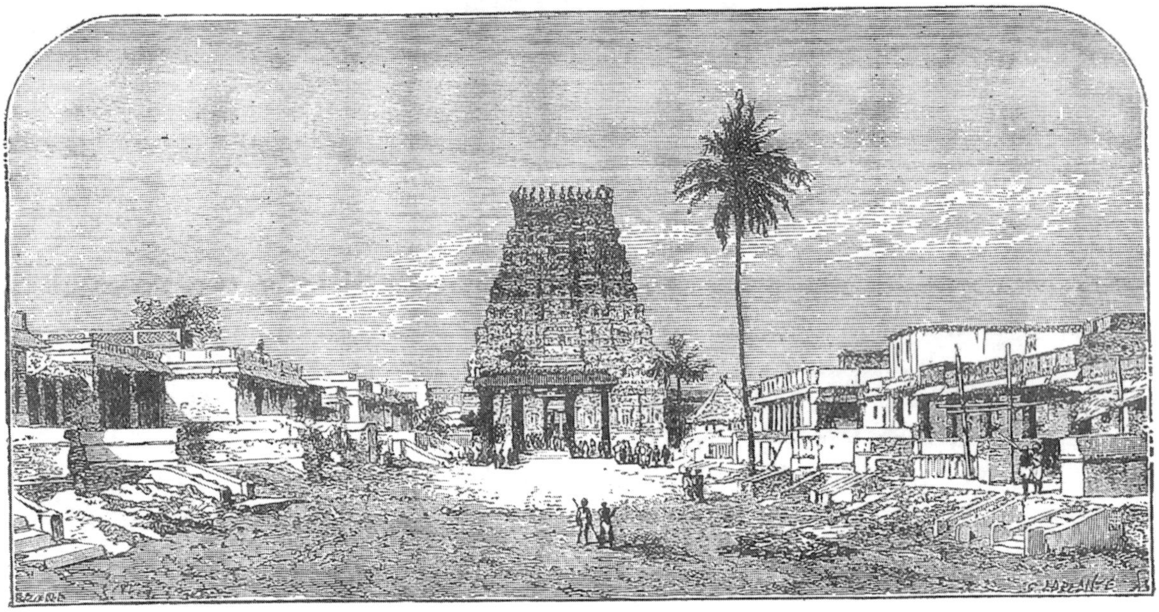

ENTRANCE TO THE PAGODA, CONJEVERAM.

Southey, in his *Curse of Kehama*, refers to this legend of a submerged city thus :

" For many an age
Hath ocean warred against his palaces,
Till overwhelmed beneath the waves—
Not overthrown—so well the awful chief
Had laid their deep foundations. . . . .
Their golden summits in the noonday light
Shone o'er the dark green deep that rolled between,
Her domes and pinnacles and spires were seen
Peering above the sea, a mournful sight.
And on the sandy shore, beside the verge
Of ocean, here and there a rock-cut fane
Resisted in its strength the surf and surge
That on their deep foundations beat in vain."

Mahavalipur is, according to Mr. Fergusson, a petrified Buddhist village, applied to the purposes of another religion, but representing Buddhist forms in the seventh century, when Buddhism was dying out. Doubtless it had some connection with Ceylon. The people who carved these curious monuments seem, says Mr. F., suddenly to have settled on a spot where no temples existed before, and to have set to work at once to fashion the detached granite boulders they found on the shore into nine raths or miniature temples. They pierced the side of the hill with fourteen caves, carved two long bas-reliefs, and then abandoned them unfinished. The raths are close together on the sandy beach south of the hill of caves. The roofs are ornamented with ranges of little recesses or simulated cells, which characterize the

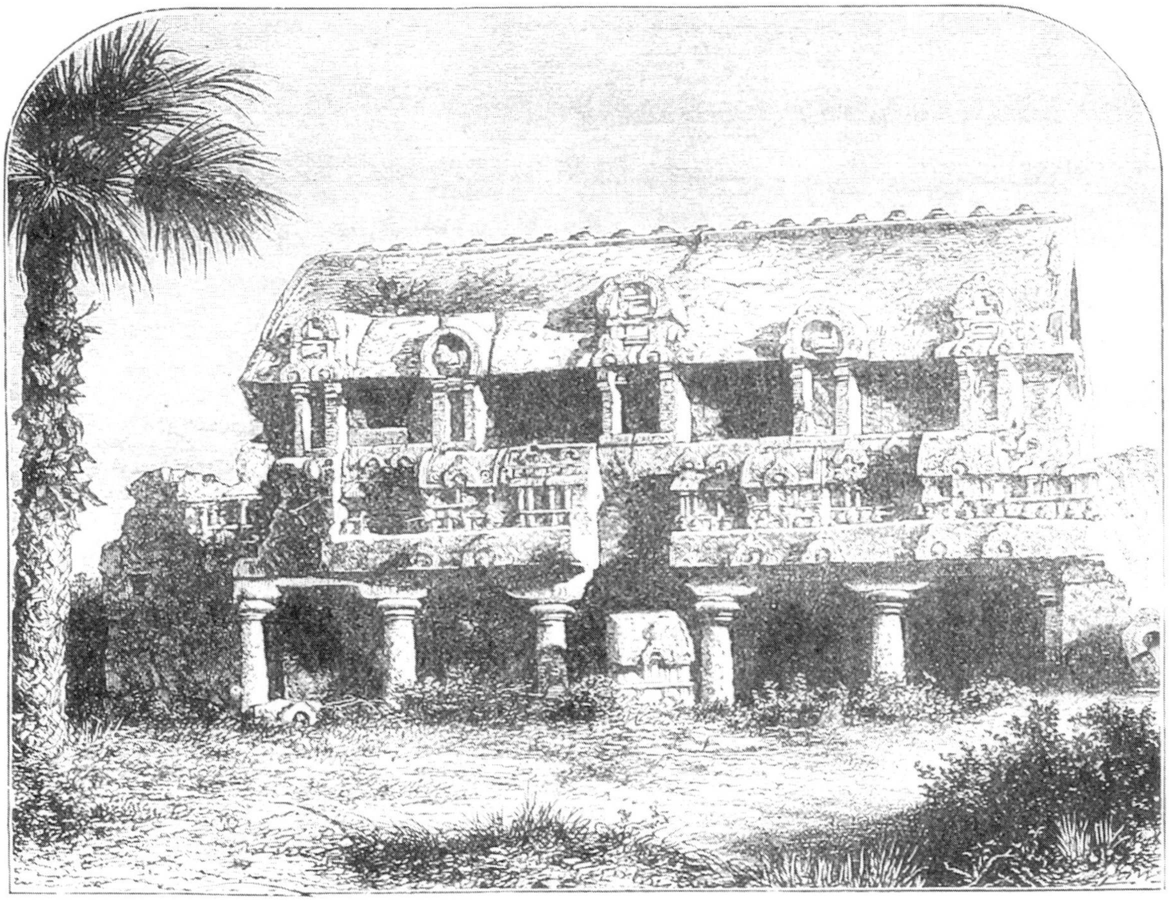

MAHAVALIPUR : THE CHAITIYA.

Dravidian temples, and are surmounted by a dome, an equally universal feature. These singular ruins, while they are memorials of Buddhism in its decay, throw light upon the history of the Dravidian buildings, which probably were originally of wood, and from about the seventh century began to be constructed in stone. Regarding the Hinduism of Southern India, as embodied in these temples, Dr. Monier Williams says : " Religion is even more closely interwoven with every affair of daily life, and is even more showily demonstrative in the south of India than in the north. A distinction must be pointed out between Brahmanism and Hinduism. Brahmanism is the purely pantheistic and not necessarily idolatrous creed evolved by the Brahmans out of the religion of the Veda. Hinduism is that complicated system of polytheistic doctrines, idolatrous superstitions, and caste usages which have been developed out of Brahmanism after its contact with Buddhism and its admixture with the non-Aryan

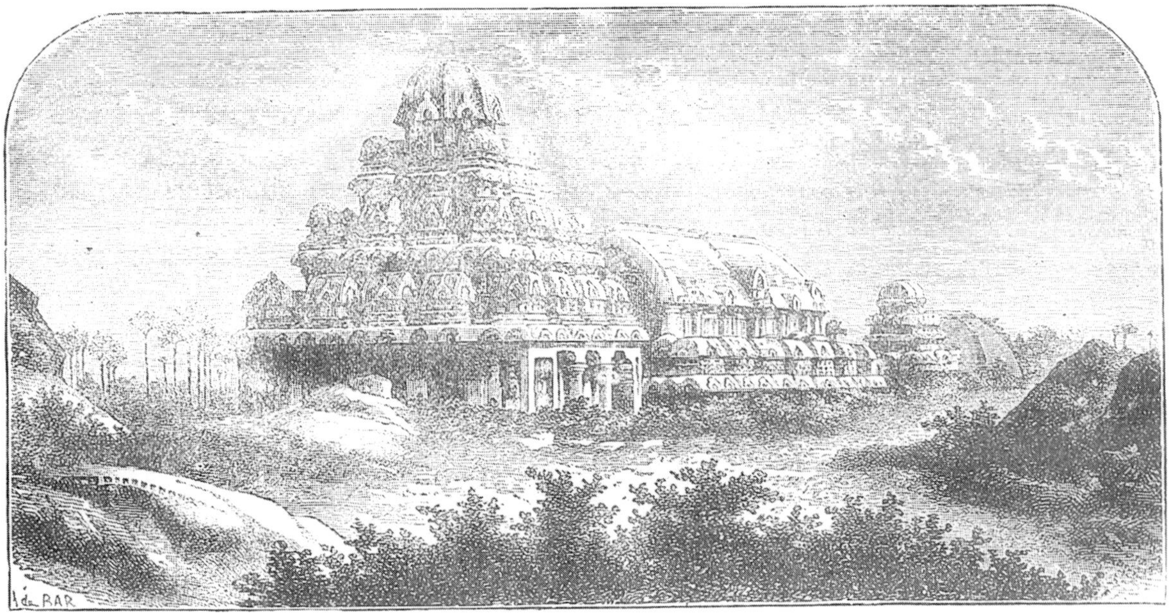

GREAT RATH AT MAHAVALIPUR.

creeds of the Dravidians and aborigines of Southern India. Brahmanism and Hinduism, though infinitely remote from each other, are integral parts of the same system. One is the germ or root, the other is the rank and diseased outgrowth. . . . . Vaishnavism and Saivism, or the worship of Vishnu and Siva, constitute the very heart and soul of Southern Hinduism. As to Brahma, the third member of the Hindu Triad, and original creator of the world, he is not worshiped at all, except in the person of his alleged offspring, the Brahmans. Moreover, Vaishnavism and Saivism are nowhere so pronounced and imposing as in Southern India. The temples of Conjeveram, Tanjore, Trichinopoly, Madura, Tinnevelly, and Ramessveram are as superior in magnitude to those of Benares as Westminster Abbey and St. Paul's are to the other churches of London. Furthermore, it must not be forgotten that although a belief in devils, and homage to *bhutas*, or spirits of all kinds, are common all over India, yet what is called 'devil worship' is far more systematically practiced in the South of India and in Ceylon than in the North. The god Siva is constantly connected with demoniacal agencies, either as superintending and controlling them, or as himself possessing, especially in the person of his wife Kali, all the fierceness and malignity usually attributed to demons. . . . . All honor to those noble-hearted missionaries who are seeking by the establishment of female schools to supply India with its most pressing need—good wives and mothers—and are training

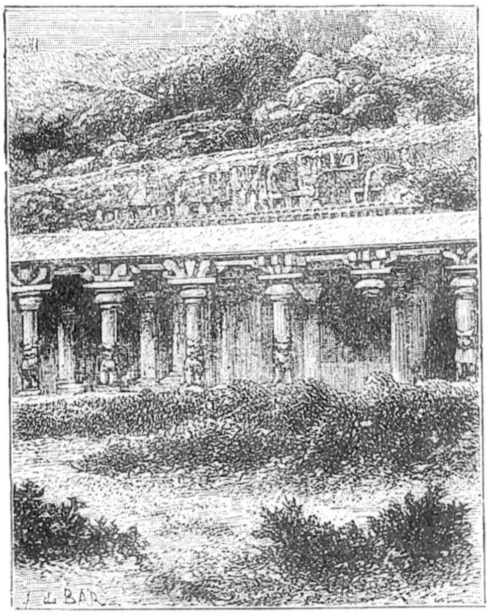

DETAILS OF ENTRANCES TO SUBTERRANEAN TEMPLES, MAHAVALIPUR.

girls to act as high-class schoolmistresses, and sending them forth to form new centers of female education in various parts of Southern India."

No city, perhaps, in the world has a site so utterly unpropitious and disadvantageous as MADRAS. On a coast exposed without shelter to the northeast monsoon, with a barrier of sand lashed continually by a surf passable in fine weather only by native boats of singular construction, manned by native boatmen, and in foul weather insurmountable even by these, with no navigable river flowing into the sea, it spreads along the border of a wilderness of barren sand in the torrid zone, exposed to the unsheltered glare of a scorching sun. The first British settlement was at Armagan, sixty miles north, but in 1639 was abandoned for the miserable spot, granted in irony by a native prince, upon which Fort St. George was built. Nothing more strikingly illustrates the power of British pluck and enterprise than the present aspect of Madras. Along that inhospitable coast for a distance of nine miles, and covering that sandy waste, there now stretches a thriving city, with an area of twenty-seven square miles, and a population of four hundred thousand. Along that unprotected roadstead the ships of all nations ride at anchor to take in or discharge cargo; and from the city the iron horse wends its way northwesterly across the continent, eight hundred miles in forty hours, to Bombay, and sends its tracks southward almost to Cape Comorin. The meridian of Madras now gives its time to the entire railway system of India.

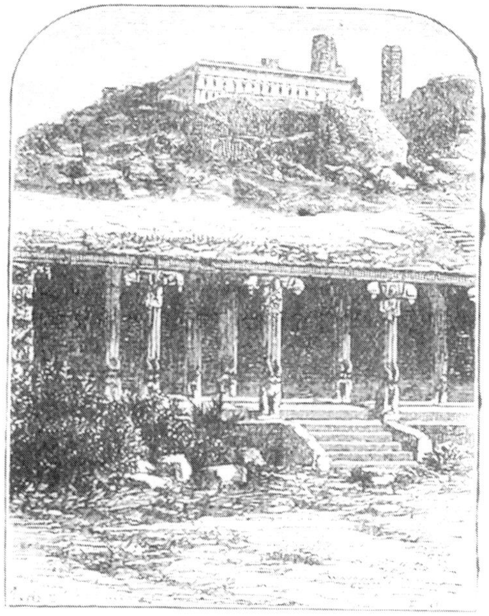

ENTRANCES TO SUBTERRANEAN TEMPLES, MAHAVALIPUR.

Spreading over this wide area, Madras is an aggregation of no less than twenty-three towns and villages, with public buildings, European residences, warehouses, and even shops, in park-like inclosures, filling up the intervening spaces. Beginning with the north, there is Royapuram, with the Tinnevelly settlement; then the Black Town, defended from the encroachments of the sea by a strong stone bulwark, and with seven wells of water, filtered through the sand, pure and wholesome. The population of these two is one hundred and fifty thousand. Next comes Fort St. George, the first nucleus of the city, strongly fortified, containing the arsenal, council house, and the Fort church, with its monument to the missionary Schwartz; and beyond, the island and the Governor's house and gardens. Then southward, Triplicane, the Mohammedan quarter, with eighty thousand souls; and beyond this St. Thomé, the traditional site of the martyrdom of the Apostle Thomas. Inland, beyond the Fort and the Black Town, are Chintadrepettah and Vepery, in which stands the church where the Lutheran missionary Sartorius preached for many years, and where the London Mission has its compound. The view from the lighthouse, one hundred and eleven feet high, is extensive; one sees the entire city, and the shore for miles. The houses for the most part are yellow, covered with the stucco called chunam, which when dried and polished has the appearance of the finest marble. The grounds round the European houses are well planted, and the country now presents a green and cheerful aspect. Mount Road, running south and inland, leads to many bungalows and hotels. The drive along the beach to the Capper House is the pleasantest in Madras. Here one meets the sea breeze, appropriately called by the residents "The Doctor." Here we pass the most imposing of the public buildings of the city, in particular the University. It was strange to see on the Sunday the punkas swinging during service in the churches. Like huge weavers' beams with heavy curtains, they are kept in motion by means of cords pulled from the outside by two natives, who keep each other awake. However strict a Sabbatarian, the minister as well as the people must have the punka kept going over his head throughout the service.

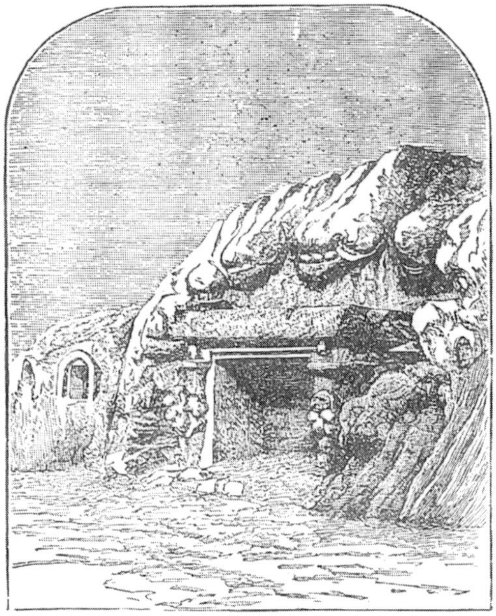

TIGER CAVE, MAHAVALIPUR.

In Madras we visited two large hospitals; the one in the Foreign Town supported by Europeans and conducted upon the English system, the other in the Native Town and under native superintendence. The general hospital in the Foreign Town is a very large and well-ventilated building. It has spacious corridors, wide and shady verandas, and noble wards. The doors were open on every hand, mainly toward the verandas; and a refreshing breeze, passing gently through, relieved the heat, which in this climate is so oppressive to the patient. In every ward freshness and cheerfulness seemed to bespeak a cure. Hopefulness was upon the countenances even of the most afflicted, and pleasant pictures and beautiful flowers gladdened the eye. The matron is a lady, clever and kind. Her apartments are at the top of the building, on which a garden is laid out, and which commands an extensive view. The other hospital, that in the Black Town, was, I regret to say, a contrast to all this. It is called the Choultry Poorhouse and Hospital. Here mute misery was written on every face. The patients had no bedclothes. The paupers lie on a mat on the floor. The portion set apart for lepers presented a most painful spectacle. Those who were in the early stages of the disease were all oiled, and were sitting on their haunches, rubbing and scratching themselves uneasily. Two young men, brothers, presented two different types of the disease. The one was not in the least disfigured; the other was frightfully so, the face being covered with blotches. But whatever the form it assumes, the disease is incurable. In its later stages ulcers appear, and eat off fingers and toes, features

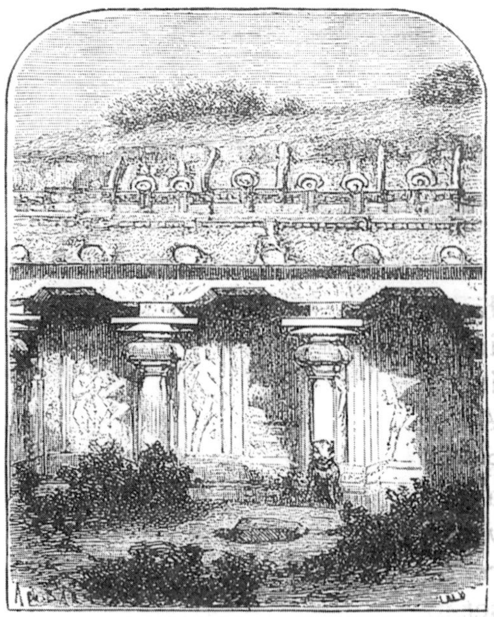

ENTRANCE TO ROCK TEMPLE, MAHAVALIPUR.

and limbs. Several poor wretches in great suffering were plastering their own sores, the materials for doing so being handed to them at the point of a long wand. It was a revolting sight. Most of the sufferers were natives, but a few knew English. To these I spoke a few words about the Lord Jesus and the lepers. It was all one could then do. Sickened and saddened, we next went through bare and comfortless wards for aged and infirm men and women, who here drag out the residue of their days of sorrow. There is also a foundling ward. The foundlings seemed to be in great wretchedness. In this hospital there were 250 patients, and the average was at that time ten deaths a week.[1]

During the awful famine of 1878, there were nine thousand inmates kept in a sort of camp, and an average of thirty deaths a day. The dead were burnt in heaps

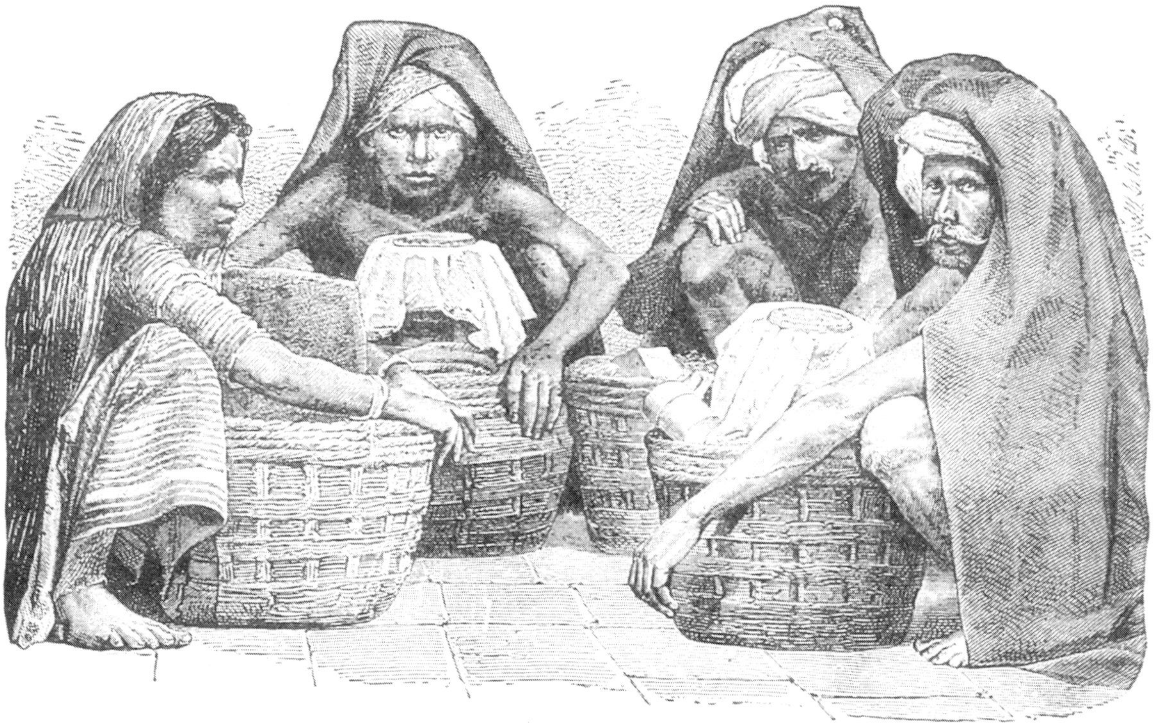

SELLERS OF MILK, MADRAS.

by contract daily. In this lazar house there were, when we visited it, 250 patients in hospital, 265 in the almshouses, 42 in the Rajah's Choultry, and 250 lepers; making a total of 817 souls. The horrors of that famine year are untold and untellable. As the wagons of grain passed from the shore to the railway, they had to be guarded with a strong military force; but the starving would risk blows and sabers and horses' hoofs to pierce the sacks, so that the grain might trickle out; and afterward hundreds might be seen eagerly picking up the grains that had fallen upon the road. In punishment for this offense all who could be captured were driven into pens set up upon the shore, and confined there without food or water, and under the blaze of the sun, for four and twenty hours. Thus many perished. And this was not in remote districts, but at the headquarters of British power, pomp, and fashion in South India—in Madras itself! Inland, they died of famine by hundreds. "I do not

[1] Great advance has been made in India, latterly, in all departments of medical work. I visited 208 lepers in one hospital where everything was scrupulously neat and where the only odor was the perfume of flowers.—Ed.

know," said an eye witness, a government dispenser of relief, "I do not know what we should have done without the dogs and vultures."

No account of Madras would be complete without a reference to the Free Church College, which stands first among the educational establishments of Southern India. It was begun in 1837 by the well-known missionary, Dr. Anderson, whose name is in the south what the name of Dr. Duff is in the north, and within a year there were two hundred and seventy scholars. But then it was suddenly broken up by the agency of "that hydra-headed monster," Caste. Two Pariah boys were admitted, and the rest left. Dr. Anderson was entreated to dismiss the Pariah boys, but he was firm, and he gained the victory. By-and-by the youths returned, and Pariah and Brahman might be seen sitting side by side on the same bench, learning the same lessons. This was a blow given to caste that has been felt throughout Southern India, and felt to the present day. The numbers soon rose to five hundred, and ever since the college has maintained its position as the most efficient in Madras. It is a striking fact that the three Presidency cities in India—Madras, Calcutta, and Bombay—possess colleges organized by Scotchmen, which have accomplished greater results in producing an enlightened and well-trained body of natives in India than any other society, nay more, than the Government itself.

At Tirupetty, about fifty miles from Madras, there is an old temple much frequented by pilgrims, and very interesting to the student of Indian architecture. Pursuing the path up the hill, we go through three towers curiously carved. The hill is two thousand five hundred feet high, and has seven summits, on the last of which is the pagoda. Along the top are ruined houses, forming a quadrangle, with stone wall inclosure. A tower rises above these, and around is a broad belt of mango, tamarind, and sandal trees. It is said to be one of the oldest Dravidian temples.

West of Madras about sixty miles is Arcot, the famous town which Clive pounced upon in 1751, that he might relieve Trichinopoly. The garrison, seeing Clive's troops marching on steadily in the teeth of a thunder storm, thought they were fireproof, and abandoned the place. Entering it, Clive held the place during a fifty days' siege, and repelled the assaults of Mohammedan troops. Arcot is now a large and prosperous town.[1] Beyond lies MYSORE, one of the most flourishing of the native tributary states in India, occupying a table-land, lofty, well-wooded, and cool, where is the famous Seringapatam, now almost in ruins, and Bangalore, one of the healthiest cities in India, with a large British settlement. Scattered over the table-land are many huge isolated rocks called *drûgs*, four thousand feet above the sea, and formerly used as fortresses. Coorg is a mountainous district, thickly wooded, with extensive coffee and tea plantations. Worthiest of record is the name of a native, Samuel Flavel, a man of great originality, intellectual power, and untiring zeal, who for twenty years, 1826–1847, was instrumental in spreading Christianity, with its civilizing influences, in Mysore.

The coast voyage from Madras to Calcutta occupies eight days, and gives an opportunity of seeing the main ports, the steamer calling daily at some place on the way, and stopping four or six hours. Of the entire voyage the most difficult and disagreeable part often is the passage over the surf from the shore to the ship. The

[1] Occupied by the American Board in 1851. Dr. Henry Martyn Scudder started the mission. He was afterward pastor in Brooklyn and Chicago. Seven sons of John Scudder, M. D., became missionaries in the land of their birth.—ED.

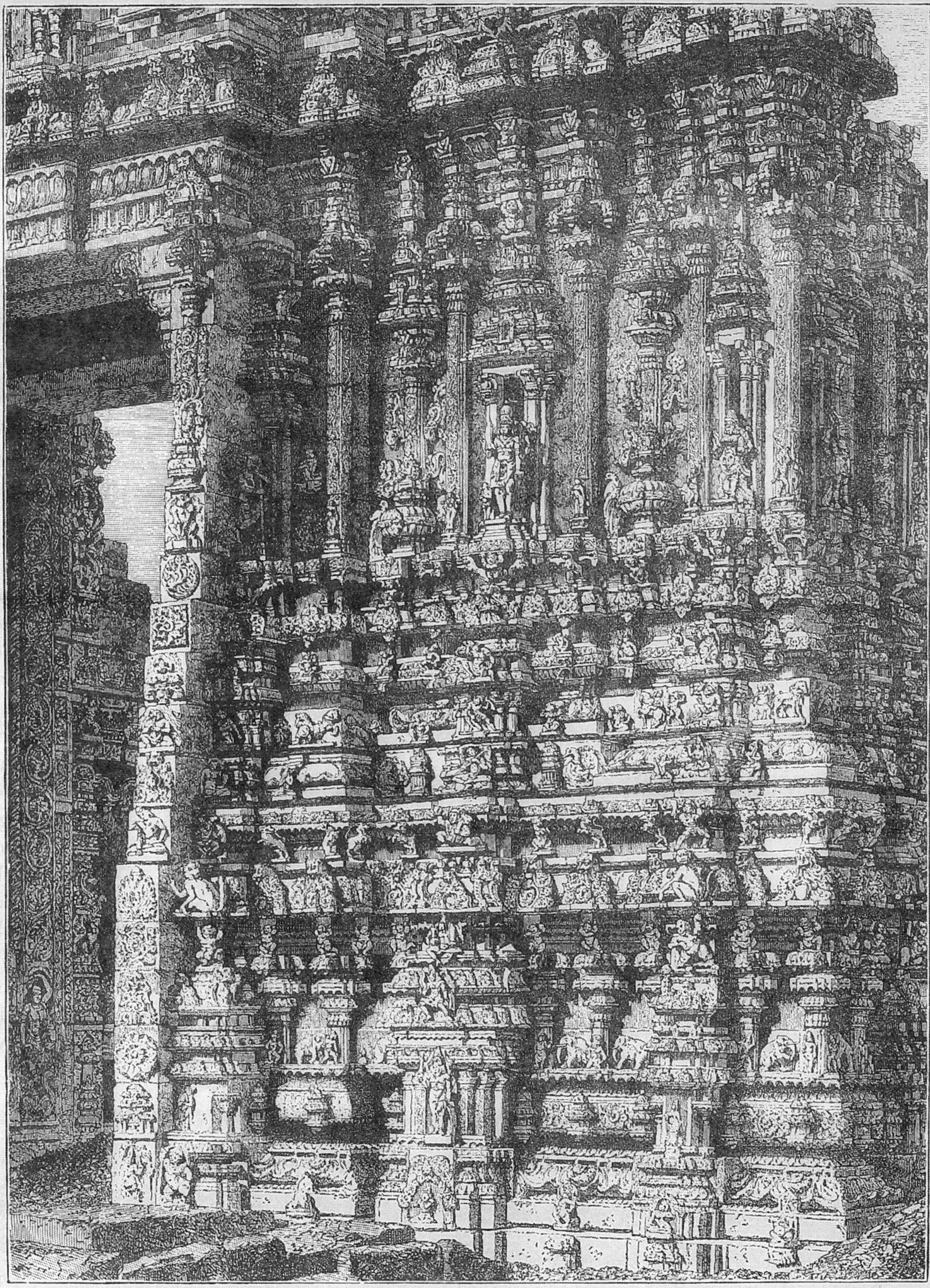

PORTION OF GOPURA AT TIRUPETTY.

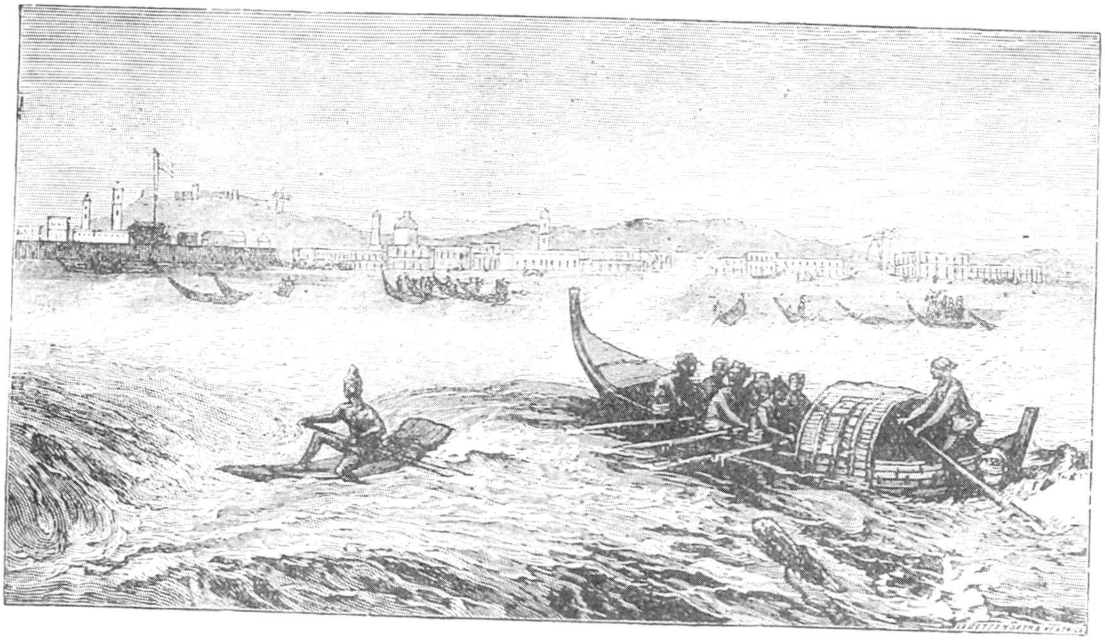

MADRAS SURF.

morning was calm ; yet the huge billows were rolling in in all their majesty and strength. There lay our Masulah boat waiting to receive us. These boats are twenty-five feet long, eight feet broad, six feet deep, flat bottomed, pointed, and curved up high at either end. They are exceedingly light, drawing only three inches of water. There is not a nail in them nor a rib of timber. They are sewn together with cocoanut fiber, and padded inside with straw, outside with tow. They yield to the force of the wave and to the bump of the shore. As they lie on the sand, they seem to you immovable; but the native boatmen, twelve in number, soon push their obedient and easily managed craft into the advancing lip of the wave; it is carried out as this retreats, and they dexterously jump in, lay hold of their paddles, and pull with their might. The helmsman steers with a long and powerful oar, and thus keeps the bow to the waves. And now you see approaching the next yawning wave high above you, and threatening to engulf you ; but meeting it, the sloping bow mounts up perpendicularly, shipping perhaps a quantity of spray, but springing first to the top and then over the crest of the huge billow, and down again into the shallow water left as the wave rolls on. In calm weather only three of these huge billows are dangerous, and these surmounted you are safe. But the boatmen have been trained to the work from boyhood, and handle their craft with marvelous skill. Though a daily feat, the novelty seems never to wear off. They are all excitement, and cheer over each leap and plunge. Besides the Masulah boats, another kind of craft is used by the natives, called a catamaran, which is simply a raft constructed of three pieces of timber ten or twelve feet long, tied together, the middle one being longer than the others and curved upward at the ends. It is driven through the surf by a man with a paddle, who is often washed off, but is so well practiced that he leaps on again in an instant. With these amphibious creatures the catamaran keeps on its way where a boat would inevitably be lost. It took us half an hour in the Masulah boat to reach our ship, the boatmen keeping time to a monotonous song.

The first port off which we anchored on our coasting voyage northward was Masulipatam, a very old city, of forty thousand inhabitants, situated in the Telugu District, between the deltas of the two mighty rivers, the Krishna and the Godavery. Telugu is the most melodious and soft of the Dravidian languages, and is spoken throughout the portion of the Madras Presidency extending northward to Orissa. It is also spoken far inland in the Nizam's dominions. The great rivers the Krishna and the Godavery form the characteristic physical features of the country. Both rise in the Western Ghauts, seventy miles northwest of Bombay, and sweep across the vast table-land from west to east, flowing right across the Indian peninsula, winding their way by deep defiles through the Eastern Ghauts, and spreading over the country in immense deltas as they empty themselves into the sea. Formerly these rivers were a peril to the country, overflowing their banks and sweeping whole villages away.

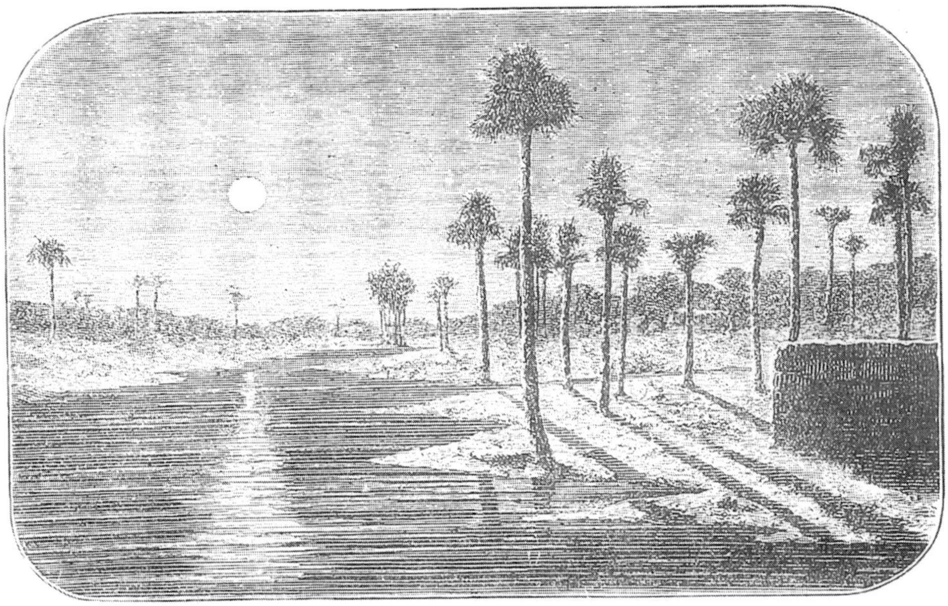

PALMYRAS IN THE GODAVERY.

But the irrigation works of modern enterprise "have turned the furious streams into ministering angels." Colossal *anicuts*, or dams, have with immense labor been thrown across them, and the water is carried by canals over the whole country, which has thus become one of the richest grain-producing districts in India. Masulipatam possesses a cotton manufacture, distinguished for the bright and beautiful colors of its cloth. In the center of the city, where the streets meet, are thirty-three huge limestone slabs covered with alto- and bas-reliefs brought from the ruins of a neighboring pagoda. Masulipatam is the center of the operations of the Church Missionary Society in this part of India; the noble high school for the thorough education of young Hindus is distinguished in influence and success, and its pupils are to be found in almost every department as sub-magistrates, schoolmasters, and even deputy collectors. Inland, at Guntur, the American Lutherans have a flourishing mission. In this district are the Buddhist topes of Amravati, fragments of which are in the British Museum. The rails are the most richly ornamented in India, and furnish a series of pictures of Buddhism, "unsurpassed" says Fergusson, "by anything now known to exist in India."

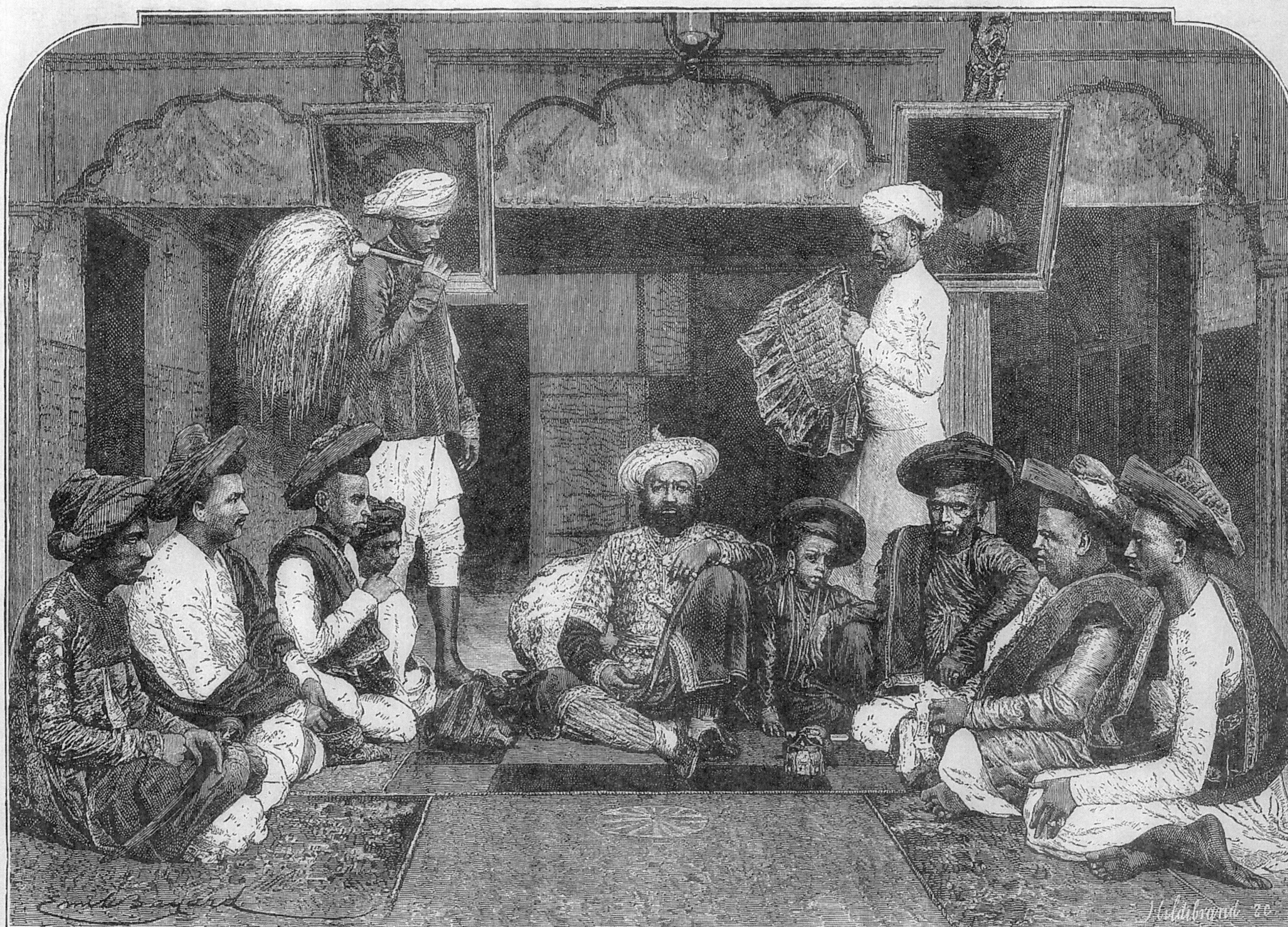

DURBAR OF A NATIVE PRINCE IN THE SOUTH OF THE DECCAN.

Another night's vogage brought us northward to Cocanada, north of the river in the Godavery District, where we spent our second day. Landing in the morning, we made our way to the compound of the Canadian Baptist Mission, delightfully shaded with banyan and pipul trees, and there we heard much of the marvelous conversions at Nellore and Ongole, where eight thousand natives had in one month embraced Christianity, owing to Christian kindness during the famine. Here we traveled inland about five miles in coffin-like palanquins, with twelve bearers to each,—who went dolefully along on the high banks of a canal, keeping time with their voices in the heat of the day,—to a lonely pagoda whose high tower is a revolting sight. It is,

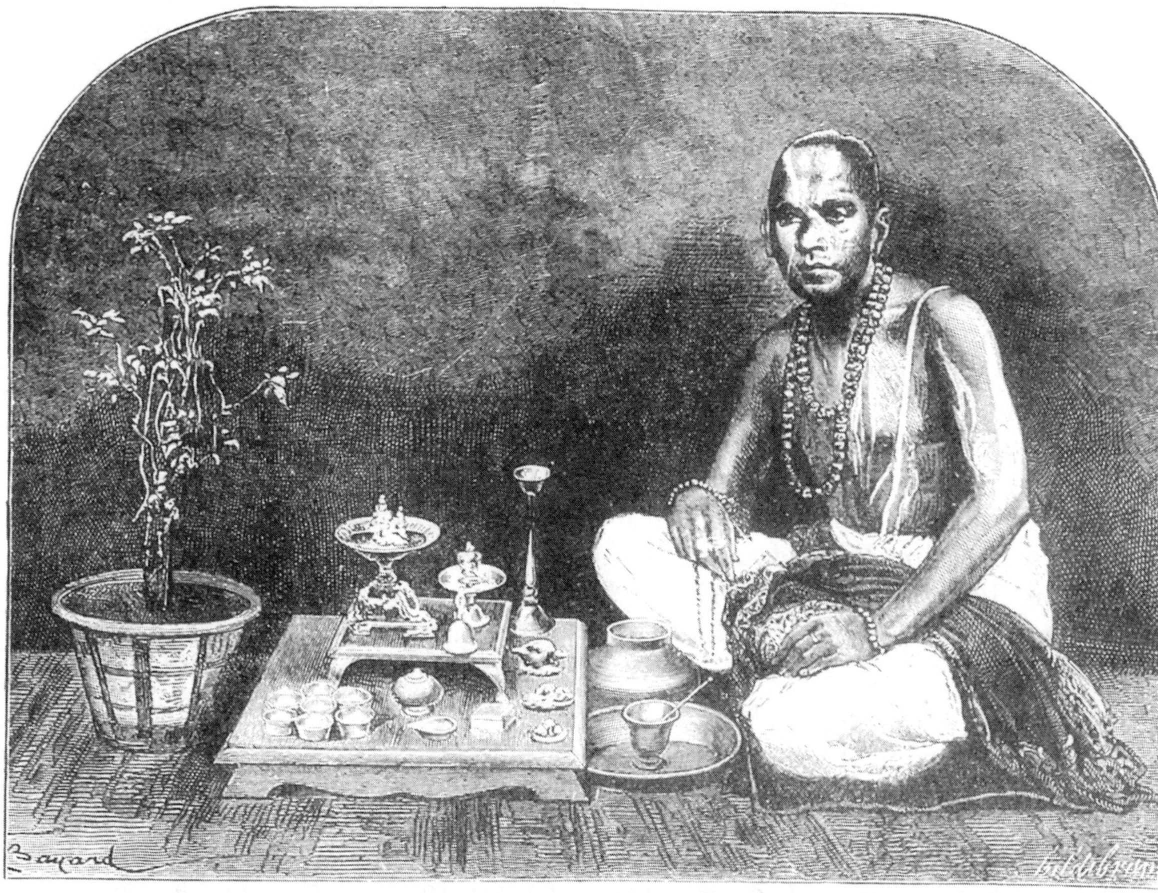

BRAHMAN PREPARED FOR PRAYERS.

in fact, a mass of obscenity cut in stone, such as one could hardly imagine depravity itself capable of inventing. Yet this is part and parcel of the religion of Brahma, that religion upon the excellency of which some Sanscrit professors expatiate! One sight of this temple at Cocanada would suffice to disabuse them of their fine pictures of Hinduism and of the elevating power of the Vedas. A few pet quotations are always at hand when one would praise Brahmanism. They are, in the oldest Vedas, grains of wheat in the bushel of chaff. If we would learn what the Hindu religion really is, and what are its practical fruits, we must visit the temples of India.

Next morning we reached Vizag. The headland, one thousand seven hundred feet, as approached from the south, is called the Dolphin's Nose; there is a huge cave on the sea-line, and the cliffs are imposing. On the hill above the creek three striking buildings meet the eye: a heathen temple, a Mohammedan mosque, and a Roman Catholic church. As we landed, we saw crowds of poor women working as porters, and carrying huge boxes of cargo. Vizag is in the province called the Northern Circars, extending about five hundred miles along the Bay of Bengal, and among the earliest possessions of the East India Company. The natives are a fine class of men, both in physique and in character, and live under the simple form of village government. The London Mission here was founded in 1805, at a time when the Company discountenanced missions. But it has held its ground, and its missionaries have translated the Scriptures into Telugu. I met the venerable John Hay, the chief translator and master of the language, who has been here for forty years. The Telugu language is, Mr. Hay says, in its primitive forms, much simpler than in its more modern development. On account of its soft accent and musical tones, it has been called by Europeans the Italian of the East.

Eight miles from Gopalpur is Berhampur, chief town of the district of Ganjam. Here there is a flourishing Baptist Mission. This district forms the extreme north of the Madras Presidency.

Inland, and behind the strip of the Madras Presidency, running up thus far north along the coast, are two large tracts of territory, the CENTRAL PROVINCES, now belonging to Britain, and HAIDARABAD, belonging to the Nizam of the Deccan. The district called the Central Provinces is not thickly peopled, the country being hilly and forest land. The chief town, Nagpur, contains about eighty thousand inhabitants. There are extensive coal-fields, and cotton is much cultivated. The Deccan is a name applied to the entire central plateau of the Indian Peninsula, of which Haidarabad forms the northern portion. The Vindhya Mountains, running east and west, form a great wall, separating the Deccan and the Ganges valley. They extend from Mount Parasnath in the east to Mount Abu in the west. Near the city of Haidarabad is the British settlement called Secunderabad, eighteen hundred feet above the sea, where are the largest barracks in India. The Godavery river flows though this district eastward, and it is crossed by the railway connecting Madras with Bombay. Not far from Haidarabad is Golconda; and near the fort, on the top of a conical hill, the tombs of the kings are well worth a visit. Their vastness and solidity are most impressive. The diamonds of Golconda were merely cut and polished here, being found at Partial. Chanda stands amid charming scenery. The Free Church of Scotland has flourishing missions at Nagpur and at the settlement called Jalna, a British cantonment in the Nizam's dominions.

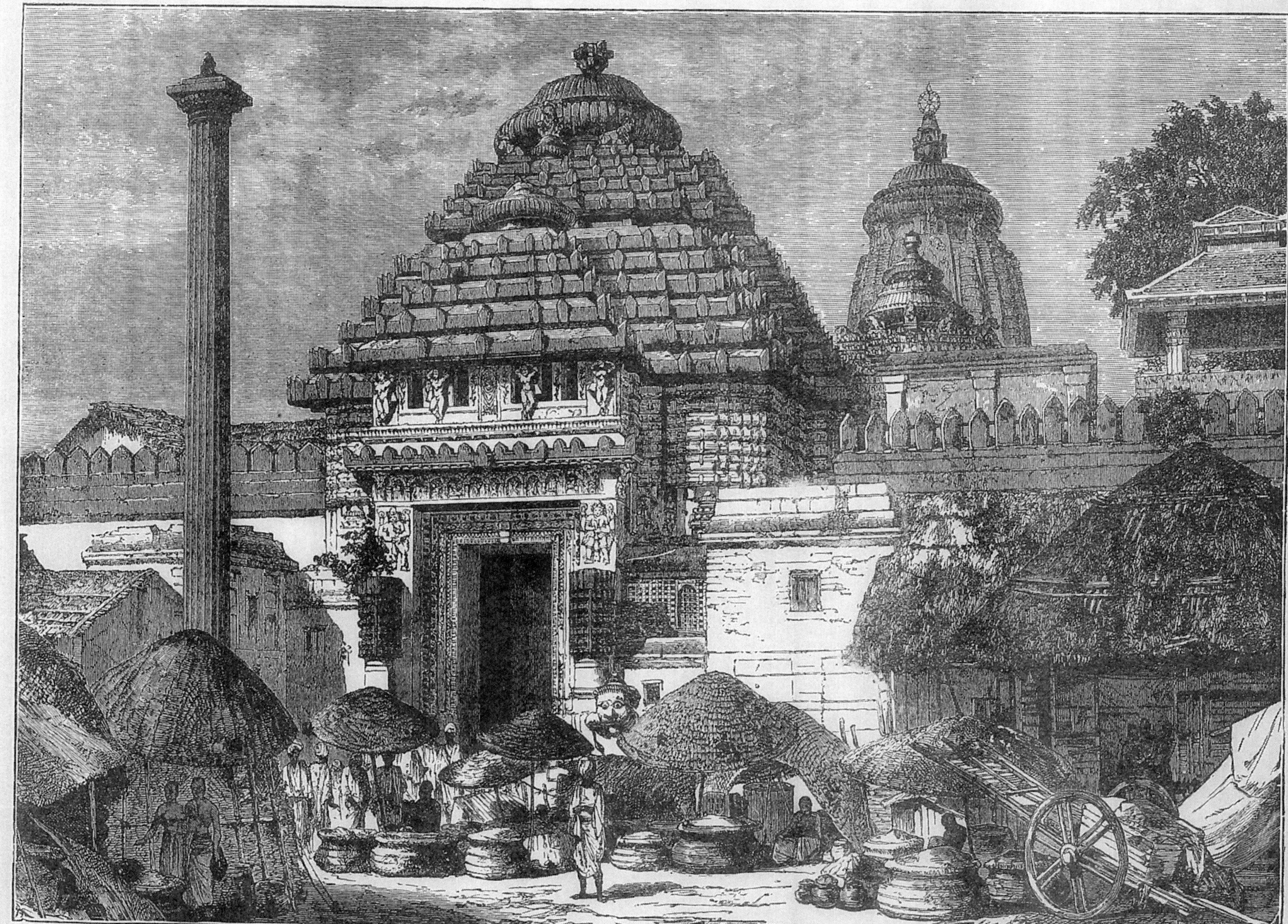

TEMPLE OF JUGGERNAUT.

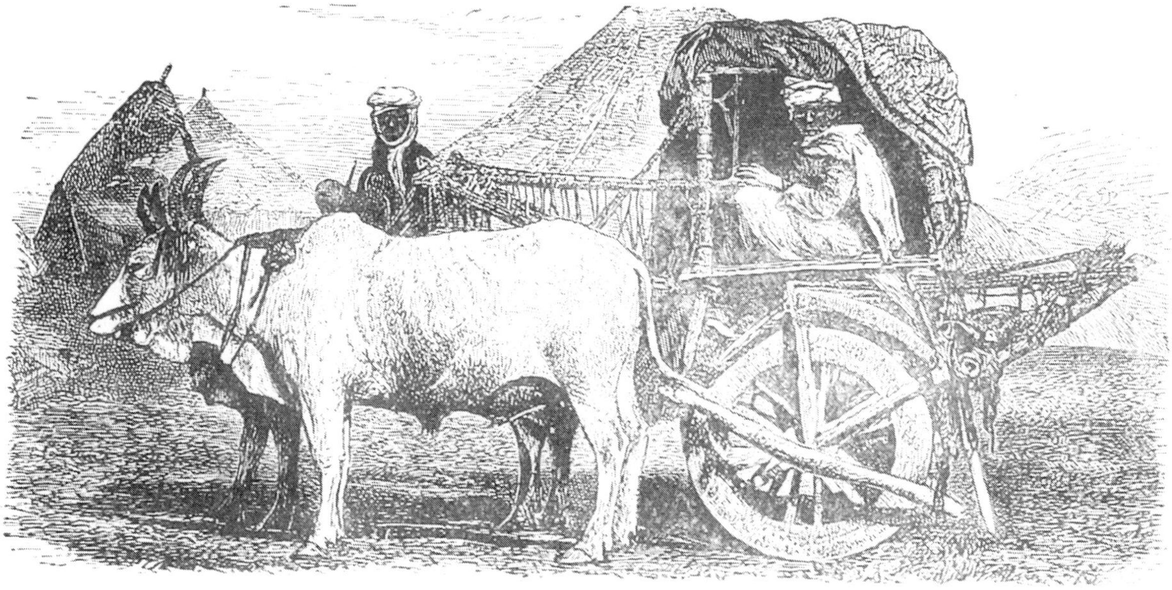

THE BENGAL PROVINCES.

ORISSA AND JUGGERNAUT—CALCUTTA AND ITS SURROUNDINGS—BARRACKPORE—SERAMPORE—DARJEELING AND THE HIMÂLAYAS—THE GREAT GANGETIC PLAIN.

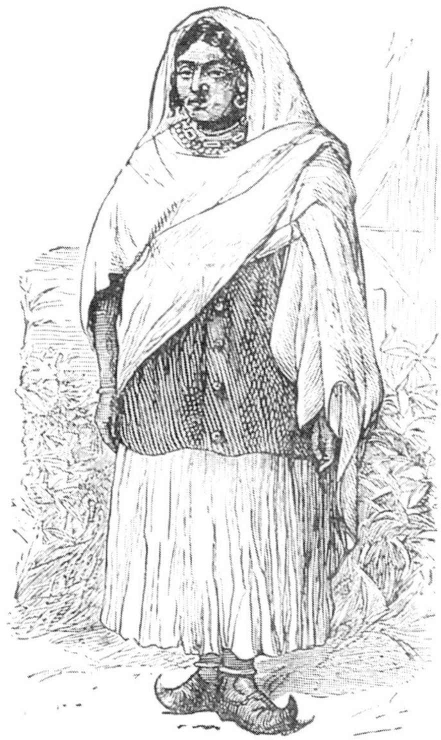

HIMÂLAYAN WOMAN.

IN the coasting voyage from Madras we have the Madras Presidency still on our left, northward as far as Gopalpur. Here the country of the Northern Circars ends, and the coast of Orissa begins. The maritime part of Orissa forms the British district of Cuttack, called by seamen the Orissa Coast. The shore is flat and dreary, and inland appear several "saddle-hills" terminating in a chain of mountains running south. The extensive Chilka Lake is joined to the sea by a narrow strait.

After leaving Gopalpur, our good steamer, keeping near to shore, brought us next morning to Puri in Orissa, and the far-famed Temple of Juggernaut. This part of the coast is considered healthy, and the sea breeze is found very refreshing. The houses of English residents are on the seashore, and the native town and temple, surrounded by high wall and luxuriant vegetation, lie a little inland. The temple inclosure measures four hundred and twenty by three hundred and fifteen feet, and the height of the great tower is one hundred and ninety-two feet. "Whitewash and paint," says Mr. Fergusson, "have done their worst to add vulgarity to forms already sufficiently ungraceful, and this, the most famous, is also the most disappointing of Northern Hindu temples." It was erected in A. D. 1174, and is the latest of the Orissa group of temples. It is dedicated to Vishnu, and pilgrims are continually on their way through Bengal to and from this temple. It is calculated that ten thousand pilgrims annually die either of disease or fatigue and want at Puri, or on the return journey. Those who live bring back with them umbrellas made of cane and palm-leaves, bundles of painted rattan canes, and backbones of cuttle-fish, to show that they have been on the seashore. These fish bones are called by the poetic name of "ocean foam." The street leading to the temple is full of sacred buildings, and the inhabitants of the town number thirty thousand. Three wooden images of revolting aspect, six feet high, represent the god Juggernaut, his brother, and his sister. Once a year, in the month of March, these are taken through the town, each idol in its car, that of Juggernaut being thirty-four feet high, with sixteen wheels. On these occasions a hundred and fifty thousand pilgrims are assembled. The English Government has interfered to put an end to the self-immolations beneath its wheels. Mounted police, armed with heavy whips, accompany the car in its progress, and when a frenzied devotee throws himself in its way the whip is applied, and he immediately jumps up and runs away, forgetting that if he is willing to be killed he should be willing to bear the lash. The tradition of a bone of Krishna being contained in the image is regarded as a Brahmanical form of Buddhist relic worship, and the three images are supposed to be only the Buddhist Trinity—Buddha, Dharma, Sanga. The idol is, in fact, an imitation of the Buddhist emblem. Buddhism formerly existed in Orissa, and the tooth-relic of Buddha was preserved at Puri. Everything at Puri is redolent of Buddhism. Another significant vestige of this system is the absence of all recognition of caste during the festivals. In the neighborhood of Juggernaut, on the coast, is the so-called Black Pagoda at Kanarak, of which only the beautiful three-storied porch remains, carved with elegance and variety. Orissa, indeed, abounds with temples, all of the same type, and very different from those of Southern India. The towers, or vimanas, have a curved outline; they are not storied, and the buildings have no pillars. The Temple of Juggernaut is the latest, and the oldest is supposed to be the great Temple of Bhuvaneswar.

"The Temple of Bhuvaneswar is," says Fergusson, "perhaps the finest example of a purely Hindu temple in India." It is three hundred feet long by seventy-five broad. It consisted of a vimana, or tower, and a porch. It has a singularly solemn and pleasing aspect. Its height is one hundred and eighty feet, wholly of stone, and every inch of the surface is covered with elaborate carving. "Infinite labor bestowed on every detail was the mode in which a Hindu thought he could render his temple most worthy of the deity; and, whether he was right or wrong, the effect of the whole is marvelously beautiful."

On Sunday, as we were passing Juggernaut Puri, our ship's company of passengers and officers were quietly gathered on deck to offer our common prayers to the great Father in heaven, to read His Word and to hear His Gospel. Again it was my lot to conduct service at sea, and the heaving of the ship formed an accompaniment to the lessons and the sermon. On board was an officer high in rank, and inspector of military schools, who spoke of what he had seen of the brutal treatment of the natives. A passing Hindu, he said, was rudely taken to task by Captain —— for not making a salaam to him. "Why should I?" said the man; "you have con-

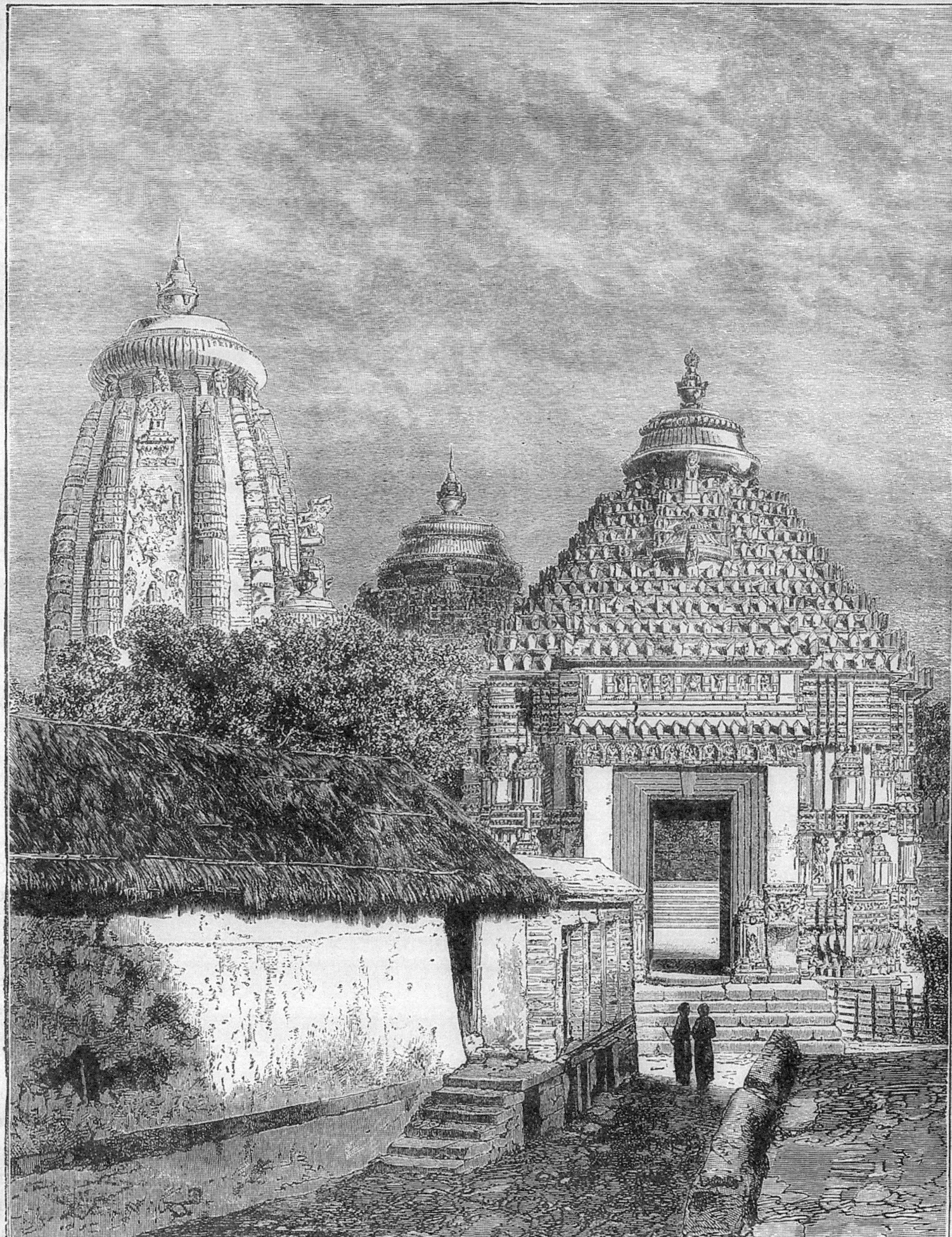

BLACK PAGODA AT KANARAK, ORISSA.

quered our race, and I won't salaam." "Let us see the general," said the captain. The general said, "Make a salaam, sir." The man still firmly but calmly refused, and the general seized him by the neck, threw him to the ground, buried his face in the dust, and ordered the man fifty lashes. Thus by sheer brute force was this

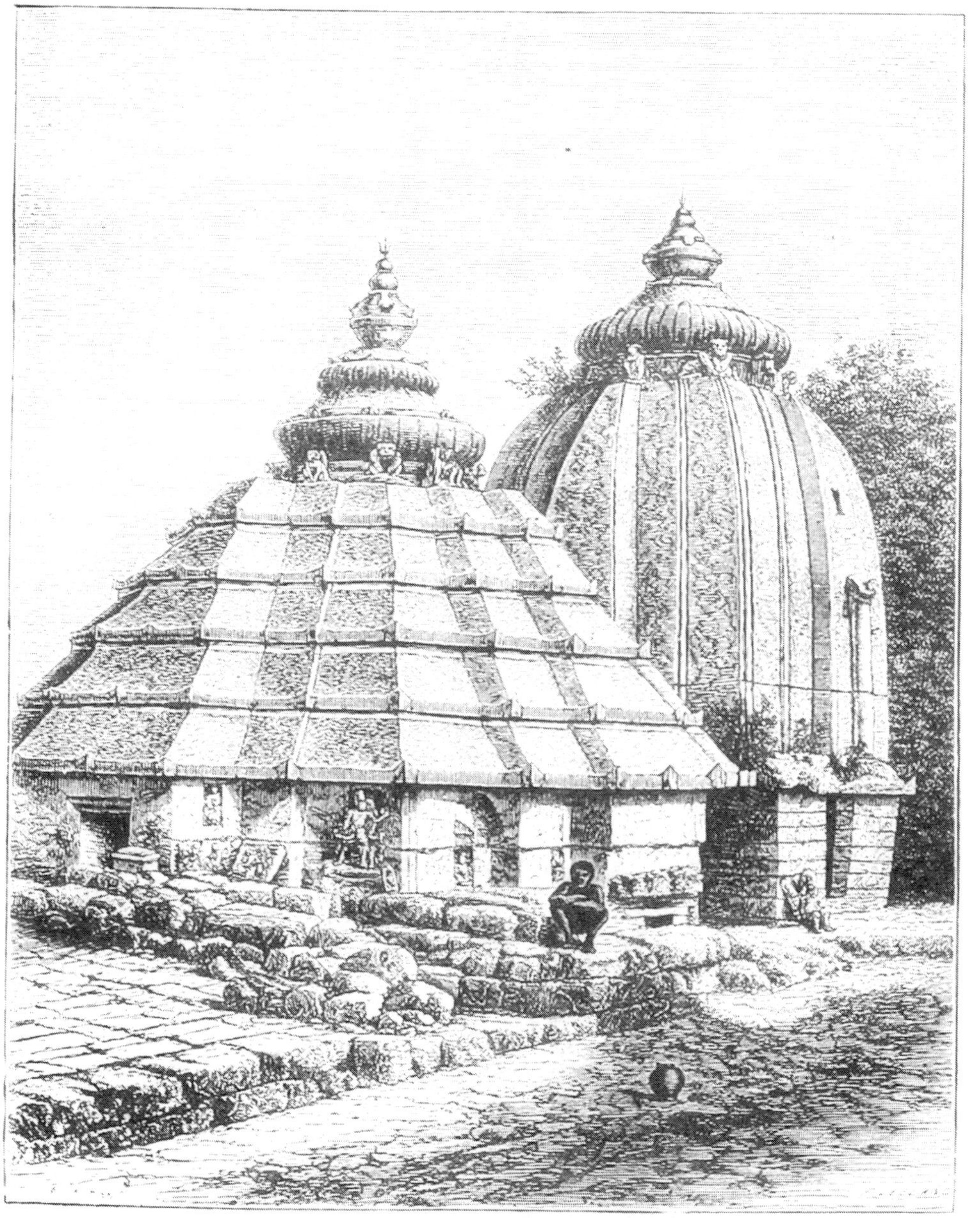

PAGODA, NEAR CUTTACK.

Hindu punished for an independence which we should honor in an Englishman. The mild Hindu submits to the English as to a conquering race, and all he can do is to be patient and bide his time. If not subdued by justice and kindness, he will seek his revenge some day.

In the afternoon we anchored at False Point, outside the mud-locked harbor at the mouth of the Mahanadi River. It is a dismal spot, with a house on the beach and a lighthouse in the distance. A few cargo boats and native vessels were swinging at anchor and rolling lazily with the tide. From this place a steam-launch runs, or rather crawls up the river to Cuttack, the capital of Orissa, whither some of our passengers were bound. When Akbar built Attock, or Attack, on the Indus, *Kattack* and *Attack* were spoken of as the two extremes of the Mogul Empire. Seventy miles beyond Cuttack is the famous Barmul Pass, eight miles long, between peaked ridges and hills covered with jungle, through which the Mahanadi flows rapidly. The scenery is said somewhat to resemble the Lower Danube.

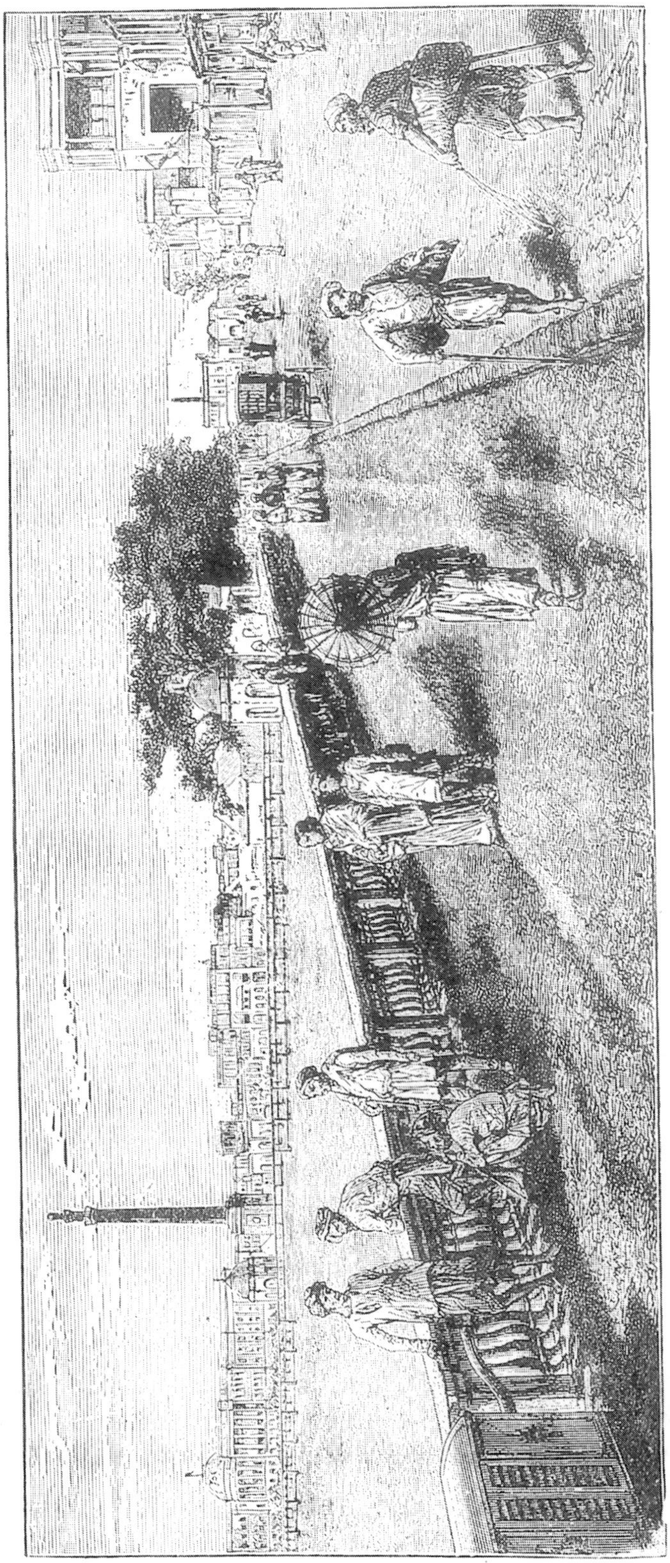

THE MAIDAN AT CALCUTTA.

And now weighing anchor, and taking our pilot on board, we started up that narrow and dangerous branch of the Ganges called the Hoogly. After stopping at Diamond Harbor, a turn or reach in the river with its signal flagstaff, where particulars are given as to the height of the tide at the bars, we made our way cautiously up past "James and Mary," the most dangerous of the rapids, all hands on board being in readiness to let go the anchor if we should ground. At Garden Reach our ship was turned round, and was steamed stern foremost up to Government House, CALCUTTA, amidst a crowd of shipping reminding one of Liverpool.

Calcutta, City of Karli, ninety miles from the sea, and on the east bank of the Hoogly, which here flows directly south, is a city not two centuries old. It was founded by Job Charnock, who set up a factory here in 1690, married a Hindu wife, and as to religion led a Hindu life. In 1742 the famous ditch was cut to protect the settlement against the Mahratta cavalry. It ran along the ground now marked by the Circular Road. The settlement, in spite of this, was captured by the Nawab, when, on the 19th of June, 1756, a hundred and forty-six Europeans were imprisoned

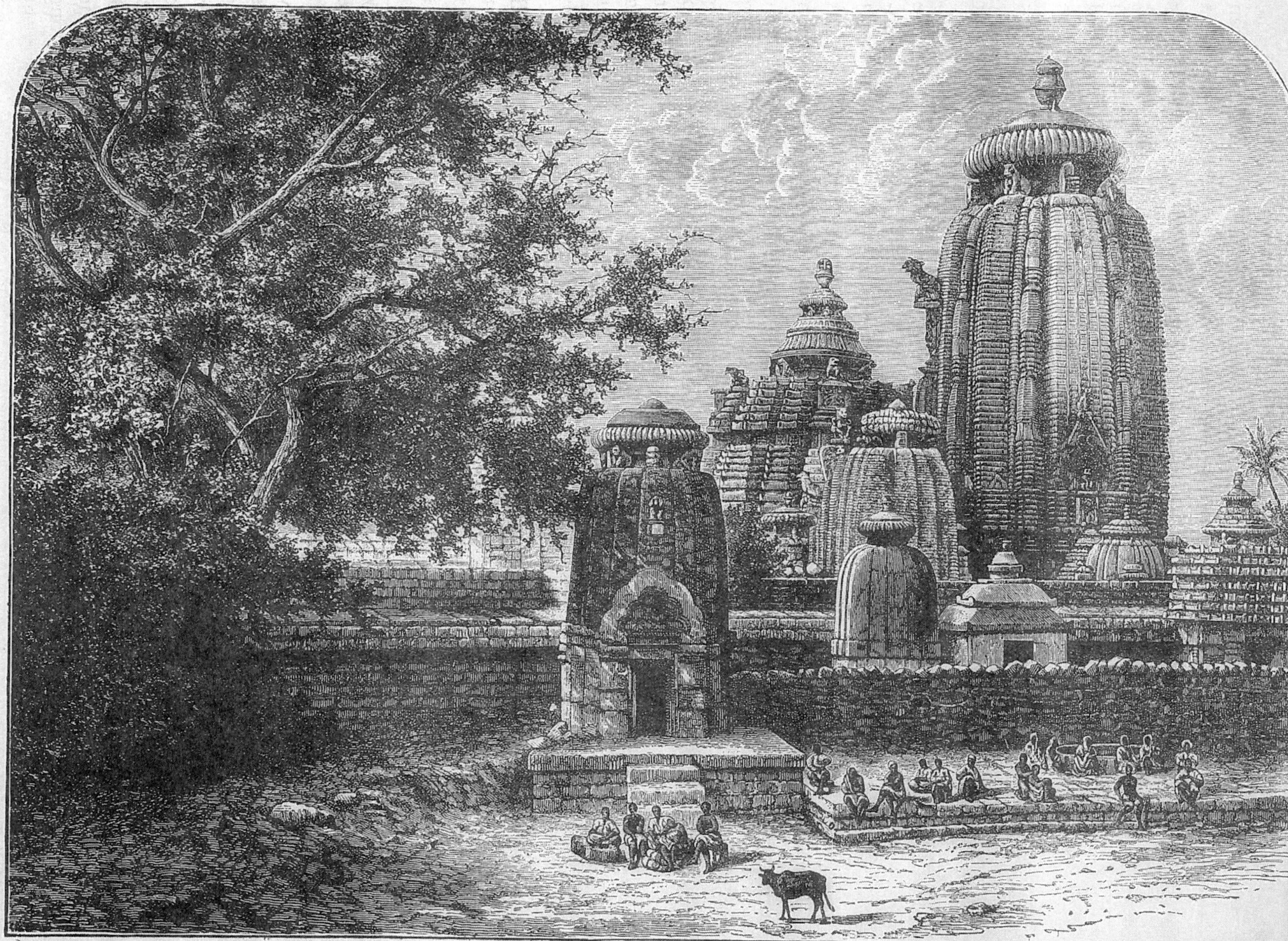

GRAND TEMPLE OF BHUVANESWAR.

in the Black Hole, a small chamber eighteen feet square in the Fort, and one hundred and twenty-three were smothered to death. The Black Hole was destroyed in 1818. In January of 1757 Clive won back the settlement; and the place has gradually grown in size and importance until now it is the center of Government, the seat of the Viceroy, and, if we include Howrah, on the opposite bank of the river, now connected with the city by a bridge, it numbers nine hundred thousand inhabitants.

The Government House is a huge and imposing building, and in it is that famous Council Room, with the portraits of Hastings and others on its walls, where the welfare or fate of millions of souls has often hung in the balance. In the immediate neighborhood are the modern and majestic Law Courts, with towers and fretted roof. Behind, rises the dome of the Post Office, a noble building; and

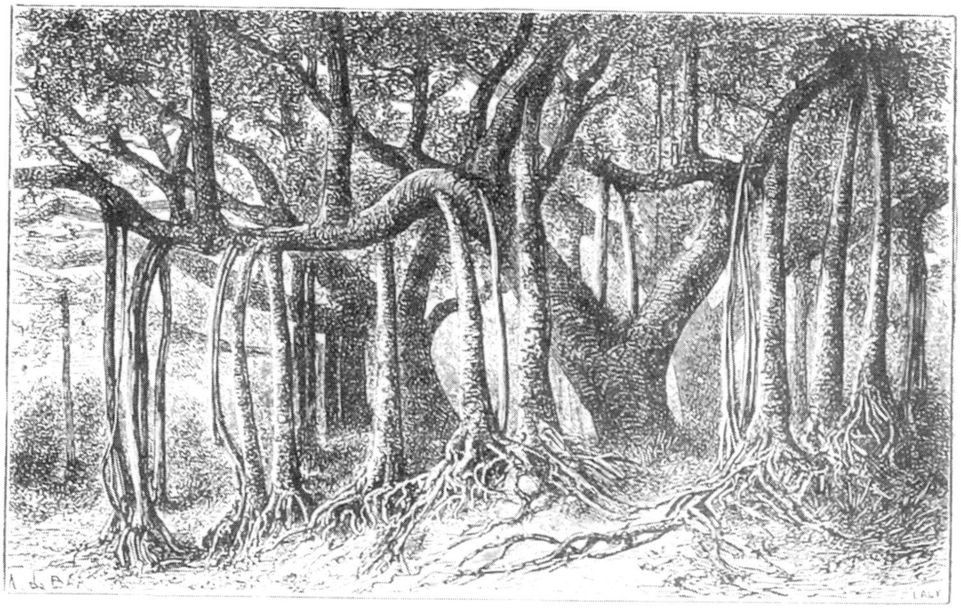

BANYAN IN CALCUTTA BOTANIC GARDENS.

along the road called Chowringee, looking out upon the Maidan, or common, six miles in circumference, are the large houses, each within its gardens or "compound," that have won for the place the name "City of Palaces"; while the ravages of climate upon the health of European residents have suggested the parody, "City of Pale Faces." There are many statues and monuments about the Maidan, the creatures of official inspiration. To the west is the river, with its forest of masts; and Fort William, which covers some acres between the Maidan and the river to the south, is an imposing barrack with a very noble church. To the north runs the Chidpore Road, through the Black Town, full of natives and native shops, and parallel with it Cornwallis Street, noted for its charitable and educational institutions. These institutions all over Calcutta stand as the memorials of illustrious names. Here it was that Bishop Wilson toiled, and here stands his church, St. John's. Here, too, in a conspicuous position, stands the Scotch Church, where the zealous and self-denying Dr. Duff labored. In Cornwallis Square is the College which he first founded, now in the hands of the Scotch Established Church; near it is the Free Church College, afterward built by Dr. Duff, in which he taught for many years, and where a thousand young men and boys are daily assembled for religious and secular education. It is a giant building, and in the center hall, where the school is wont to assemble to hear the Scriptures every morning, now stands a bust of that noble presence, placed there in loving remembrance of the founder. Not far off, on the banks of the river, is the Burning Ghaut, in the native quarter, where the process of cremation may be witnessed every day.

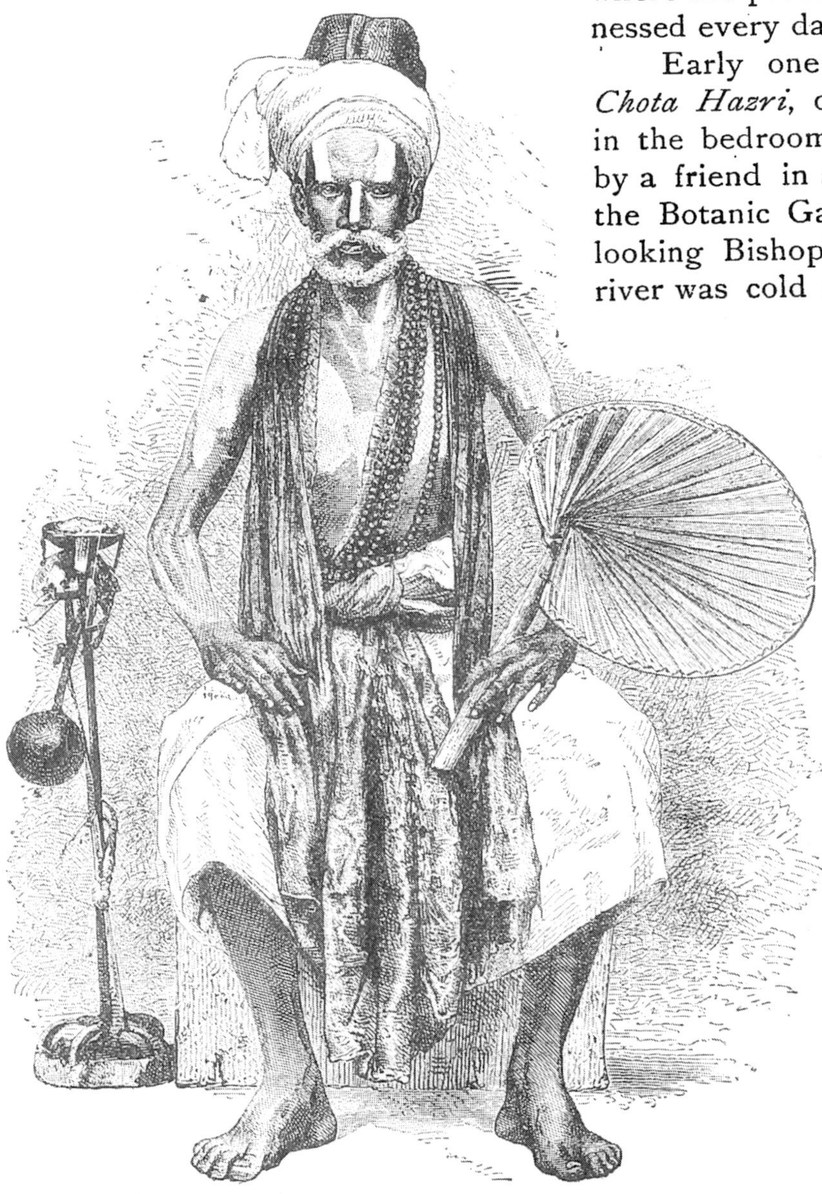

RELIGIOUS MENDICANT.

Early one morning, after the usual *Chota Hazri*, or "little breakfast," served in the bedroom before rising, I was taken by a friend in a boat down the Hoogly to the Botanic Gardens, beyond the deserted-looking Bishop's College. The air on the river was cold and damp, reminding one a little of London fog, a strange contrast to the noonday heat of the city. A few boatmen were plying their craft lazily along. Opposite was the palace of the deposed monarch of Oude, who keeps tigers in his grounds. Landing at a wharf on the west bank, we at once entered the gardens, which cover three hundred acres, and happily combine the natural with the artificial; they contain beautiful specimens of the Mauritius, the talipot, the sago, and other palms, a large variety of crotons, and, above all, a great banyan tree, with a girth of eighteen yards, whose branches and descending roots extend to a circumference of three hundred yards. The same day we visited Kalighat, which gave its name to Calcutta, and is situated on the bank of an old bed of the Ganges, four miles south of the city. The legend is that when the corpse of the goddess Kali, wife of Siva, was cut in pieces by order of the gods, one of her fingers fell here, and a temple was raised in her honor. The present temple was built three hundred years ago, and renewed in 1809; its priests are called "Haldar," and amass great wealth from the daily offerings of pilgrims.

There are many festivals, to which immense crowds resort, especially on the second day of the *Durja Puja*, the great Bengali religious festival in honor of the goddess, held at the autumnal equinox. The street off which the temple lies is full of shops for the sale of idol pictures, images, and charms. When we arrived, sacrifices were being offered in the midst of an excited crowd. In an area before the temple stood the priest, and beside him the executioner, sword in hand. We saw three kids and two buffaloes sacrificed. The head of the victim is fastened in a wooden vise, its body is held up by the hind legs, and the sacrificer strikes with his sword. If the head is severed with one stroke, the victim is considered acceptable to the goddess, and its blood is collected by the priest, carried into the shrine, and sprinkled upon her huge projecting tongue. We could see in the distance the hideous idol within, its tongue streaming with blood. If the head of the animal is not severed with the first stroke, it is considered unacceptable, and is cast aside. The officiating Brahman, almost naked, with the sacred cord round his neck, was a fierce-looking, but very shrewd man. He could speak English. We found that he had been, when a boy, five years at the Bhowanipore Mission School, and that a near kinsman of his was a convert to Christianity and a missionary. Upon my saying, "How can you carry on these revolting rites? You know that they are vain, and a pretense," he replied, "Yes, I know it; but the people will have it, and I must get my living." The man evidently disbelieved in his heathenism, and might be a professor of Christianity, if he saw it would pay. It was strange and saddening to see these bloody, exciting, and degrading rites amid a huge gathering of devotees, within a few miles of English civilization and fashion. Only a mile away is the large college and compound of the London Mission. Two miles nearer town stands the cathedral of St. Paul, in Gothic style, with its library and statue of Bishop Heber. And in the evening the fashionables of Calcutta, pale and listless, might be seen rolling in gay equipages, in lines three deep, across the Maidan, and by the shipping along the river-side, and gathering round the band in the Eden Gardens. In the temple area at Kalighat, around the shrine of Kali, you see Hindu caste and idolatry in all their proud and devout barbarism; the same day, at evening, in the Eden Gardens, around the band, you may witness the pomp and vanity of Anglo-Indian caste, from the haughty Collector, who lives upon the taxes, to the industrious tradesman who pays them. Brahman and Sudra you find alike in both assemblies; and it is not easy to decide which is the more unreasonable and inexcusable, the heathen or the official pride.

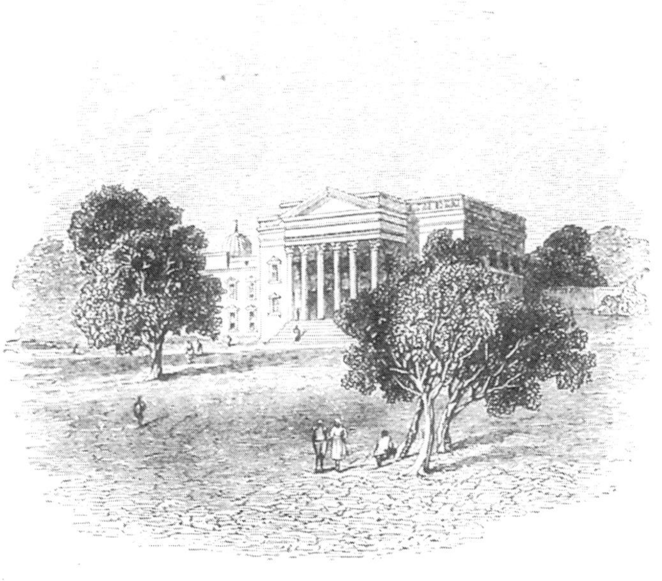

SERAMPORE COLLEGE.

The Mohammedans of Calcutta have a large educational establishment, called the Madrisa, where the pupils are instructed in languages and Mohammedan law, and graduate at the Calcutta University. The new theistic sect called the Brahmosomaj has a mandir, or church, for the "Progressive Brahmos," as the party headed by K. C. Sen is called. They have normal and adult schools, and a small girls' school. The Hindu College, in College Square, is a handsome building of the Ionic order.

Starting one morning early by railway from Sealdah Station, we traveled about eighteen miles north to Samnuggur, where we were taken over a cotton factory, and found the rooms as airy as in Lancashire, though, of course, hotter. The

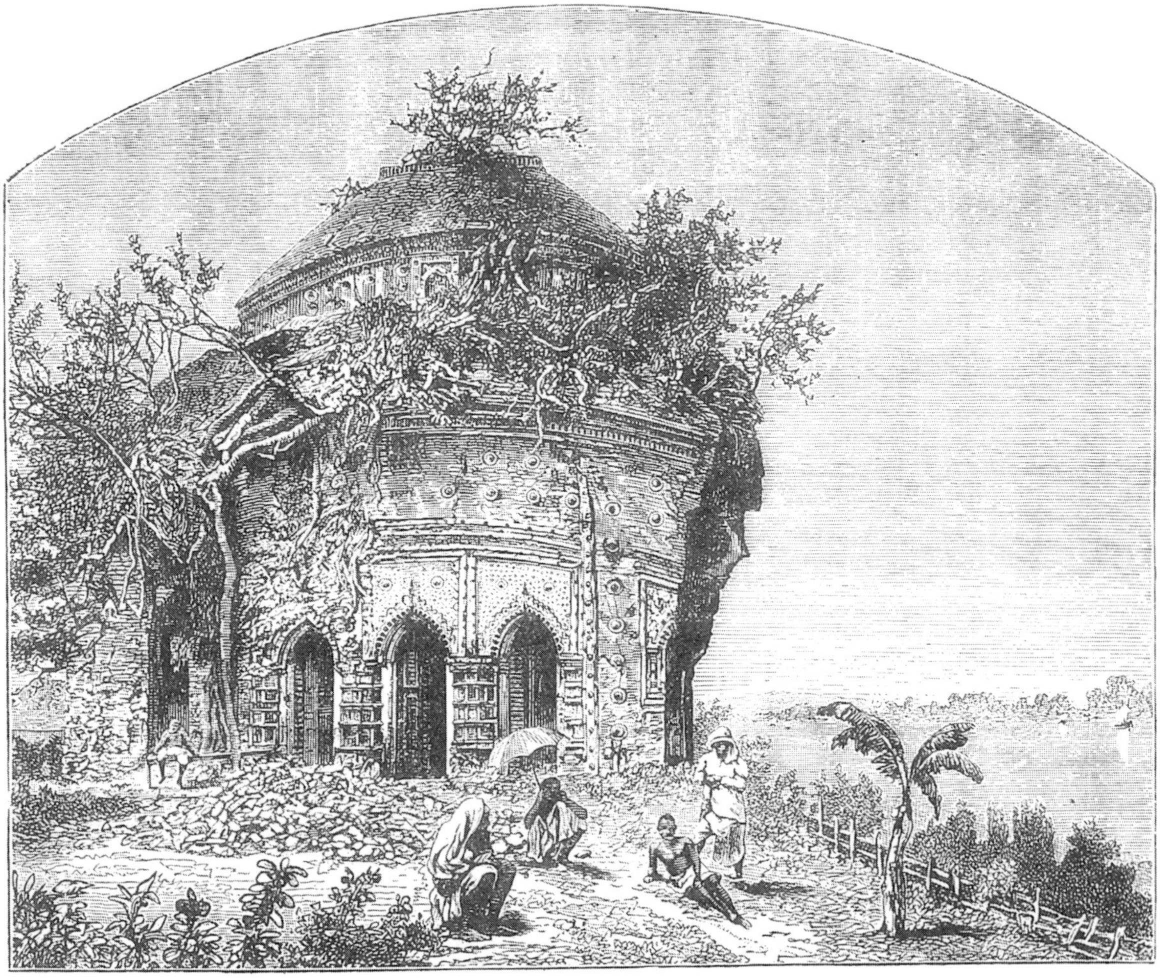

MARTYN'S HOME, ALDEEN, SERAMPORE.

workpeople looked healthy and content. The average wages per month are, for a girl, ten shillings; a woman, sixteen shillings; a man, thirty-two shillings. The Hoogly, which flows close by, is deep and wide, and there is an interesting old temple, with beautifully carved stone, in the neighborhood. The view is very picturesque, commanding a reach of the river, teeming with rural beauty. Farther up are Hugli and Bandel, where is a monastery said to be the oldest in Bengal, dating from 1599. Returning to Barrackpore, on the same line, we drove through the park, a charming, quiet retreat, not unlike Kew Gardens, on the banks of the Hoogly, whither the Viceroy usually comes to spend the Sunday. The house commands a noble prospect six miles down the river. A short distance off is Lady Canning's tomb, which occupies a charming spot on the banks of the river. Her remains have long since been removed to England. The park contains many good trees, palms of various kinds, banyan trees, lovely pine-like casuarinas, and graceful bamboos. In the neighborhood are the filtering-beds, through which the waters of the Ganges pass to supply Calcutta.

Immediately opposite, on the west bank of the river, is Serampore,—once a Danish settlement,—thirteen miles from Calcutta, where are the famous Baptist College and the scenes of the labors of Carey, Marshman, and Ward. Carey landed at Calcutta in 1793, and after some struggles for subsistence set up a printing press. His colleagues came in 1797; and they would all have been reshipped by the authorities, had they not found refuge at Serampore, under the protection of the Danish flag. The college is a substantial building, with a noble staircase, and possesses a fine library, in which is an interesting collection of Bibles in Oriental languages, and some valuable manuscripts. One of Carey's, a ployglot dictionary of Sanscrit words, with the corresponding word in six languages, is beautifully written, and shows the toil and perseverance of its author. The burial-ground is about half a mile distant, where lie the mortal remains of Carey, Ward, and Marshman. Carey's tomb has this inscription:

WILLIAM CAREY.
Born, 17th August, 1761;
Died, 9th June, 1834.

A guilty, weak, and helpless worm,
On Thy kind arms I fall.

The tombs of all three missionaries have domes, supported on pillars; but the ground has the air of neglect and decay, and the wall near Carey's tomb is broken down. We next drove to the Danish church in which Carey preached. It is now in the hands of the Establishment. Near the mission chapel a large jute factory has been erected. Not far off, on the river side, at Aldeen, stood the pagoda where another eminent missionary, Henry Martyn, took up his abode on his arrival in India in the year 1806, and where he spent many hours in learning Hindustani and translating portions of the Scriptures. It is a picturesque spot. He thus speaks of it in his journal: "The habitation assigned me by Mr. Brown is a pagoda in his grounds, on the edge of the river. Thither I retired at night, and really felt something like superstitious dread at being in a place once inhabited, as it were, by devils; but yet felt disposed to be triumphantly joyful, that the temple where they were worshiped was become Christ's Oratory. I prayed out aloud to my God, and the echoes returned from the vaulted roof. Oh! may I so pray that the dome of heaven may resound! I like my dwelling much, it is so retired and free from noise; it has so many recesses and cells that I can hardly find my way in and out." The building has in part been washed away by the river.

Serampore has a calm and cheerful aspect, with its clean, shady roads. It is a pleasant suburban retreat, but factories are gaining ground, and the mission has the air of decay. Carey's Botanical Garden of six acres, which contained three thousand species of plants and trees, is now jungle, and has recently been sold for business purposes. There is a considerable silk manufacture here. It is sad to see the scenes of many years of Christian labor, and the fruits of missionary enterprise associated with revered names, thus on the decline. The headquarters of the mission, it should however, be remembered, have been removed to Calcutta. Twelve miles farther on is the French settlement of Chandernagore, dating from 1688, pleasantly situated on the river side. It consists of a long row of white buildings interspersed with trees. But, as has been quaintly said, "it looks a little out at elbows, and has about it a shabby genteel sort of air."

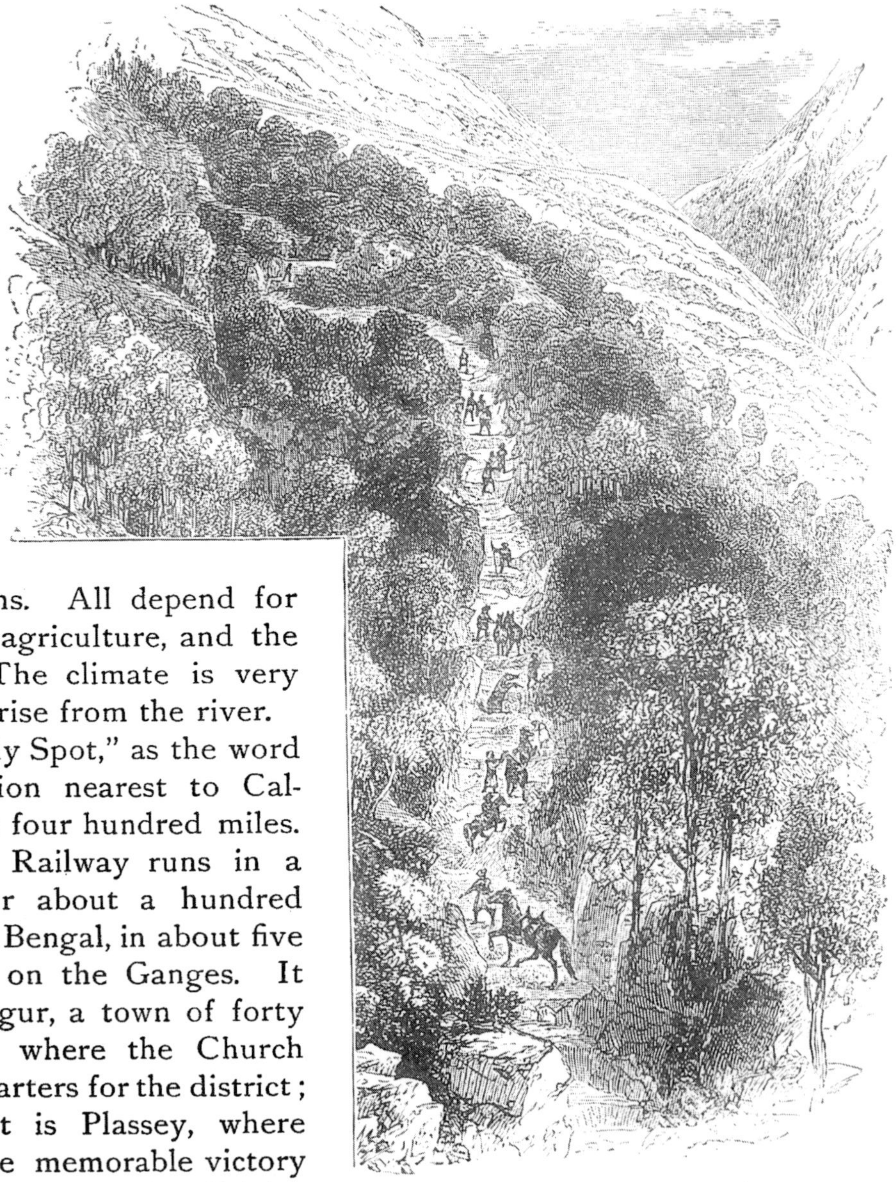

ON THE WAY TO THE HIMÂLAYAS.

ASSAM, with its capital Shillong, in the Khasi Hills, includes the fertile Brahmaputra valley, with its rich black soil. Its hills in the east contain limestone and coal beds, and tea is largely cultivated on their lower slopes. The population is four millions, chiefly Hindus and Mohammedans. All depend for their livelihood upon agriculture, and the staple crop is rice. The climate is very humid, and fogs often rise from the river.

DARJEELING, "Holy Spot," as the word signifies, the hill station nearest to Calcutta, lies north about four hundred miles. The Eastern Bengal Railway runs in a northerly direction for about a hundred miles over the plains of Bengal, in about five hours, to Damookdea on the Ganges. It passes near Krishnuggur, a town of forty thousand inhabitants, where the Church Mission has its headquarters for the district; and thirty miles west is Plassey, where Clive won, in 1757, the memorable victory from which virtually dates the British supremacy in North India. A large steam ferry conveyed us across the Ganges from Damookdea in forty minutes. It is a perilous passage, owing to the strong current and the shoals; two men were taking soundings, one on each side the vessel, all the way across. At Sara Ghat, we again entered the train, and traveled all night, two hundred miles, stopping at many stations, till we reached the temporary terminus, Silliguri, at about 10 A. M. Here, with much difficulty, and after some hours' delay, we obtained wretched ponies to take us on to Kursiong, half-way to Darjeeling; but our ponies traveled so slowly across the Serai, or swamp of low-lying jungle, the seat of malarious fever, which forms a deadly belt along the foot of the hills across the north of India, separating the

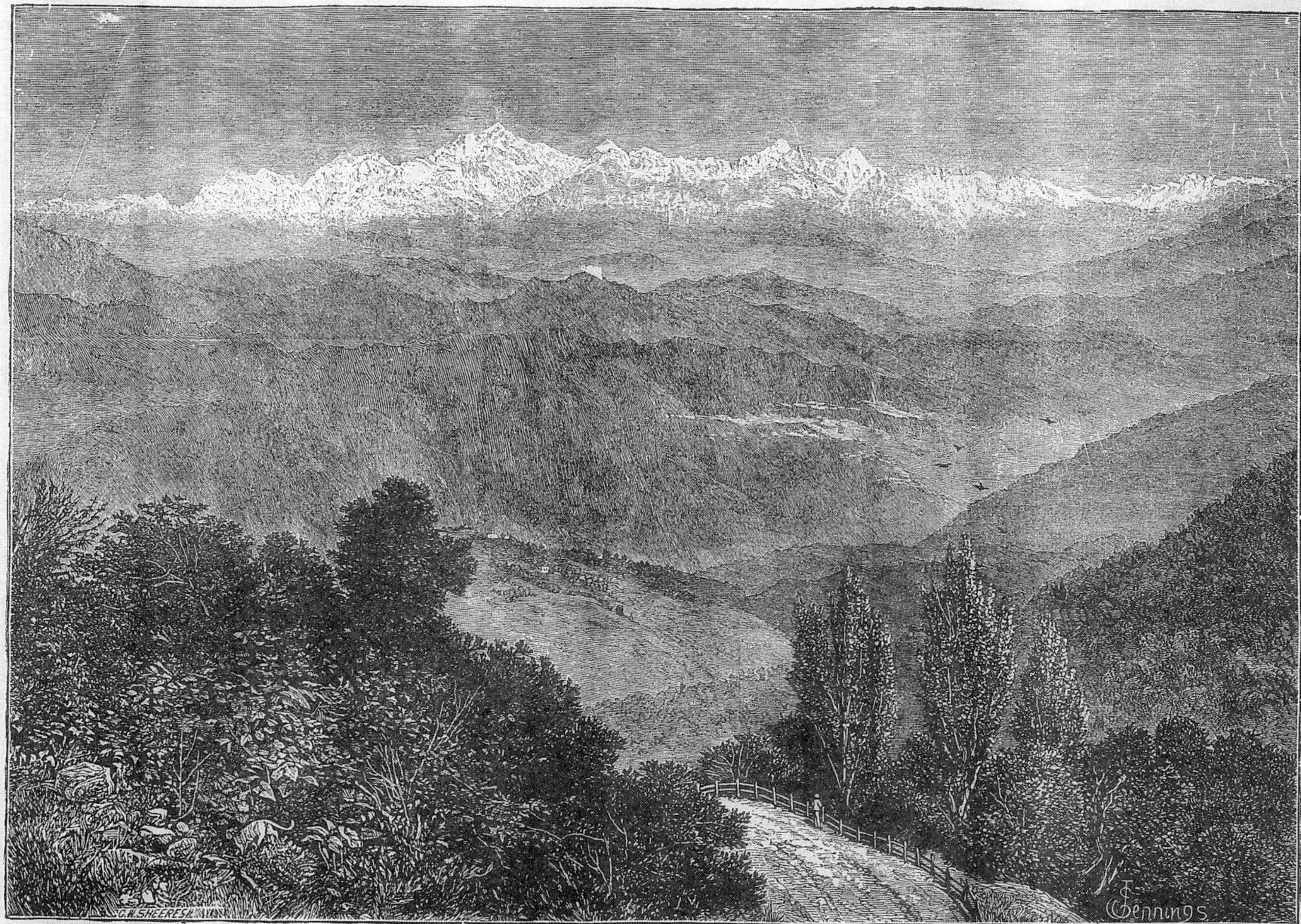

KINCHINJUNGA, FROM DARJEELING.

Himâlayas, that darkness came on before we began to ascend, and we rode in faith along the road, which at the time was undergoing repair, till we reached the Dak Bungalow of Chambattie, where we put up for the night.[1]

The Dak Bungalow is an Inn, or Rest House, provided by Government for travelers, one-storied, with verandas, often perched on a knoll; with scanty furniture and scantier fare. It is in charge of a native called a *Khansamah*, who locks it up when empty, and appears on the ground to open it when you call. A tariff of prices,—very moderate,—a list of rules, a list of articles provided, and a carefully drawn map of the district hang on the walls. After some delay we got candles and chocolate and bread; but it was too late to procure the usual repast of roast fowl, or "sudden death," as this dish is called in the East, the creature being usually killed and dressed

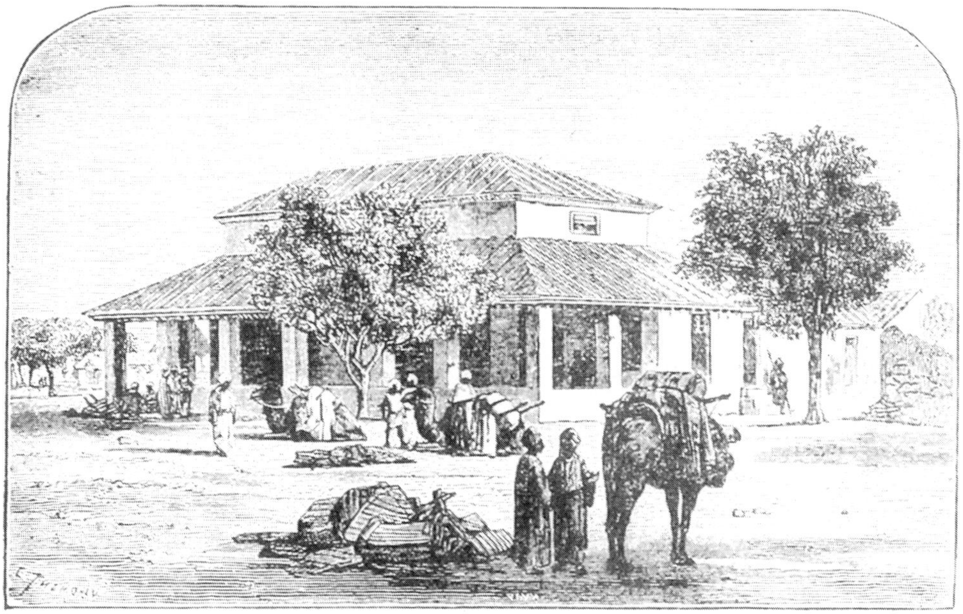

TRAVELER'S BUNGALOW.

within half-an-hour of your arrival. We turned in, after giving directions to the khansamah to look after our ponies, and to prepare an early morning meal. The silence of the hills was impressive: here and there a firefly; here and there, across the valley, or through the trees, the twinkle of the light in a native hut.

At daybreak next morning we were again in the saddle, and rode ten miles, over lovely hills with wooded sides and varied ravines, clad in forest and brushwood, to Kursiong. The views were fine, and the verdure beautiful. The air was delightfully clear and cool, and peasants of the native tribes were passing to their work along the mountain paths. Kursiong is four thousand six hundred feet above the sea, a village perched on the ridge of a hill; and here we had our first sight of the Himâlayas. Kinchinjunga, the second highest of the range, twenty-eight thousand feet, was full in view, though sixty miles away. The sight was grand and impressive. The air became more keen and bracing, and after the refreshment of breakfast in a comfortable inn, we mounted fresh ponies and started on the remaining twenty miles. The road is lovely in the extreme, skirting the flanks and rounding the spurs of the mountains,

[1] The time from Calcutta to Darjeeling, 379 miles, is now about twenty-four hours, all rail.—[ED.

carried by bridges over deep ravines with roaring torrents, and adorned with luxuriant tropical vegetation, splendid orchids, graceful tree-ferns, flowering creepers, and noble trees. After crossing the ridge called "the Saddle," we came through the barracks used as a convalescent depot, and rode on to the delightfully placed lodgings which we had beforehand engaged, distant just fifteen minutes' walk from the Observatory Hill and the Mall, and with the sublime snows towering high before us—a spot much frequented by Calcutta officials during the hot season.

At sunrise on Sunday morning I walked round the Mall and up to the Observatory, which commands a full view of the stupendous scenery. Never did I understand so fully the force of the apostle's expression, "depth and height," as now that I had before me the giant mountains, and looked down into the depths, deeper and deeper still, six thousand feet, into the forest-clad ravine of the Great Ranjit river, and then slowly raised my eyes higher and higher, through the successive ridges of foliage and rocks, till they reached the eternal snows, and still far up and up to the peaks soaring into the sky. From the lowest point which the eye can reach in the Ranjit valley to the highest peak of Kinchinjunga, the vertical height is not less than five miles—such a thickness of the earth's crust being probably nowhere else visible on the earth's surface. More than twelve peaks can be counted which rise above twenty thousand feet. The air was cold and bracing, the grass was crisp and white with frost; the sun shot his rays across in dazzling splendor, and in the stillness and brightness of the scene one felt as if transported to another world. After morning service in the little English church, I went down to the square bazaar, or market-place, which is crowded on Sundays with strange nationalities. Here were the old aborigines, the LEPCHAS, with Mongolian type of face, oblique eyes, high cheek-bones, clad in striped cotton garments; the men with pigtails like the Chinese, the women with nose-rings and large silver ornaments, some with strings of rupees. They are a small, plain, but powerful-looking race, inured to hardship, nomadic, but amiable. Their besetting sin is gambling. They are a merry and careless people, with but little thought of the morrow. They are very fond of quoits, using pieces of slate for the purpose, which they throw with great dexterity. They always wear a long knife, curved like a sickle and stuck in the girdle, which serves them to fell trees, skin animals, build huts, pare their nails, sever their food, and even pick their teeth. Rice is their staple food. Their language is a Thibetan dialect, and their religion a corrupt Buddhism.

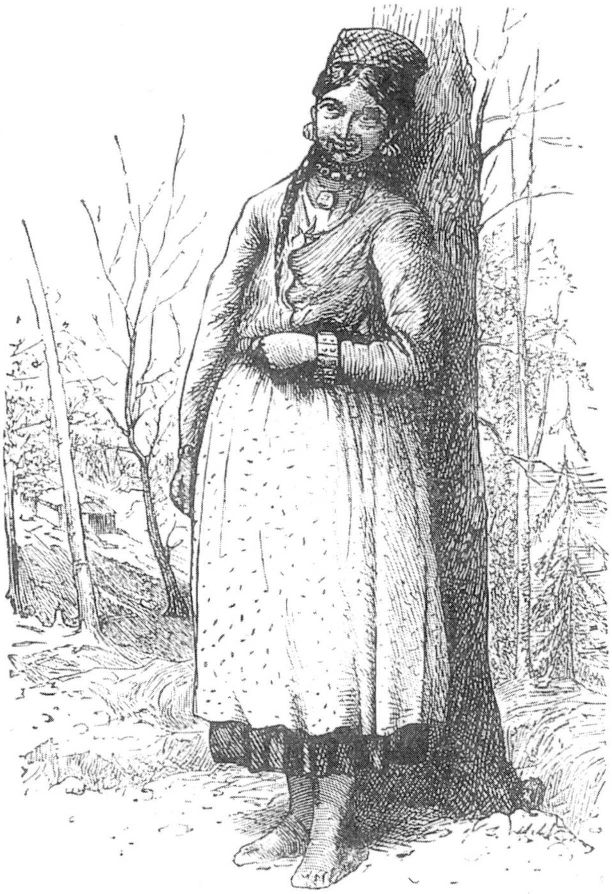

HIMÂLAYA HILL GIRL.

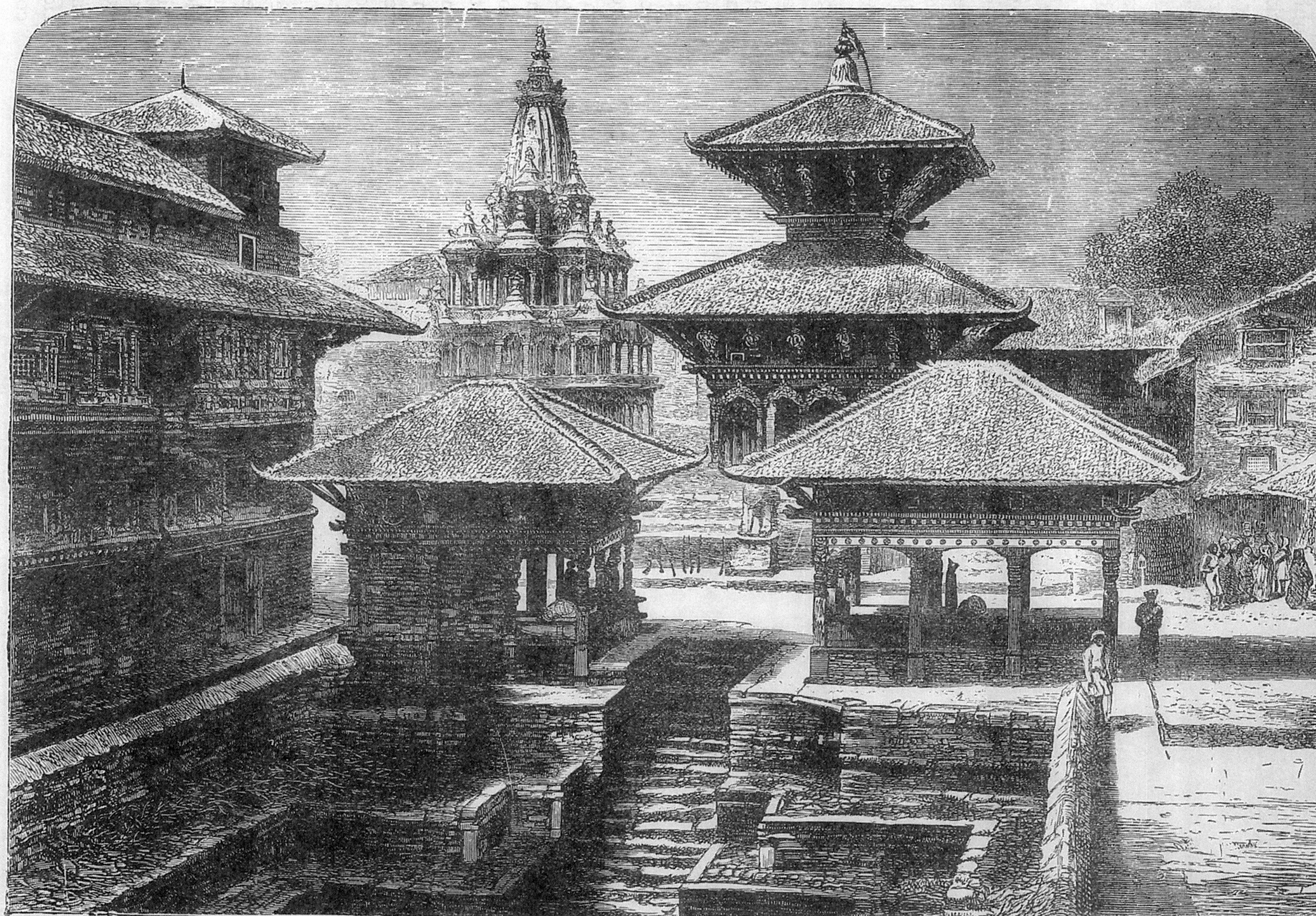

TEMPLE AND SACRED TANK, NEPAL.

Here, too, in large numbers, were the Bhooteas, tall and robust, sturdy, flat-faced people, weather-beaten, with broad mouths and flat noses; their complexion whitish yellow, but incrusted with dirt, and tar, and smoke. They seldom wash. They are dressed in loose blankets, girt about the waist with a leather belt, in which they place their brass pipes, their long knives, chopsticks, tinder-box, tobacco-pouch, and tweezers, with which they pluck away all trace of beard. They wear stout woven boots—boot and stocking in one. The women have their faces tarred, and their hair is plaited in two tails, the neck loaded with strings of coral and amber, large, heavy, round earrings dragging down the lobe of the ear. They are always spinning. The Bhooteas are Buddhists, and believe in the efficacy of praying-machines. When crossing mountains they hang little scraps of rag on the bushes, as a prayer for safety, and place grains of rice along the hill-side to propitiate evil spirits They bury their dead on the mountains, raising cairns over them.

Here, again, one might see the light and agile Nepalese, with intelligent and pleasing countenances, active and enduring, and brave to a degree, as the Nepal war of 1816 witnesses. Their secluded valleys are rich in forest and minerals, and on the frontier indigo is largely grown. Their dogs are yellow-fanged, wolf-like, fierce, surly creatures, but invaluable watch-dogs. Nepal proper is a small valley twelve miles by nine at the foot of this part of the Himâlayan range, but the country extends west from Sikkim to Kumaon. The ruling race are called Ghûrkas. Here Buddhism and Vaishnavism are found side by side. The temples are of wood, and remind one of those of Japan. The temple of Mahadeva at Patan presents both styles of architecture, the Hindu and the Thibetan, or Turanian, side by side. The capital of Nepal is Khatmandu, and contains a beautiful temple in the Chinese style. The view of the Himâlayas to the northeast is very grand. The ragged Lama mendicant is also to be met with, and Sherbas and Thibetan beggars, jovial, but easily excited. Intermingled with these native mountain tribes were stolid Chinamen, proud Mohammedans, and graceful Hindus. In the midst of the bustle and bartering, the missionary had his open room, or shed, into which the people came to hear hymn, or prayer, or Scripture. In the Bhootea village there is a small, dirty Buddhist temple called Bhootea Bustee. The Lamas, or priests, are also of a low type—unctuous, sly, insolent. They sell praying-machines and use them in their worship, continually turning them round. Indeed, you enter the temple between two huge cylinders, like pillars, two feet in diameter and six feet high, which are gigantic praying-machines, turned by means of a winch. Here we met many Thibetans returning to their country with heavy burdens.

Rising one morning while it was yet dark and starlight, we mounted our ponies, and, with guides, started for the ascent of the SINCHAL MOUNTAIN, eight thousand three hundred feet, six miles from Darjeeling. Riding through the military sanatorium to "the Saddle," or Johr Bungalow, we began the ascent up a steep winding track through the jungle, and after an hour's climb reached the Chimneys—the ruins of the first military station—perched upon a ridge, or shoulder, of Sinchal, where Kinchinjunga and its neighbor peaks burst on our view, kindled with the rays of the rising sun. The air was perfectly clear, and the sky cloudless. Here we dismounted, and scrambled through brushwood and snow to the summit, which is specially celebrated because of the glorious prospect it commands—the sweep of the Himâlayan range, including Everest itself, the presiding monarch of them all, the highest mountain in the world. There he rose to our view, of sugarloaf shape, far off, but clear cut against the sky. The entire range, "Pelion on Ossa piled," was now before us as far as the eye could reach in a clear atmosphere and a cloudless sky. It was like looking from a Pisgah across the valleys and over mountains to a

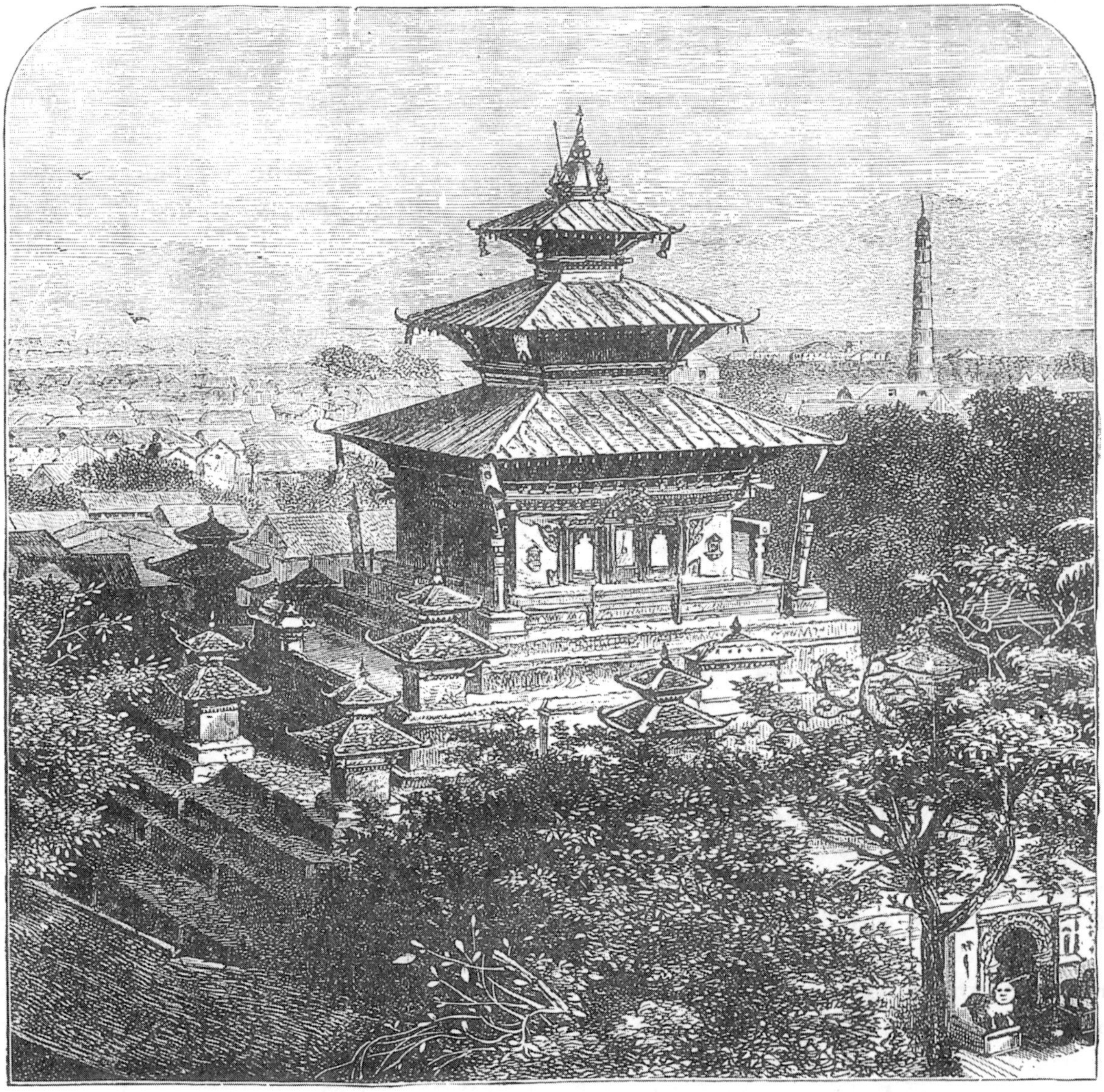

PALACE AND TEMPLE, KHATMANDU, NEPAL.

new and loftier country. Here one is overwhelmed with the majesty of Nature and the power of the Almighty. The deep blue sky, the pure white snows, the clear-cut precipices, the dark, shady ravines, the dense primeval forests, all impress the spectator with the presence of God. Having filled the eye and mind with the sublimity of a prospect never to be forgotten during two hours spent on that green, but now frost-whitened mountain, we reluctantly descended to the shoulder where our ponies were, and returned thankful and exultant that we had been so favored in the weather; for these grandeurs are often enveloped in mist or cloud for days together. The annual average rainfall at Darjeeling is nine feet eight inches—one hundred and sixteen inches—June to September being the wettest months.

The descent from Darjeeling to the Ranjit river, which separates it from the Himâlayan range, is six thousand feet in eleven miles, and the river is crossed by one of those cane bridges which are peculiar to this part of the world. The main chains supporting the bridge are branches of trees and rattan canes; the sides are of split canes, hanging from each main chain, two feet apart. Into these loops the foot-path is laid, composed of three bamboos, the thickness of a man's arm, laid side by side, the section of the bridge resembling the letter V, in the angle or base of which the traveler finds footing. The piers of these bridges are generally two convenient trees through whose branches the main chains are passed and pegged into the ground beyond. Only one traveler can pass over at a time, and the spring and oscillation are considerable, but strong bamboos are placed underneath and connected with the main chains by split rattan ropes to prevent the bridge from collapsing with the weight.

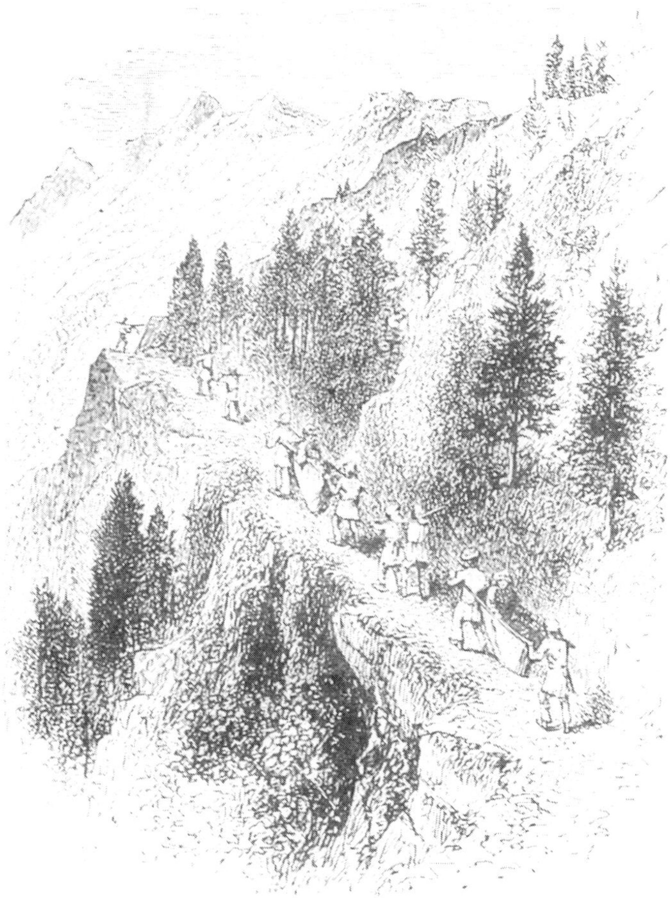

DANDY TRAVELING, HIMÂLAYAS.

At the lower edge of the great forest which clothes the Sinchal lies a botanical garden, lonely and lovely, the Rungaroon Garden, where we found roses, scarlet geraniums, verbenas, and many English plants and flowers in the midst of tropical luxuriance. The garden is to be devoted to such indigenous plants, epiphytes, orchids, and gingers, which are not likely to thrive in the moister and more shady forest sections. The path leading to this spot is rich in forest beauty. Beyond are some of the tea and cinchona plantations for which Darjeeling is famous, and which, as the slopes are cleared, mar in some degree the beauty of the nearer hills. The tea gardens are laid out in the most unromantic fashion, acre upon acre planted with straight rows of bushes, two feet high, with small glazed dark green leaves, and in the center the manager's bungalow, flanked by long ranges of low buildings, where the process of drying, sorting, and packing is carried on. The Bhootea coolies, both men and women, may be seen carrying chests of immense weight up the steepest hills. They leave the railway porters of England far behind. A story is told that one of these sturdy women actually brought up a grand piano on her back from Kursiong to the station. The work on the plantations is not so laborious. It consists mainly in deep hoeing between the lines of trees as weeds appear, and careful hand weeding. In November of the third year, when the plant is four feet high, it is pruned down to twenty inches, that the young leaves may be plucked easily; and six weeks afterward, when the tea plant is said to "flush," or throw out new shoots six inches high, the picking is repeated, and so on at intervals of twenty days for eight months. Tea can be made only of these young and tender leaves, and the plucking requires gentle touch, women and children being employed. For sorting, rolling, drying, etc., machinery is generally used.

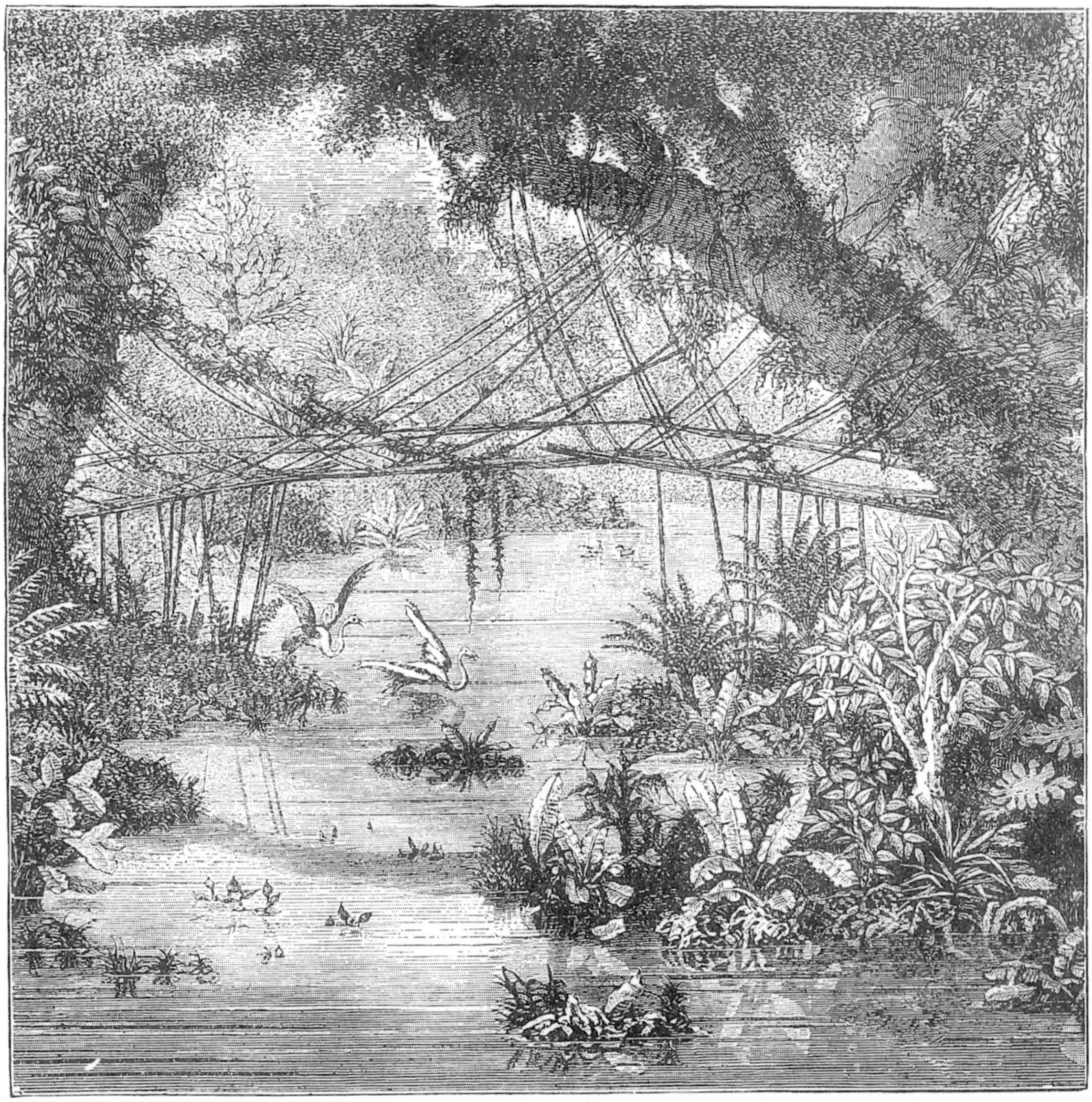

BRIDGE OVER THE RANJIT RIVER, DARJEELING.

The cinchona (quinine) plantations in the Darjeeling district cover nearly two thousand acres, stocked with about three million cinchona trees. The quinine comes from the bark. Quinidine, or cinchonidine, chiefly from the red cinchona, is a good substitute for quinine. It is produced in large quantities, and is obtainable at a much more moderate cost.

Language cannot describe the glory of the Himâlayas seen from Darjeeling lit up by the rays of the setting sun. From the Observatory more than twelve peaks can be counted, which rise above twenty thousand feet, and none are below fifteen thousand. Against the azure sky, in an atmosphere far clearer than we ever see in England, the snowy range reflects the colors of the sunset, ever changing and deepening in richness from bright yellow to pink, from pink to crimson, and long after the sun has set to us. One writer speaks of the view as "something to be treasured as one of the most noteworthy moments of his life"; and another of "the deep happiness of a sojourn in this enchanted land, sentineled by the everlasting mountains." And the contrast from these "abodes of snow," to the luxuriant

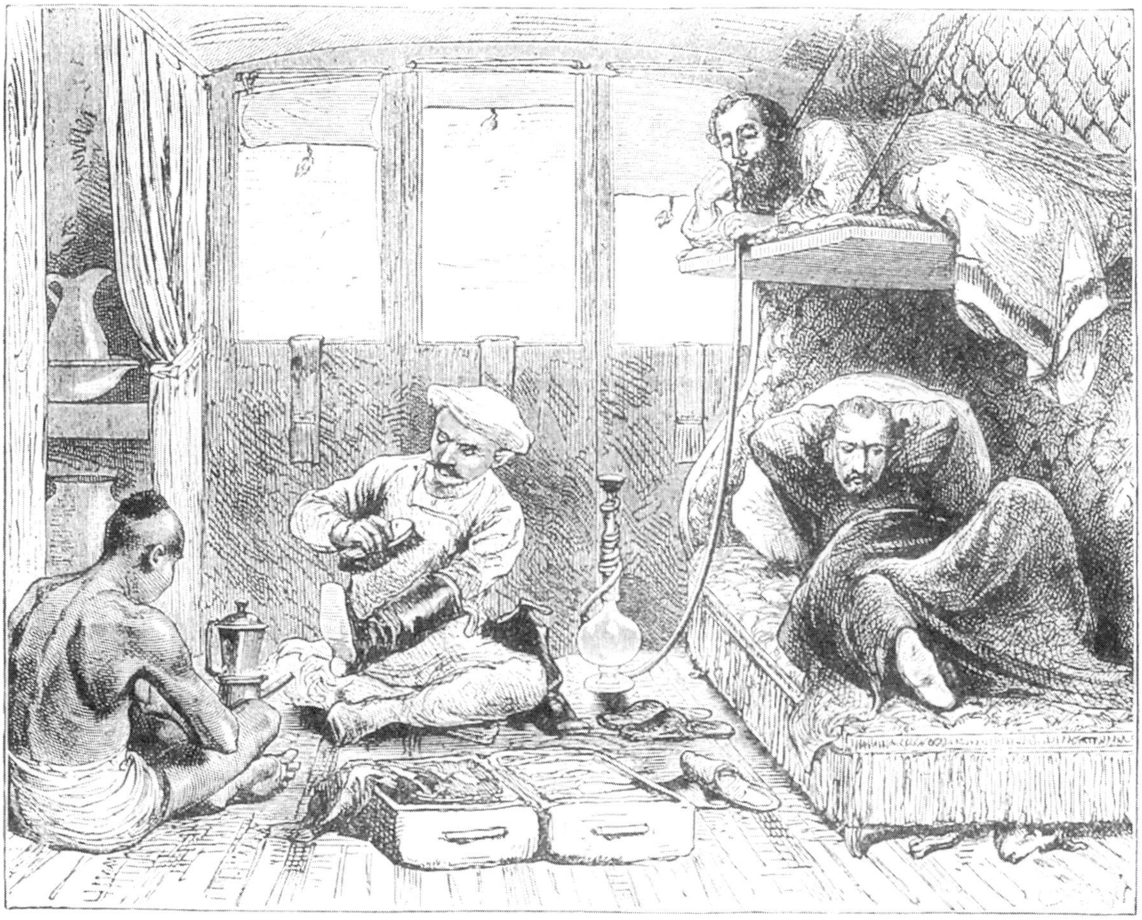

RAILWAY TRAVELING.

tropical vegetation surrounding us on every hand, clothing the richly wooded hills through which we drive, is hardly less striking and impressive. The natives are loth to stir early, for they feel the morning cold, and are ill prepared against it as to clothing; but with the Himâlayas now bright with the rising sun we succeeded in starting by Tonga Dâk, a sort of dog-cart, at 8 A. M., reaching Kursiong at 11 A. M. and Sillijuri in time for the evening train. The transition—as we drove along from snow and frost to firs and oaks, then to rhododendrons, india-rubber trees, tree-ferns of immense size, golden ferns with stems three feet high, and wondrous orchids, white, yellow, and purple; banks studded with stag-moss and yellow calceolarias, scented magnolia and magnificent bamboos—gives an exhilaration and excitement not to be had to the same extent in any other part of the world.

The East Indian Railway runs northwest from Calcutta up the Ganges valley nine hundred and fifty-four miles to Delhi; and at Delhi it meets the Scinde Punjab and Indus Valley State Railways, which complete the iron road by Lahore away still northward to Peshawar, and southward to Karâchi, that important and rising port at the mouth of the Indus, one thousand one hundred and sixty-nine miles from Delhi. Thus the railway journey across India from Calcutta to Karâchi is two thousand one hundred and twenty-three miles, and from Calcutta to Bombay, branching south from Allahabad, is fourteen hundred and nine miles. The River Ganges, with its tributaries, drains an area of three hundred and ninety thousand

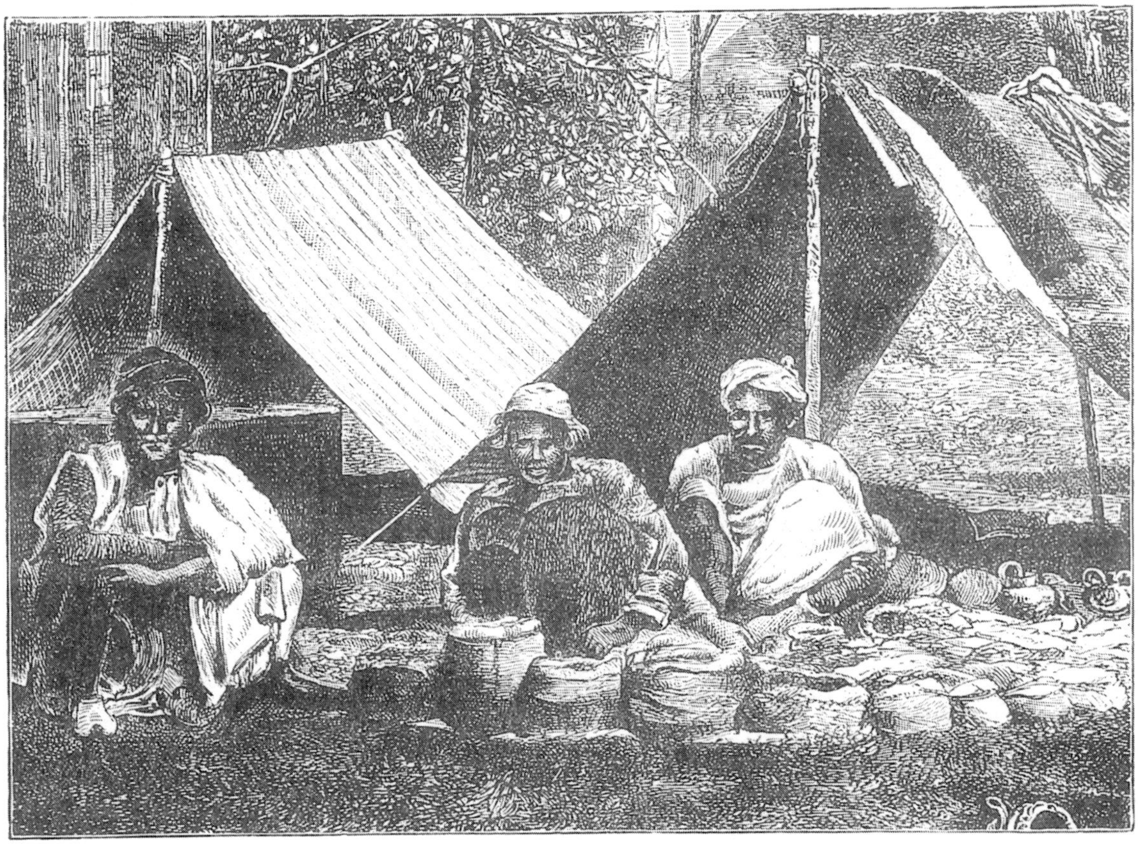

GRAIN SELLERS.

square miles, including the Lower Provinces of Bengal, the Northwest Provinces, and Oude. Here the Aryan race, entering from the northwest, attained their full strength and development. Hindi, Hindustani, or Bengali is their language, with the written character called Nagari, resembling the ancient Sanscrit. The population is estimated at sixty millions. Their life is for the most part a struggle for existence by the tillage of the soil—rice, plantains, cocoanuts, and the cultivation of indigo, hemp, cotton, and the opium poppy. The land is not, as in England, parceled out into farms. There are wealthy proprietors, who hold large tracts by grant, purchase, or hereditary succession; but the tenants are literally children of the soil. Wherever a village nestles among its plantains or mango groves, the land is parceled out among the villagers. The villagers or immediate cultivators of soil are called *ryots*. The land-owners are called *zamindars*. A large proprietor does not reckon up his farms, but he counts his villages. Often between the zamindars and the ryots there are middle-men or lease-holders, *patnidars*, who are sometimes indigo planters. Having got the village on lease, you summon the tenants, show them their rent account, and get them to agree to cultivate a certain percentage of the land in indigo. The compact being made, the ryots are your slaves forever. The sowing of every year goes to pay the debt of the last, and the debt must be paid off by so many bundles of the indigo plant. The planter's bungalow is a fine-looking house, with an immense compound. In front of it is the factory, and at some distance miserable huts in which the coolies live.[1] In the cultivation of the land, bullocks are used for draught and carriage. The Bengal plow is much the same as the Greek or Roman one. "The English have no idea," says Sir J. B

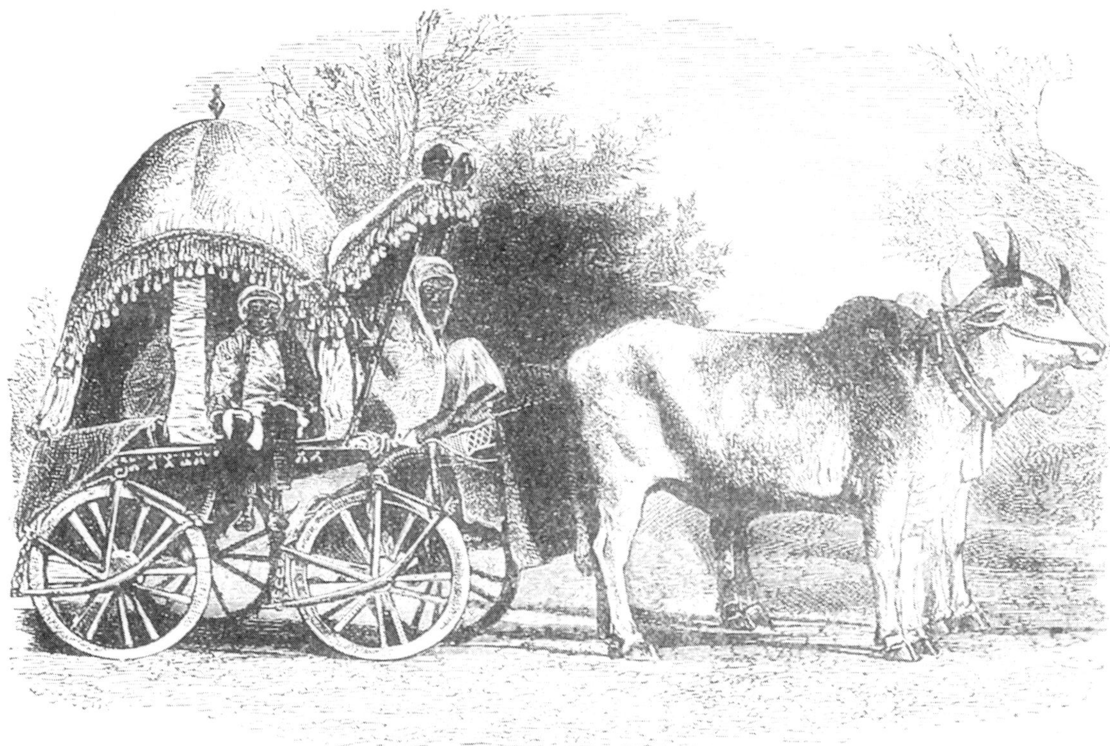

BULLOCK CARRIAGE.

Phear, "of the extreme poverty of the bulk of the Bengal population. Seven rupees a month will support a whole family. Food is the principal item, and probably one rupee eight annas a month will suffice to feed an adult man, and twelve annas a woman." Yet the salt tax alone averages annually a hundred and twelve annas per head upon the entire population. "Famine," says another experienced writer, "is the horizon of the Indian villager; insufficient food is the foreground. And this is the more extraordinary, since the villager is surrounded by a dreamland of plenty. Everywhere you see fields flooded deep with millet and wheat. The village and its old trees have to climb on to a knoll to keep their feet out of the glorious poppy and the luscious sugar-cane. Sumptuous cream-colored bullocks move sleepily about with an air of luxurious sloth. Everything is steeped in repose. The bees murmur their idylls among the flowers; the doves moan their amorous

[1] Any one who would learn what Indian village life is, should read *Bengal Peasant Life*, by the Rev. L. B. Day; and *The Aryan Village*, by Sir J. B. Phear.

complaints from the shady leafage of pipal trees; out of the cool recesses of wells the idle cooing of the pigeons ascends into the summer-laden air; the rainbow-fed chameleon slumbers on the branch; the enameled beetle on the leaf; the little fish is in the sparkling depths below; the radiant kingfisher, tremulous as sunlight, in mid-air; and the peacock, with furled glories, on the temple tower of the silent gods. Amid this easeful and luscious splendor the villager labors and starves. While he has to maintain the glorious phantasmagoria of an imperial policy, while he has to support legions of scarlet soldiers, golden cuprassies, purple politicals, and green commissions, he must remain the hunger-stricken, over-driven phantom that he is."[1] What with income tax, license tax, succession tax, salt tax, feast tax, and fast tax, his hookah—his "hubble-bubble," so called from the gurgling noise of the water inside the cocoa-nut-shell—is his only solace amid the privations of his wretched life. When he would protest, he dies of famine; this is his revenge.

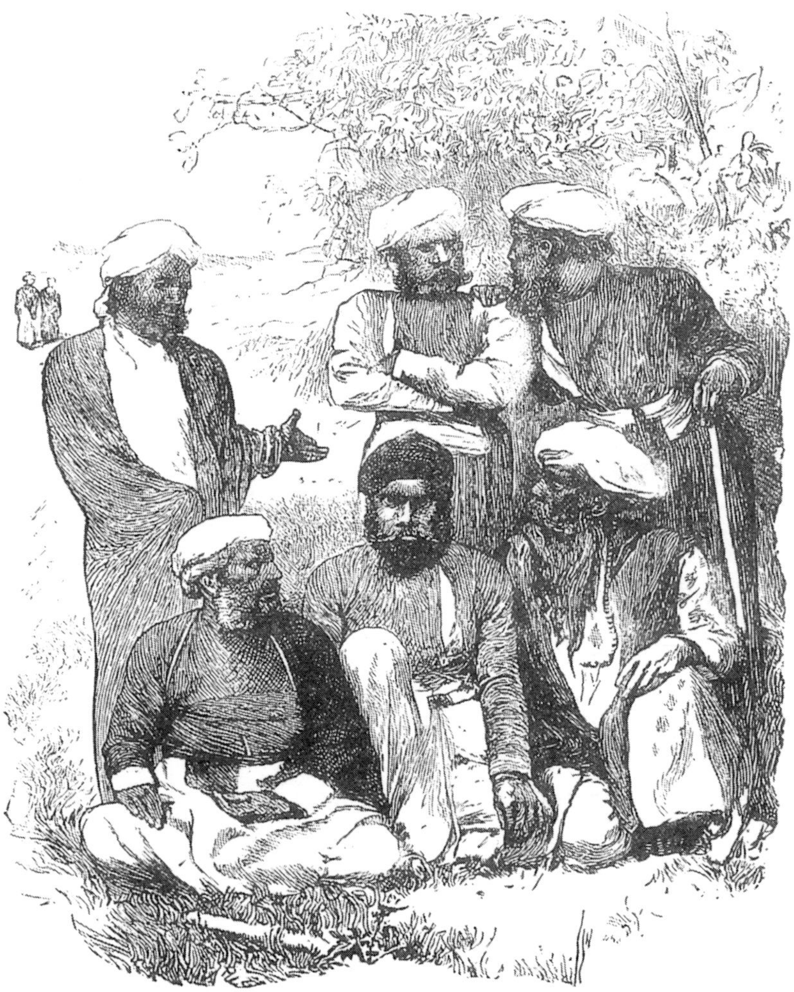

THUGS.

Through this vast district the railroad now wends its way. Before it came along the great trunk road travelers were often attacked, robbed, and even murdered in the days of Thug notoriety. The Thugs, who abounded chiefly in the forests, were fanatics, who made highway robbery part of their religion, and declared that their victims were sacrifices to the goddess Kali. Disguised as peaceful travelers, they would first engage in simple and friendly greeting, looking gentle and unassuming, and then suddenly they would throw the handkerchief-noose round the neck of the wayfarer, strangle him in a moment, and rifle him of all he possessed. Sometimes a girl appeared sitting at the wayside weeping. The traveler, in pity, might stop to speak to her; but if so he was doomed. She soon had the noose round his throat and strangled him on the spot. Since 1830 Thuggism has been suppressed, but the instinct possesses the thieves still, and the sight of the noose will cause the calm features to blaze with fury. In the school of industry at Jabalpur, some aged Thugs, proud of

[1] *Twenty-one Days in India*, by G. A. Mackay.

their race and profession, may still be seen. A visitor, anxious to understand their mode of strangling, submitted his neck to be operated upon, but at the great risk of his life; for with the kindling instinct of the Thug, the illustration threatened, in another moment to become a reality. Datura poisoning is still practiced by the same class of people. An old man and his son were lately poisoned for the sake of a new blanket by a gang of Thugs. The railroad now conveys us in ease and security over these vast plains. About a hundred and twenty miles from Calcutta we pass through Ranigunge, where there is the largest and most important coalfield in India. The miners are Bhowries and Sontals, low of stature, and great toilers,

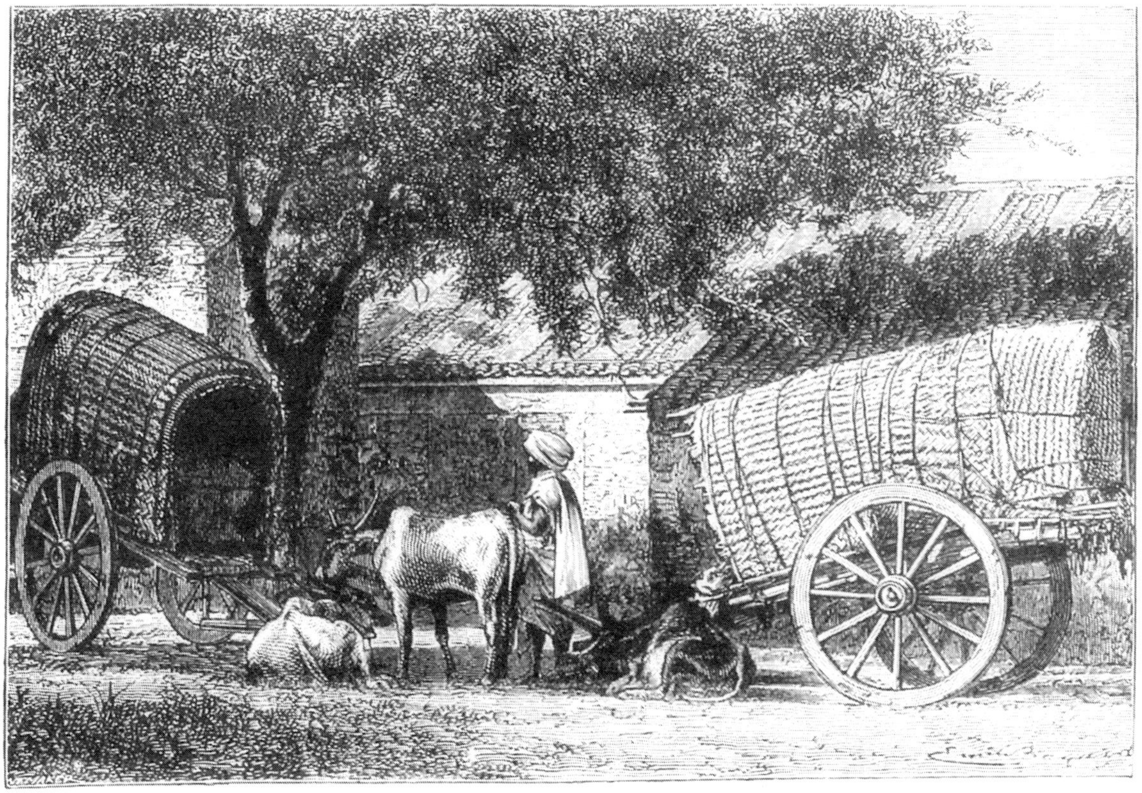

TRAVELING WAGONS.

the former using the pick, the latter only the crowbar in getting the coal. The mines are not deep, and they are free from fire-damp. In this district is Parasnath, the highest peak in Bengal proper, four thousand six hundred feet above the sea. It is a place of great sanctity to the Jains, who make yearly pilgrimages hither, and who strongly opposed the sanatorium for sick soldiers, now erected on it. The mountain commands a grand panorama of the surrounding country, with its winding rivers and its wooded hills. The Sontals have made their way north to Raj Mahal, where by industry they have established themselves. Their villages are quite distinct and separate from those occupied by Hindus.

The chord line carries us between Chotia Nagpur on the south, and Behar on the north. Chotia Nagpur is a mountainous province inhabited chiefly by Dravidian tribes, the Kols and Oraons, among whom the Lutheran missionaries labored successfully for many years. It is a succession of high tablelands called *Pats*, three thousand feet above the sea. In Behar we have the Patna district, which is famous for its rice, and the Gaya district, famous for its Buddhist remains. Behar, indeed, is the cradle of Buddhism, and the name is only a corruption of *Vihara*, a cave or temple. Near Gaya is the site of the famous Bo-tree, under which Gautama Buddha taught; and the Elephant Rock, on which he sat with his disciples, is still pointed out. Here it was that Gautama learnt that the path to salvation lay not in penance and self-torture, but in preaching a higher life to his fellowmen. Here he became "the Buddha," the Enlightened, and began a ministry of love that lasted till his death at the age of eighty. In front of the Bo-tree is the Buddh Gaya Temple, dating from the seventh century, and the Buddh Gaya rails are supposed to be the oldest Hindu sculptures hitherto found. There are several groups of cave temples, more or less ruined, in the neighborhood, and bearing date from Asoka, B. C. 250. Hindu pilgrims come hither to adore the footprint of Vishnu on a rock. Shraddhas, *i. e.*, offerings in honor of departed relatives, are performed here at the Vishnu-pada temple, situated on one of the ridges and built of black stone with a lofty dome and golden pinnacle. Various offerings are placed by the pilgrims around the footprint, the object being to help the progress of the souls of ancestors departed to heaven, and the time occupied in the rites being at least eight days.

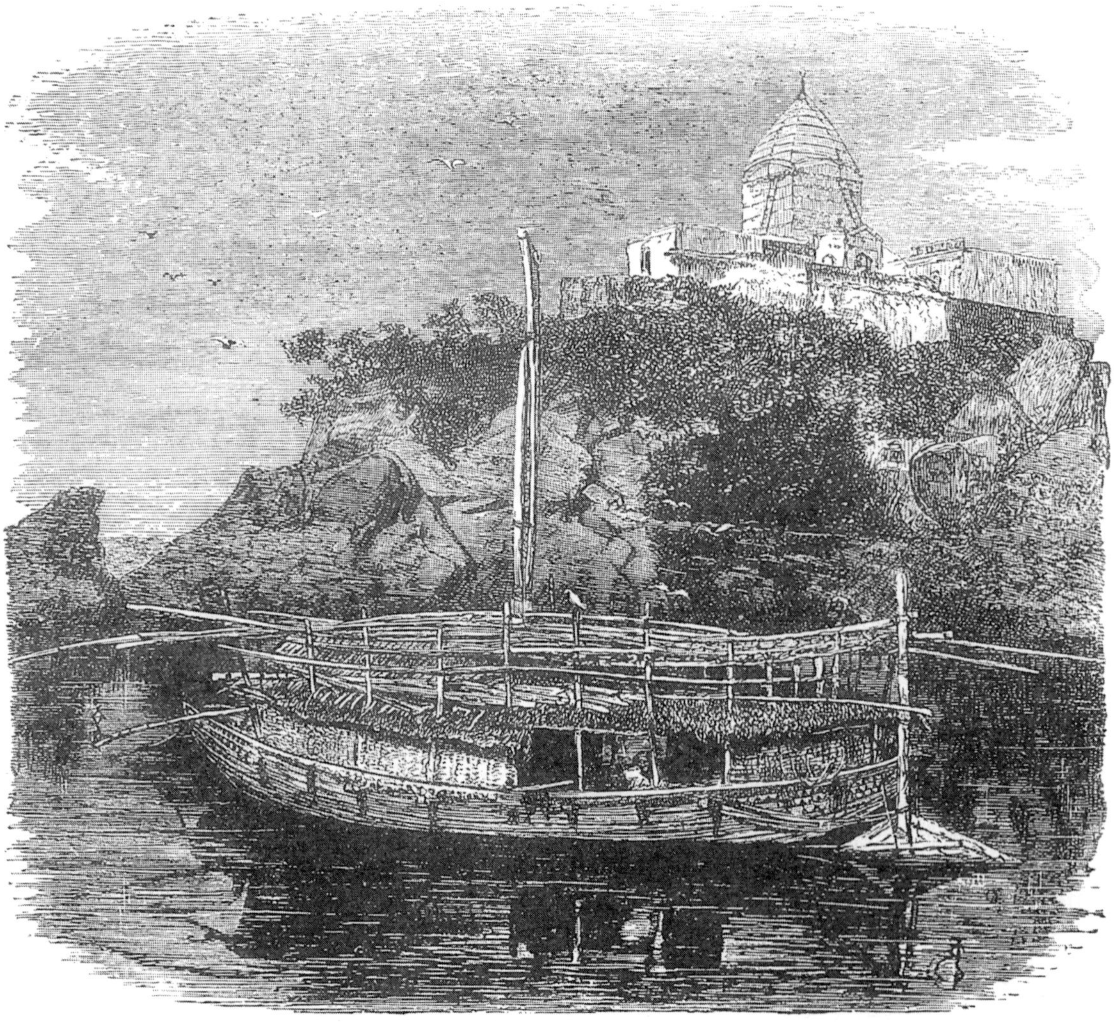

COLGONG ROCKS, GANGES.

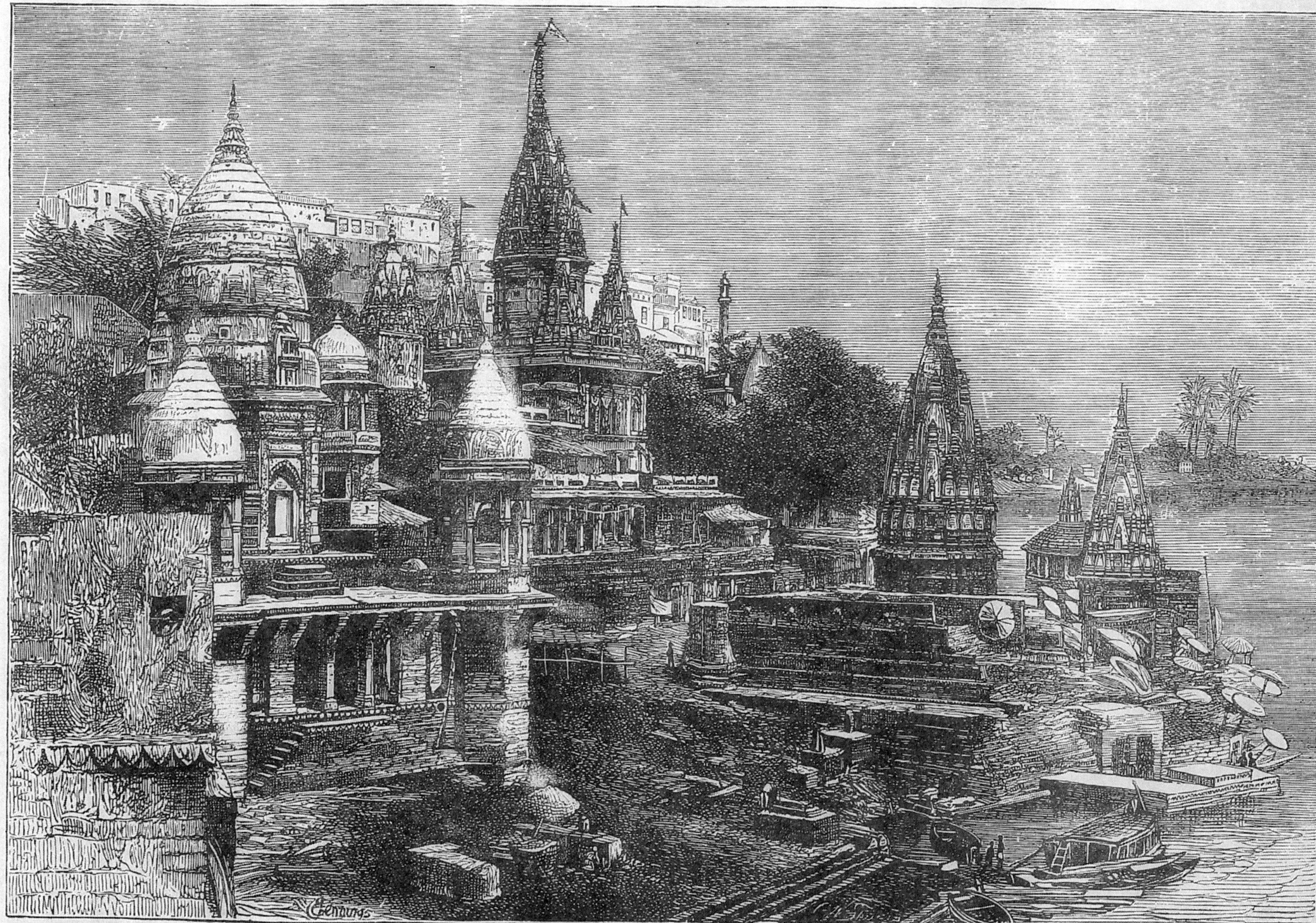

HINDU TEMPLES, BENARES.

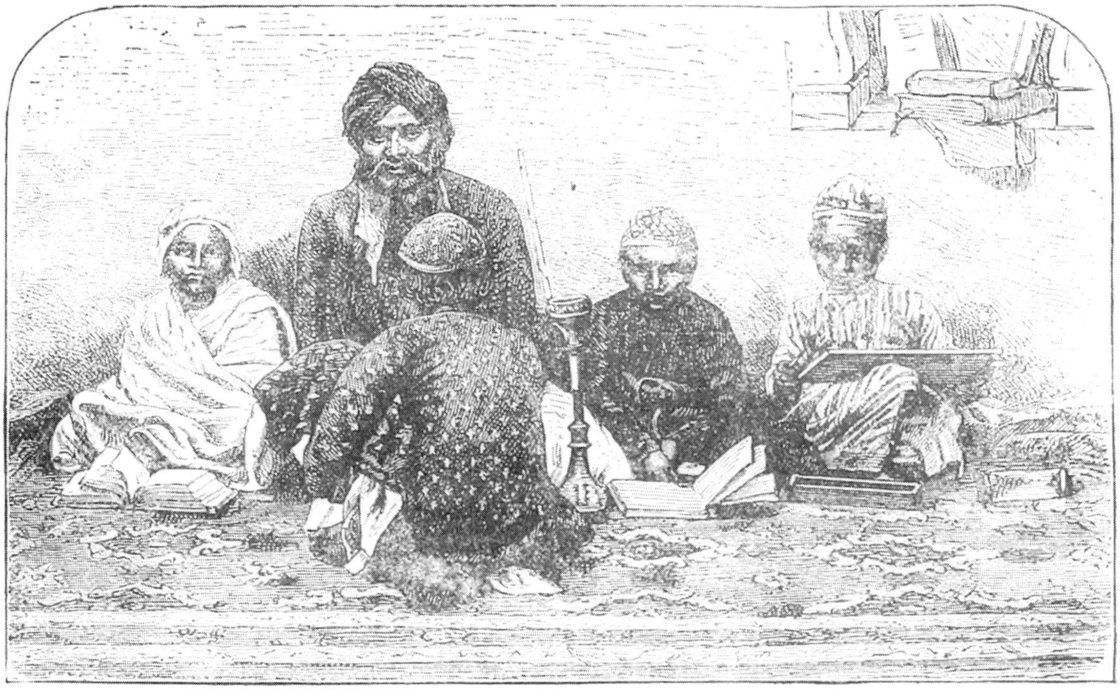

MOHAMMEDAN SCHOOL, ALLAHABAD.

THE NORTHWEST PROVINCES AND OUDE.

BENARES, THE HOLY CITY — THE MUTINY CITIES: LUCKNOW AND CAWNPORE—THE MOHAMMEDAN CITIES: AGRA AND ALLAHABAD.

HOW pleasant, after a long, wearisome railway journey of five hundred miles across the plains of Bengal, on reaching the terminus opposite the great stronghold of heathenism, Benares, the sacred city of the Hindus, with the mighty Ganges flowing between, to find Christians and friends waiting to receive you. So was it with us when, on our arrival, a *sayce*, or footman, from the mission, conducted us across the bridge of boats and through the city four miles to the European settlement and to our hotel; and when presently that eminent Oriental scholar and missionary, the Rev. M. A. Sherring, whose premature death has since been announced, came to welcome and to guide us in our plans for sightseeing. Having crossed the Ganges, we were now in the Northwest Provinces, and in the headquarters of idolatry in India. What Jerusalem is to the Jew, what Rome is to the Latin, what Mecca is to the Mohammedan, Benares is to the Hindu. It contains fourteen hundred Hindu temples, idols innumerable, and twenty thousand Brahmans. Like Paul at Athens, the Christian's spirit is moved within him as he sees the city wholly given to idolatry. Troops of pilgrims are continually thronging its streets, and swarming up and down its *ghats*, or flights of steps leading down to the Ganges, along which the city stretches for three miles, rising gracefully upon the solitary cliff, up the face of which it is built tier upon tier.

In Benares we see what Hinduism practically is. Students of the *Vedas* may restrict the term Brahmanism "to the purely pantheistic and not necessarily idolatrous system evolved by the Brahmans out of the partly monotheistic, partly polytheistic, partly pantheistic religion" expressed in those sacred songs. But it is the polytheistic element which has become its life and soul, embodied as this is in the Hinduism of India. Hinduism is, in fact, idolatry of the basest kind, the worship of *Vishnu*, the preserver, and *Siva*, the destroyer, represented by numberless idols and symbols of the most revolting character. Here in the Northwest Provinces, and above all in Benares, Hinduism has acquired a stony compactness, and a solidity almost impenetrable. Here Brahmanism and caste hold sway. The Hindustani—stalwart, tall, strong-limbed, independent, solid—proudly rests on his good breed, good blood, and the associations of antiquity. He adores the social hierarchy; and all the great events of life—births, marriages, deaths, occupations, professions—are interlaced and enchained with the overgrown fabric of his idolatry. And Benares is the center of all this. It is a very ancient city, and is frequently alluded to in early Sanscrit literature. For the sanctity of its inhabitants, of its temples and reservoirs, of its wells and streams, Benares has been famed for thousands of years. Here, to quote the high authority of the lamented Rev. M. A. Sherring, "Idolatry is a charm, a fascination, to the Hindu. It is, so to speak, the air he breathes. It is the food of his soul. He is subdued, enslaved, befooled by it. The nature of the Hindu partakes of the supposed nature of the gods whom he worships. And what is that nature? According to the traditions handed about among the natives, and constantly dwelt upon in their conversation, and referred to in their popular songs—which, perhaps, would be sufficient proof—yet more especially according to the numberless statements and narratives found in their sacred writings, on which these traditions are based, it is, in many instances, vile and abominable to the last degree. Idolatry is a word denoting all that is wicked in imagination and impure in practice. Idolatry is a demon—an incarnation of all evil—but nevertheless as bewitching and seductive as a siren. It ensnares the depraved heart, coils around it like a serpent, transfixes it with its deadly fangs, and

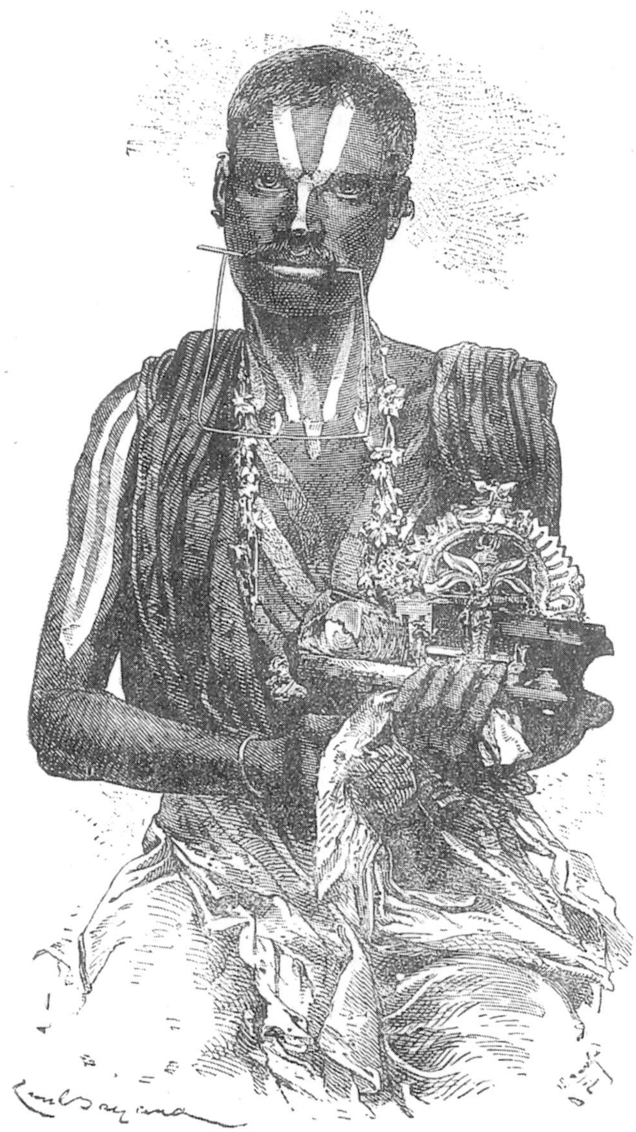

A VISHNUVITE FAKÎR.